| 6 '84 | DATE DUE | | |
|---|---|---|---|
| FEB 15 993 | | | |
| MAY 11 1984 | | | |
| | | | |
| | | | |
| | | | |
| | | | |
| | | | |
| | | | |
| | | | |
| | | | |
| | | | |

# MONEY
# AND JUSTICE

# MONEY
# AND
# JUSTICE

*Who Owns the Courts?*

---

## Lois G. Forer

W · W · NORTON & COMPANY

NEW YORK   LONDON

Copyright © 1984 by Lois G. Forer
All rights reserved.
Published simultaneously in Canada by Stoddart, a subsidiary of
General Publishing Co. Ltd, Don Mills, Ontario.
Printed in the United States of America.

The text of this book is composed in Avanta, with display type set in Baskerville. Composition and manufacturing by The Haddon Craftsmen, Inc.

First Edition

Library of Congress Cataloging in Publication Data
Forer, Lois G.
   MONEY AND JUSTICE: WHO OWNS THE COURTS?
   Includes bibliographical references and index.
   1. Equality before the law—United States. 2. Courts,
—United States. 3. Legal assistance to the poor—United
States. 4. Justice, Administration of—United States.
I. Title.
KF4764.F67 1984      347.73      83-25004
                     347.307

ISBN 0-393-01869-5

W. W. Norton & Company, Inc., 500 Fifth Avenue, New York, N. Y. 10110
W. W. Norton & Company Ltd., 37 Great Russell Street, London WC1B 3NU

1 2 3 4 5 6 7 8 9 0

To Dylan,
who watched many of these trials with wondering young eyes
and questioned the justice of law.

# CONTENTS

We all have reasons
for moving
I move
to keep things whole

   —Mark Strand

# ACKNOWLEDGMENTS

A ll decisions are influenced by the experiences of the decision makers. Judges are no exception. Judicial beliefs and values are derived from libraries, courtrooms, and one's individual encounters with the social order. Many judges and lawyers who preceded me have struggled with the Procrustean task of equalizing justice among unequal litigants and their unequal counsel. I have been awed by the courage, intelligence, and successes of Anglo-American law. But I have also been mindful of Walter Pater's admonition to maintain a kind of candid discontent, even in the face of the highest achievements.

The titans of the past, my colleagues at the bench and bar, my own clients, and the lawyers and litigants who have appeared before me have all contributed to my education and the development of this book. I owe special debts of gratitude to several people whose endurance, encouragement, and assistance enabled me to write this book while maintaining a full case load in a very busy trial court. My husband was patient and understanding during its Gargantuan period of gestation. My daughter has been unfailingly encouraging. Susan Wallack diligently and cheerfully checked innumerable references. Andrea Vartanian Jamison uncomplainingly typed and retyped the manuscript. Evan Thomas encouraged me to undertake this book. George Brockway, my editor, has been enormously helpful in requiring me to clarify and sharpen my vision and expression. And always, I am grateful to the people of Philadelphia, who have have shown their faith in me by permitting me to serve them for many years.

# MONEY
# AND JUSTICE

# INTRODUCTION

What doth the Lord require of thee, but to do justly,
and to love mercy and to walk humbly with thy God?

—Micah VI:8

"I wrote for the common man, hoping I could help
them see the main contours and seeing them, better
understand the high vantage point we have reached with
our form of government.

—William O. Douglas

It was the case of Kevin Wallace[1] that compelled me to write this book. For many years I had been dismayed by the fact that certain cases were allocated only fifteen to twenty minutes of trial time while others were given virtually unlimited time. On this day in August 1982 I was sitting in a felony courtroom. Sixteen cases were listed to be tried or disposed of by guilty plea on that day.

Kevin Wallace was the fifth defendant. His attorney announced that Kevin wished to plead guilty to burglary. Kevin was represented by the same public defender who represented eleven other defendants. Kevin had been properly arraigned when he was arrested. He had had a preliminary hearing at which $500 bail had been set. Kevin could not raise the $50 cash required (ten percent of the bail). He had no real property to post as bail. He did not meet the criteria for release on his own recognizance. When he appeared before me, he had been in jail for five months awaiting trial. It was a hot day and the dirty courtroom was sweltering. When the ancient window air conditioner was turned on, I could not hear the witnesses. When it was off, we could scarcely breathe. The defender recited for the fifth time that morning the litany of rights that

Kevin would be relinquishing by pleading guilty. At appropriate moments, Kevin was asked, "Do you understand?" He then turned to the defender, who nodded, and Kevin replied "Yes." When the prescribed questions had been asked and answered, I turned to Kevin and asked him, "Are you pleading guilty because you are guilty?" Again he turned to the defender, who nodded to him, and Kevin uncertainly replied "Yeah."

"Did you go into that apartment with the intent to steal something?" I asked him.

Kevin answered, "No. The door was open and I seen other people coming out carrying things away. It looked like nobody lived there. So I went in. I didn't take nothin'."

Burglary is defined as the unauthorized entry into a building or portion of an occupied building with intent to commit a crime, in this case, larceny.

"I can't accept the guilty plea. You have a defense," I told him.

The police report indicated that the lock on the door to the apartment had been broken, that Kevin had no tool with which he could have broken the lock, and that he had not tried to flee. He did not have any stolen goods in his possession. The defender was dismayed.

"Your Honor, will the Court indulge me for a few minutes while I confer with my client?"

A groan went throughout the courtroom. The prosecutor, the defender, the court officers, the friends and relatives of the defendants in the other cases, and the witnesses knew that this would cause a delay. We might sit until six o'clock. The last cases on the list might not be heard at all. These other defendants would have to remain in custody until their cases could be relisted for another day, perhaps six weeks in the future. The witnesses would have to lose another day of work.

Of course, counsel should have had a long discussion with Kevin before coming to court. But the van bringing the prisoners to the courthouse from the prison had been late. It was impossible for one attorney to interview twelve defendants in the half hour between 9:00 and 9:30, when court opened.

Kevin was nineteen years old, a slim, gentle, uneducated soft-spoken black boy. He had attended a school for retarded educables until he quit in the tenth grade. When asked whether he could read and write the English language, he had replied, "Not too good." I had the court officer hand him the morning paper and asked him to read the headlines. He managed to stumble through. The whereabouts of Kevin's father were unknown. His mother was at home sick. Why couldn't I just accept the guilty plea, put him on probation, and let him go back to his job, as his mother and everyone in the courtroom wanted me to do?

If Kevin's story was true, and it appeared to be corroborated by the police report, he was not guilty. A conviction for a felony could have serious consequences for Kevin. It would be more difficult for him to get another job. If he was arrested again and was convicted or pled guilty, under a mandatory sentencing law he would have to serve a prison term. These were practical reasons that could be outweighed by the benefits of an immediate release. If I did not accept the plea, he could not be tried before me, since technically I knew matters that were hearsay and would have to be proved in court before he could be convicted. All the other judges hearing felony cases had long lists and probably could not hear Kevin's case on this day. The police officer who would have to testify had been excused from the courtroom to go back on his beat in anticipation of the guilty plea. Kevin would probably remain in custody several weeks more before he could be brought to trial. Balancing possible future harms against the present benefit of immediate release, the gut reaction of all the people in the courtroom to accept the plea was right and I knew it.

But I am a judge. Before going on the bench, I had spent years defending accused people, taking cases to the Supreme Court, arguing the supremacy of the rule of law. I had been an officer of the American Civil Liberties Union. I had taught law school. I had taken an oath to uphold, protect, and defend the Constitution. Kevin was poor, deprived, uneducated—one of the most disadvantaged people in our society. But in a court of law Kevin was supposed to be the equal of the millionaires who had appeared before me the preceding weeks. Kevin was entitled to the presumption of innocence, to a fair trial, to his day in court. I could not accept his guilty plea knowing that he had a good defense to the charge.

Three weeks later Kevin appeared before another judge, pled guilty, and was sentenced to time in. He was released that day. But he had a criminal record and a sentence of almost six months that he had already served.

During the months before Kevin's case, I had been sitting in civil court, in a clean, well-ventilated courtroom. I had heard several jury trials, each of which took approximately two weeks to try. One equity matter had taken forty-three trial days. It involved a dispute among partners who had a multimillion-dollar business. Why, I asked myself, were those litigants—who were only seeking an award of money damages—given so much court time, while Kevin Wallace and countless other persons accused of crime were accorded so little?

These cases are not unusual or anomalous. People like Kevin Wallace are rushed through trial in every city and state while wealthy individuals and corporations pursue their rights and remedies in court for weeks, months, and even years.

This problem had disturbed me during the twelve years I had been a trial judge. Every action, every decision of a judge is supposed to be in conformity with the laws and constitution of the state in which he[2] sits and of the United States Constitution. The Fourteenth Amendment provides that no state shall "deny to any person within its jurisdiction the equal protection of the laws."

Equality can be measured in many ways. Most appellate opinions examine the denial of equal rights in a complicated fashion. Is one person denied equality of treatment because of race, religion, sex, or age? Has he or she been prejudiced? Was the discrimination intentional? Can it be proved statistically? Is the classification suspect or reasonable? To me, the issue is so clear as to be simplistic. Time can easily be measured. Discrimination is proved day after day in the courts of every state. The prejudice to the litigants is undeniable. It is an apothegm, a given in American jurisprudence, and common belief, that every person is entitled to his day in court. But why should that day be so elastic that for Kevin and thousands of people like him it is a scant twenty minutes and for others it is many months? Are my colleagues and I violating the Constitution? I wondered what other judges, lawyers, and scholars thought of this epidemic problem. What were they discussing and doing to enforce equal protection of the laws?

I began to research the statutes, cases, and legal literature. Surely in more than 200 years some enterprising lawyer must have raised this issue and some court must have ruled on it. In an age of record keeping and statistics, there must be information on the length of trials and the cost to the public. In the vast legal libraries and in the more than 170 accredited law schools in the United States, scholars must have considered the question and supplied a rationale—a logical, reasoned explanation for these gross disparities in trial time.

The longer I searched, the more dissatisfied I became. In the masses of statistics, data as to the length of trial time were either ignored or expressed in terms of averages. To average Kevin Wallace's twenty minutes with the thirty-seven-day trial of John Hinckley gives grossly misleading information. I could not find an opinion of an appellate court discussing the question of equal trial time. Nor could I find any meaningful discussions by legal scholars or evidence of concern in the remarks of leaders of the bench and bar.

Many of these eminent people criticize the situation in the courts. They deplore overcrowded calendars, trial delays, the quantities of judicial opinions, and the lack of time for justices of the Supreme Court to consider adequately the difficult questions presented to them. But I could find little comment or concern for this problem—the gross disparity in trial time accorded the rich and the poor.

The president of the American Bar Association admits that the public distrusts the legal profession.[3] The chief justice of the United States declares that the judicial system is on the verge of collapse.[4] Able judges resign from the bench. Big law firms grow bigger; the cost of litigation soars. More civil claims are processed through the court system; proportionately fewer cases are tried. More defendants are accused and convicted or plead guilty. Overcrowded prisons are bursting with tried and untried prisoners. The picture presented is of a legal system that has run amok. No one relates these alarming conditions to the use of trial time. No one asks what cases are consuming the bulk of the time and energies of the judiciary or why some litigants have such a preferred status over others.

Many suggest better management as a remedy for overcrowded dockets. Most courts and many law firms have engaged professional managers. The leaders of the bench and bar urge lawyers and judges to educate the public to understand the legal system. Many courts and law firms have hired public relations personnel to improve their public image. Proposals abound to add judges, create new courts, and divert litigation to nonjudicial bodies. Alternative dispute-resolution systems handled by nonlawyers are touted as a new panacea. Studies proliferate. One reads these jeremiads and proposals with a sense of bewilderment. The lawyers, judges, political scientists, and sociologists appear to be like the proverbial blind men describing an elephant. Each is concerned with only a small part of the leviathan. Why should one individual attempt to deal with such an overwhelming problem? Why me? There are several thousand state trial judges who preside over cases similar to those I try. However, the combination of my experiences as a lawyer, a judge, and a law teacher have given me an unusual opportunity to see the legal system from many perspectives. During the twelve years I have been on the bench, I have sat on both civil and criminal cases. During the many years I was in private practice, I tried civil, criminal, probate, and domestic relations cases. As an attorney with the state and federal governments I prosecuted cases in many jurisdictions. I have appeared in courts of all levels. In the 1960s, I was attorney-in-charge of an antipoverty law office defending thousands of indigent children. In all those years, I had faith in the ability of the legal system to promote a more just and civilized society. I believed that through law and the judicial process disputes could be resolved fairly and peaceably, that the parameters of government could be properly delimited and the rights of the individual protected, that through litigation continuing adjustments necessitated by complex new technology and rapidly changing social conditions could be made while still preserving the basic principles of our Constitution.

In the 1960s, many in the legal profession shared this optimism. We thought that providing lawyers for the poor would give them equal access to the courts, that through energetic enforcement of individual and public rights society would become more just and our increasingly fragmented and hostile society would become unified. Two decades later those bright hopes have faded, despite extraordinarily rapid developments in the law.

As a result of persistent litigation by dedicated lawyers, forthright decisions by courageous judges, and actions by the Congress and many state legislatures, it is now a legal requirement that the indigent be furnished legal counsel in all serious criminal charges and in some civil cases. Those accused of crime have a new panoply of procedural rights. Children, tenants, and consumers of goods have new legal protections. Counsel who represent litigants in successful actions against the federal government are entitled to receive adequate fees from the public treasury. However, despite these newly articulated rights the legal system has become more costly and less accessible to the poor. The elaborate procedures designed for those accused of crime are essentially verbal formulae to propitiate the appellate courts but meaningless to most defendants. Civil litigation is so costly as to be a tax deductible service provided for the wealthy, rather than an entitlement for the entire population.

In 1968, the Kerner Commission declared, "To continue present policies is to make permanent the division of our country into two societies: one, largely Negro and poor, located in the central cities; the other, predominantly white and affluent, located in the suburbs and in outlying areas."[5] Thanks in large measure to the legal profession, America today is not a society of apartheid based on race. However, the legal system is divided into two separate and unequal systems of justice: one for the rich, in which the courts take limitless time to examine, ponder, consider, and deliberate over hundreds of thousands of bits of evidence and days of testimony, and hear elaborate, endless appeals and write countless learned opinions; the other for the poor, in which hasty guilty pleas and brief hearings are the rule and appeals are the exception.

I preside over both systems alternately. Most judges do not. In many communities there are separate courts or separate assignments for probate, civil, criminal, and juvenile cases. Judges often sit exclusively on one or another type of case. Judges of local courts seldom, if ever, have a lengthy trial or one in which several counsel participate. Appellate judges who write opinions for the rich and the poor do not see the litigants. They do not see either the lonely misery of the poor or the smug security of the rich surrounded by learned, deferential counsel. They do not hear the inarticulate pauses of the semiliterate or their dubious affirmations that they understand the rights they are relinquishing. Federal trial judges seldom see indigents or poor litigants or children. Such people, except for unusual class actions and cases in which counsel have raised constitutional issues, usually appear in state and local courts.

The men and women who serve on the federal, state, and local benches are not wilfully or even consciously violating the Constitution. They are simply presiding over the cases that have been assigned to them, doing the best they can with what is presented to them by counsel for the parties. American judges, unlike continental judges under civil law, cannot investigate claims or charges and present evidence. They must rely on counsel for the parties to present the evidence and make legal argument. They can rule only on the case made out by the lawyers. I, too, am bound by these strictures.

Every day that I preside as a judge, I am confronted by the drastic differences between the two systems. On one day I may have twelve or fifteen defendants like Kevin Wallace before me, all charged with felonies. Their cases are assigned to be heard in one day. If some are not reached, they will be heard at a future date by another judge with an equally long trial list. At other times I preside over civil trials, either with or without a jury, that last for weeks or months. I pore over scores—sometimes hundreds—of pieces of documentary evidence and listen to days and days of testimony and hours of legal argument. I cannot restrict the rights of wealthy civil litigants in order to give more time to poor civil litigants and criminal defendants. Nor can I compel the counsel for those people to give their clients more meaningful representation.

"Why do you take it upon yourself to criticize the system?" colleagues and lawyers ask me. "After all, you are doing your job. Every litigant who comes before you gets a fair trial in accordance with the rules. You are only one judge. You can't change the system."

A trial judge is peculiarly situated to see the shortcomings of lawyers and legal institutions, as well as failures in other occupations and professions. People come to court only when something goes wrong. Every day doctors save patients' lives, restore sight to the blind and feeling to the paralyzed. Judges do not see these patients or doctors. We see only the cases where something went wrong—the crippled patient, the motorist whose car exploded, the factory worker whose machine malfunctioned, the purchaser of a home with a leaking roof, the tenant whose apartment is unheated. We do not see the scientists who have unlocked the secrets of the atom; we see those whose drugs cause babies to be born without hands or eyes. We do not see healthy, happy children; we judges see battered babies and teenage girls who have been raped. We do not see happy couples; we see hostile, bitter husbands and battered wives. We do not see professors who are being honored by their colleagues and universities; we see those who are fired or accused of improper conduct.

Our view of contemporary society is aptly described by Murphy's Law, "Anything that can go wrong will go wrong," and Forer's supplement to that law, "What goes wrong will become a lawsuit." Whether what is faulty is a pin on a jet plane, a probation officer's report on an offender, or a senator's acceptance of a bribe, the issue will come to trial.

A trial judge sees the failures of individuals, institutions, and government every day. It is easy to become discouraged and to lose one's belief in people and government and to forget that the norm must be honorable, upright individuals, faithful government servants, responsible businesses, competent scientists, and functioning institutions, or the courts would be even more crowded than they are. I know that in my day-to-day work presiding over trials, settling civil cases, and taking guilty pleas, I cannot restructure the ancient, unwieldy institution of courts of law. But I am also mindful of Mr. Justice Cardozo's admonition. "The judge," he wrote, "is under a duty, within the limits of his power of innovation, to maintain a relation between law and morals, between the precepts of jurisprudence and those of reason and good conscience."[6] The claims of morality and good conscience lay a duty upon a judge to afford all litigants equal justice.

Even one insignificant judge who is just one replaceable cog in an enormous machine has this duty. George Ball, former under secretary of state, was quoted as saying, in discussing nuclear war, "I have no authority to speak on the moral issues."[7] I believe that every person, regardless of office, has an obligation to speak out on the moral issues that he confronts. I believe that many judges are aware that they are presiding over a legal and legitimized system of injustice. This sense of frustration and impotence is in my opinion a major, though seldom articulated, cause of much judicial dissatisfaction. It is true that many judges are overworked, underpaid, and dissatisfied with their working conditions. But most lawyers before accepting appointment to the bench or standing for election are well aware of the low pay and the volume of work. However, they are willing to accept the office because they believe, as I do, that promoting the rule of law in a just society is a challenging and worthwhile calling, far outweighing monetary compensation and leisure. Whenever I criticize any aspect of American law, I am asked accusingly, "Do you know any better system?" The truthful answer is "No." But the fact that other nations do not accord their citizens and subjects equal rights to justice does not lessen the obligation to make our legal system consonant with due process and the constitutional guarantee of equal protection of the laws.

I have written this book because I believe that the legal system can be made to function fairly and provide equal justice for all. This book is addressed to the general public who pay taxes, support the legal system, and on occasion look to it for just treatment. The views presented are my own.

There are always shortcomings in a report by a single observer. The view is, of necessity, limited. It may be skewed by bias or prejudice or simply the narrowness of the individual's experience and vision. Difficult philosophical as well as semantical problems inhere in any discussion of justice and the role of courts in a jural society. This presentation would doubtless have benefited from discussions with philosophers and jurisprudentialists. Judges, however, do not have sabbatical leaves. We do not have research staffs. Most foundations and think tanks exclude public employees from participation,[8] although both the employees and the public might well benefit from a broader view of pertinent issues. The urgent need to examine the fairness of our present court system militates against delay in order to obtain a more leisured, multifaceted view. I hope that the immediacy of my experience will compensate for these deficiencies.

Much important statistical information is lacking. I have been forced to rely on studies by others and on federal and state government statistics. The federal government compiles information only for the federal courts. The record keeping of the several state judicial systems is not uniform or complete. In using such statistics one must attempt to correlate what are essentially disparate, noncomparable data. Although the United States government analyzed over 2,061,000 records in 1982,[9] information is lacking in many important areas. I have neither the time nor the resources to engage in national court-data gathering. It is my hope that this book will prompt others in government, academia, and private agencies to undertake this needed research.

I am moved to write because I believe strongly that the rule of law is essential to the maintenance of a democratic form of government and the freedom of the individual and that the Constitution provides enduring, valid, and fundamental principles of law. Most reluctantly, I have concluded that the members of the legal profession—lawyers, scholars, and judges—are too bemused and overwhelmed by day-to-day problems and adherence to increasingly complicated procedural rules to examine what is happening in the routine operation of the courts. Even though many criticize the high cost of legal fees and the inadequacy of legal services for the poor, they do not recognize the substantial injustice and inequality of the litigational process and the use of the courts.

To criticize one's chosen profession, to which a lifetime of labor has been devoted, is not an easy or pleasant task. I do so with misgivings. "Silence gives consent" is an old legal maxim. Since I do not consent to the continuance of the gross disparities in the "day in court" accorded to litigants, I am impelled to write this book.

# CHAPTER I

---

# THE PROBLEM

Justice shall not be rationed.
—Judge Learned Hand.

Equality is the Mother of Justice.
—Philo

W ho owns the courts?"—the question this book asks—raises not only legal but also moral, political, and philosophical issues. Although the question is grounded in the practices of lawyers and judges, it is a matter of public importance that should not be relegated to the legal profession. Every person residing in the United States pays taxes that support and maintain the courts. Every person accused of crime or delinquency must look to the courts to preserve his liberty. Every person who is aggrieved by government or private parties must ultimately look to the courts for redress. The public as a whole relies on the courts to decide public and private disputes fairly, according to law. If the courts are not available equally to all, then the fundamental basis of our jural society is seriously flawed.

It is the thesis of this book that American courts are not equally open and available to all who have legal claims and defenses—that there is turnstile justice for the poor and lengthy trials and appeals for those who can afford to pay for lawyers, investigation, expert witnesses, and documentary and physical evidence. This situation is not the result of intentional or even conscious decisions by the legislatures or the courts. John

K. Galbraith, discussing America's economic problems, observed that they did not arise by calculation. "We are," he writes, "far more in the grip of the undesigned dynamic of a great organization. . . ."[1] American courts are also in the grip of the undesigned dynamic of the legal system. Our legal system's ancestry can be traced back some 800 years. Many of the practices prevalent today long antedate the Constitution of the United States and the egalitarian principles that influenced the Founding Fathers. Until the twentieth century, Anglo-American civil courts dealt principally with property rights. There was little concern for intangible rights and injuries or for the problems of people who had no property. In criminal courts poor defendants were tried, convicted, sentenced, and executed without representation by counsel. Under this centuries-old system, the courts were in the main available only to those who could afford to use them. The declaration of Magna Carta in 1215, "We will sell to no man, we will not deny or defer to any man either justice or right," was a startling conceptual advance. As a practical matter, it was of little assistance to the medieval Englishman and his descendants.

Legal services for the poor are a contemporary innovation grafted on to a litigational structure that was not designed to accommodate or protect such litigants. The first legal aid society in the United States was established in 1876. Counsel for the poor has been provided meagerly, as an act of charity rather than a legal or constitutional right. Even in the 1980s congressional debates over funding of legal services for the poor seldom address the underlying question: whether justice is a commodity, to be bought and sold at the market price, or a constitutional right.

Americans are accustomed to paying for goods and services. There is a rough correspondence between the price and the value of commodities and services purchased. We expect a Rolls-Royce to be a better car than a secondhand Ford. No one seriously suggests that any moral or legal problem arises from the fact only a few people can buy a Rolls-Royce, that many can buy a secondhand Ford, and that some people cannot afford any car. Food and housing, like all other commodities, are also manifestly unevenly distributed. A few people can dine at the Four Seasons; many at McDonald's; and some must rely upon food stamps and soup kitchens. We accept with little question disparities in the availability of luxuries and amenities. Many people are uneasy when a significant segment of the population is denied necessities; but they view their concern not in terms of constitutional rights but rather as a humane, compassionate act of charity.

Although Americans have shown a greater awareness of the needs of the public for adequate health care than for access to justice, there is an unwillingness to confront the question of whether health care is a right or only a moral obligation, to be met by charity. The President's Commission for the Study of Ethical Problems in Medicine and Biomedical and Behavioral Research reported that society has an "ethical obligation to insure equitable access to health care." However, the commission ignored the question of access to health care as a "right" and concluded that "equity does not require equal access" to health services.[2]

When confronting inequality in the litigational system, Americans have customarily taken the soup kitchen approach. As an act of grace or charity, we provide minimal legal services for the truly indigent who meet a means test. To date no presidential commission or other high-level group has examined either the ethical or the constitutional problems inherent in the unequal access to justice.

Justice cannot be classified with food and shelter as a necessary of life. The vast majority of people in the world today and almost all people throughout history have been denied what Americans consider justice and due process of law. For all these people—past and present—accusation of wrongdoing has been tantamount to conviction. The penalties inflicted have been—and in many nations today, are—Draconian: death, torture, mutilation, forced labor camps, and exile to penal colonies. For them there is no redress against government oppression or misconduct. There is little governmentally enforceable redress for private wrongs and the enforcement of private rights. It is expected that the rich and powerful will receive preferential treatment and that the claims of the poor and friendless will be given short shrift.

How should Americans view the individual's claim to equal justice under law? Is it a constitutional right or entitlement? Is it a privilege for which one must pay? Is it the obligation of government to provide counsel for all who have legal claims and defenses? These questions are rarely asked, although the legal and moral issues have been implicit in our litigational system since colonial times.

Many factors have combined synergistically to create a crisis in the
courts in the 1980s. During the preceding three decades the numbers
of cases in all level of courts have increased dramatically, leading to what
is popularly called the litigation explosion. In part this was due to the
rising crime rate, which necessitated more criminal prosecutions. On the
civil side, new technology has taken an enormous toll in illnesses and
accidents, substantially increasing the number of claims. The civil rights
movement, the women's movement, the consumer movement, growing
interest in protecting the environment, and the rising demands from all
segments of society for protection of rights and redress for wrongs,
coupled with the availability of legal services for the poor, prompted tens
of thousands of people to litigate who had never before sought satisfaction from the courts. Government was also active in enforcing old
regulatory laws and many new statutes. At the same time some industries
and organizations resisted such regulations, forcing government to turn
to the courts for sanctions, thus occasioning many long, complex, bitterly fought cases. In the federal courts alone between 1960 and 1980
there was a 110.6 percent increase in criminal cases and a 184.7 percent
increase in civil cases.[3] Although there are no national statistics for state
court litigation, the increase in numbers of cases in the state courts have
been substantially greater. In New York City, for example, there was a
42 percent increase in the number of indictments filed in 1982 as
compared with 1980.

During these decades pretrial, trial, posttrial, and appeal procedures
in both civil and criminal cases have become far more complex, time-
consuming, and expensive. Many questions brought before the courts
are novel and difficult, requiring painstaking analysis and deliberation.
There are more appeals because the law is unsettled. Courts have to deal
with unprecedented problems involving schools, prisons, and hospitals
and monitor compliance over long periods of time. All these new demands on the courts are time-consuming.

In order to cope with the unprecedented volume of cases, courts and
lawyers have had to devise short cuts. In many criminal courts, at least
90 percent of the accused plead guilty. In civil courts judges spend a
large part of their time persuading, and sometimes coercing, parties to
settle rather than litigate their disputes. In family courts and minor
criminal courts there has been an acceleration of the trial process. Some
judges hear and decide more than a hundred cases a day. The victims

of this speedy justice are, for the most part, poor.

It must be remembered that in the United States poverty is not equally distributed among the population. There are race, gender, and age biases. Unemployment among black Americans is double the figure for whites. In some areas it is 40 percent for young black males. Of black Americans, 34 percent live in dire poverty.[4] Women are also disproportionately poor. They earn, over a lifetime on the average, less than 50 percent of the income of men. The poor, female-headed family is no longer a phenomenon but a statistic. The children of these women are abjectly poor. Almost half the children of divorce do not receive their full amount of court-ordered support. More than a fourth do not receive any support. The plight of the elderly is also well known. When poor people are denied equal access to justice in America there is inevitably discrimination against nonwhites, women, the elderly, and children. Poor people of all races and ages and both sexes do have legal problems. Poor black youths are arrested for criminal offenses disproportionately to their numbers in the population. Almost half the 400,000 prisoners in the United States are black.[5] Family courts are filled with poor children.

If discrimination in the use of the legal system were overtly based on race, the courts would have little difficulty in finding the practices unconstitutional. If the discrimination were based on age or gender, there is a good probability that these practices might be declared unconstitutional. However, the Supreme Court has held that wealth and economic status are not a "suspect classification" raising constitutional issues of discriminatory treatment in the context of equal educational facilities.[6]

Equal access to justice cannot be equated with the right to jobs, education, housing, and health care, important though they are. Equal justice is the foundation of our polity. Belief in the rule of law has been called the secular religion of the United States.[7] Despite crime waves, public corruption, unpopular wars, and a host of ills that have beset the United States, the American people have not faltered in their commitment to a government based on the concept of equal justice. But the crisis situation in American courts is betraying that faith.

Criticism of the courts is widespread. The press publishes accounts of "speedy justice," courts in disarray, and their manifest failures. Leaders of the bench and bar attack the entire legal system. They see, as I do, overcrowded courts, a costly, time-consuming method of litigation, numerous wealthy lawyers, and practices that favor the rich over the poor. The focus of their complaints is not the denial of equal justice but the legal system itself. They do not view the increased volume of cases as evidence of the vitality of the rule of law and the capacity of the courts to meet the challenges of enunciating new rights and devising new remedies for classes of people heretofore excluded from the protections of the law. Instead they charge the American people with being unduly litigious and accuse lawyers of obstructing justice.

The complaints are stated apodictically. Since the accusers are among the most successful and prominent persons in the legal profession, these charges must be examined. Chief Justice Warren Burger declares that the nation is plagued "with an almost irrational focus—virtually a mania —on litigation as a way to solve all problems." Derek Bok, president of Harvard University and former dean of the Harvard Law School, suddenly announced in 1983 that the United States has "developed a legal system that is the most expensive in the world yet cannot manage to protect the rights of most its citizens." He further states that Japan graduates 30 percent more engineers than the United States but "Japan *boasts* a total of less than 15,000 lawyers while American universities graduate 35,000 lawyers every year." (Emphasis supplied.) He also asserts that American lawyers contribute to "a stifling burden of regulations, delays, and legal uncertainties that can inhibit progress and allow unscrupulous parties to misuse the law and manipulate their victims." Lloyd N. Cutler, one of Washington's wealthiest and most prominent lawyers, writes: "The rich who pay our fees are less than 1 percent of our fellow citizens, but they get at least 95 percent of our time. The disadvantaged we serve for nothing are perhaps 20 to 25 percent of the population and get at most 5 percent of our time. The remaining 75 percent cannot afford to consult us and get virtually none of our time." All these statements appeared on the front page of the *New York Times*, [8] and have been reprinted in papers across the nation.

A casual reader of these bitter criticisms might well conclude that lawyers are the sole cause of a costly, burdensome, overly legalistic society. In the same issue of the *New York Times* (the first section of the paper, consisting of twenty-four pages) there are eleven other articles dealing with courts and court cases, all of which are newsworthy.[9] As every observer of American life from De Tocqueville to the present time has noted, law and court decisions play a crucial role in American life. The centrality of law long antedated the litigation explosion and the enormous increase in the number of lawyers. The cases reported by the *New York Times* on that one day reveal that American courts are protecting the rights of individuals and the public in many important matters. Significantly, some of these cases could not have been brought in Japan or any other nation. Among the items reported are redress for a wrongful conviction, prosecution of fraudulent researchers, and an action against the national government for wrongful conduct. Such actions and remedies are among the cherished glories of the American legal system. It must be remembered that when an accident occurs in Japan the president of the negligent company promptly apologizes to the victims of the accident and pays compensation without the necessity for each victim to file suit.[10]

During the 1960s and 1970s, litigation was initiated on behalf of the poor, the disadvantaged, and consumers. Funds were made available for legal services. Whole new classes of litigants were brought into court to seek new redress for old wrongs. A new generation of students rushed to law school and the schools rapidly expanded their student bodies and faculties and raised their tuition charges. However, the core curriculum of the law schools remained the traditional courses dealing with property rights. The aim of the law schools and their professors was, as it had been for decades, to train the brightest and the best to staff the ever-expanding elite law firms that steadily raised their fees and symbiotically served their wealthy clients. So long as litigation was lucrative, there was no incentive to cut either expenses or time-consuming procedures. In the mid-1980s, law firms, large and small, are finding that their clients are reluctant to pay large fees. Funding of legal services for the poor has been drastically slashed. There are many fewer jobs for law school graduates. It is against this background that the accusations against the legal system should be examined.

It is true that the American system of litigation is expensive. I believe that the cost and length of trials could be drastically reduced in many cases without impairing the rights of the parties. A reduction of time-consuming and expensive procedures will of necessity result in much lower counsel fees. It is not true that the American legal system does not protect the rights of most of its citizens. The rights of more Americans have been better protected by the law in the last half of the twentieth century than at any time in the history of the nation, despite many recent cutbacks on those protections.

It is true that the leading law firms devote at least 95 percent of their time to the wealthiest 5 percent of the population. But this is a matter of their choice. There is no law prohibiting them from representing less affluent clients for more modest fees. Indeed, it might be good business and good public relations for them to do so. It is doubtful that these law firms serve 25 percent or any appreciable number of indigent clients. They have done little, if anything, to represent those who have lost legal representation as a result of substantial cuts in funding for legal services.

Invidious comparisons of the American legal system with those of other countries without analyzing the social and corporate ethos of those countries is not helpful. It is more fruitful to compare the history of suffrage in the United States with the history of the equal protection clause. Both the right to vote and the right to equal protection of the laws are peculiarly American constitutional rights. Although most people in the world manage to live or subsist without either court-administered justice or the vote, both are integral to the maintenance of our form of government.

The drafters of the Constitution did not define suffrage. James Madison, however, explicitly stated his view of the nature of the electorate in the *Federalist* papers.

Who are to be the electors of the Federal Representatives? Not the rich more than the poor; not the learned more than the ignorant; not the haughty heirs of distinguished names more than the humble sons of obscurity and unpropitious fortune. The electors are to be the great body of the people of the United States.

It took almost two centuries to implement and enforce Madison's definition of the electorate. When this nation was founded only properties white males were permitted to vote. After the Civil War, racial restrictions were removed by the Fifteenth Amendment. Male sex as a voting qualification was not eliminated until the Nineteenth Amendment was ratified in 1920. Property restrictions were limited by court decision in 1969.[11] And literacy requirements (thinly disguised racial and ethnic barriers to voting) were at last abolished by the Voting Rights Act of 1965.[12] Gerrymandering was dealt a death blow by the United States Supreme Court in the famous "one person, one vote" decision in 1969.[13]

Equal protection of the laws was incorporated into the Constitution by the Fourteenth Amendment in 1868. Its ramifications (beyond blatant racial discrimination) have been only minimally explored by the courts. Denial of equal protection of the laws is less easy to discern and to remedy than denial of the franchise. Statutory restrictions on the right to vote are explicit. A violation of the right to vote can be remedied by declaring the offending statute unconstitutional on its face or as applied. Use of eligibility tests, inequitably structured voting districts, and other methods of depriving classes of people of the franchise or diluting their vote have been more difficult to prove and to eliminate. However, the knowledge of these limitations and restrictions on the franchise is widespread. They are susceptible of statistical proof. Effective remedies have been instituted by wise courts.

Denial of equal protection of the laws in the use of the courts is more obscure and subtle. It occurs in tens of thousands of unreported cases occurring each year. There is no single day on which the results of these practices are made known. The individuals whose rights are systematically denied are often only vaguely aware of the injustices done them. They cannot point to a specific statute, rule, or regulation that is the source of the denial of their rights. There is no identifiable class of litigants on whose behalf an action can be brought testing a precise, defined practice.

Even many lawyers and judges labor under misconceptions as to the nature and extent of the denial of equal protection in the courts. Some assert that the truly indigent receive not only adequate legal services but treatment superior to that of the working poor. This specious argument that the indigent receive better services is also advanced in other contexts: health, education, social services, and housing. Such an unfounded belief may assuage the consciences of the well-to-do. It also polarizes the rights of two classes of people who may both be denied equal access to many services as well as equal protection of the laws.

The competence of lawyers for the poor is only a peripheral issue, although whenever separate programs are established for underprivileged or vulnerable persons, those programs tend to be not only separate but unequal. The basic problem is that most poor people simply do not receive a due process trial in either civil or criminal courts.[14]

In civil matters, many who cannot afford the high costs of litigation simply forego their rights. Nonaffluent and poor people do utilize legal services for many civil actions when those services are available. For example, Mobilization for Youth, a legal services office in New York City with twenty-six lawyers and six paralegals, handled 5,700 civil cases in 1982. Obviously few, if any, of these clients could have had lengthy jury trials or appeals. Their cases involved significant matters such as evictions, eligibility for welfare, veterans' and social security benefits, consumer frauds, family assistance, and immigration matters.[15] Even the most brilliant lawyer would have great difficulty in handling competently more than 200 cases a year. But these clients were among the more fortunate. People with similar problems who lacked access to legal services had no remedies.

Although adequate statistics are not available, the average trial time in both civil and criminal matters is less than two hours.[16] Averages do not reveal disparities. Included in this two-hour average are quick guilty pleas, hasty bench trials, and jury trials lasting months. If one examines actual practices, not statistics, it is apparent that most people receive far less than two hours of trial time. In some misdemeanor courts more than 100 cases a day are heard by one judge.[17]

In many trial courts ten or twelve felony cases are heard and decided in one day by one judge. At issue is guilt or innocence, imprisonment or liberty. Forty or more civil cases involving small sums of money are routinely heard and decided in one day.

Most juvenile court judges hear the cases of some thirty-five children in a day. The results of these hearings may be the removal of a child from his home, family, and school and placement in a foster home or juvenile jail. The President's Commission on Law Enforcement and Administration of Justice aptly described the proceedings in juvenile court as the "five-minute children's hour."[18]

A trial day is not eight hours. If all attorneys, litigants and witnesses appear on time, trial may commence at 9:30. More often trials do not begin until 10:00. With an hour for lunch and one break of ten or fifteen minutes in the morning and another break in the afternoon, there are barely five hours of trial time per day, if the court sits until 4:30. Many courts adjourn at 4:00 or earlier.

As every reader of the daily press knows, notorious and wealthy defendants have trials lasting many weeks. The trial of John Hinckley, who shot President Reagan, took seven weeks. He was found not guilty by reason of insanity. The trial of the art dealers who were executors of the estate of Mark Rothko lasted eight months. They were found to have breached their fiduciary duties. Frequently more than a week of court time is used simply to select a jury. In the trial of Jean Harris, who was convicted of killing a Scarsdale diet doctor, 550 potential jurors were questioned over a period of three weeks. Less-publicized trials involving vast sums of money are tried for many months and even years. The IBM antitrust case lasted 672 trial days; the American Cyanamid case dragged on for fourteen years.[19] These cases are not run-of-the-mill, but they are not anomalous. Many other cases consume weeks and months of trial time.

Although there are no national statistics on the use of trial court time, certain facts are reliably documented. These figures show that in the past few years more cases are being brought in all courts. Even though the numbers of judges have been increased, there are more cases filed per judge than a decade ago. During this same period, the number of lengthy cases has increased significantly. The federal courts report that in fiscal 1971–72 only 59 of 18,780 completed trials lasted more than twenty court days. In 1982, 164 trials lasted more than twenty court days. The reports do not list the actual number of court days these 164 cases consumed, but taking into account those cases lasting several months, the number of court days utilized by a very small group of litigants is grossly disproportionate to the amount of trial time accorded to the vast majority of litigants.

One cannot draw an absolute correlation between trial time and the quality of justice. No researcher can determine whether a verdict was right or wrong. There are too many variables. Was the judge or jury governed by passion or prejudice? Were they unduly influenced by the eloquence or incompetence of counsel? Did the juries understand the judge's charge? Did they remember and properly evaluate the evidence? No one will ever know whether all the pertinent evidence was presented or whether crucial witnesses lied. Even under optimal conditions of unlimited funds and equally skilled counsel for both parties, and a learned, impartial judge, no one can know whether a just result was reached. But clearly there is a higher probability of a proper verdict under those conditions than in the hasty trials and guilty pleas that are the justice accorded most litigants.

Trial time is not a complete measure of the amount of judicial time accorded to litigants. It does not include the judge's time to consider and decide countless pretrial and posttrial motions, to read voluminous briefs that are routinely filed in lengthy cases, to hear oral arguments, and to write opinions. In the vast majority of civil and criminal cases arguments are cursory; few briefs are filed; opinions are rarely written. Only a very tiny fraction of cases are appealed. An appeal is expensive. For most litigants their justice is the trial verdict. Significantly, in those federal cases in which an appeal is taken and heard, almost one-third are reversed.

Although it is difficult, if not impossible, to quantify justice, court time and money are easily measured. A trial in most jurisdictions costs approximately $1,500 a day; a jury trial approximately $300 a day more.[20]

Simple arithmetic reveals that a thirty-day jury trial costs the public a minimum of $54,000. A one-hour bench trial about $250; a twenty-minute guilty plea approximately $75; and a juvenile hearing less than $50.

Who has decided that certain defendants are entitled to vastly more court time, paid for by the taxpayers, than most other people accused of crime? Who has decided that a dispute over money between corporations is entitled to several hundred times more court time than a case affecting the life of a child? No one. Neither the legislatures nor the courts have considered these questions.

It may seem astonishing to nonlawyers that a problem so basic to the administration of justice and affecting so many people has not been litigated and decided by the United States Supreme Court. In more than 200 years, American appellate courts have issued tens of thousands of opinions on a host of questions. Some are of great public importance. Others involve only the rights of the particular litigants.

Both the discriminatory, unequal, and unfair use of court time and the aleatory choice of issues decided by the appellate courts arise from decisions involved in bringing or defending a lawsuit and defending a criminal charge. These decisions are made by the litigant and his lawyer. Unless a case is patently frivolous, the judge cannot dismiss it. If the litigants refuse to settle their dispute, the judge must hear the case, no matter how insignificant the issues are. Although legal scholars devote much of their time to analyzing important legal issues, they rarely try cases, and they have little input in deciding which cases should be brought and which decisions should be appealed.

The factors involved in the decision to sue, to defend, or to appeal are, for the most part, economic. The plaintiff must decide whether he can afford the costs of litigation. He must calculate whether the likelihood of success is sufficient to justify the costs. Is settlement of a civil claim for a lesser sum more advantageous? Similarly, defendants in civil suits weigh the costs of a successful defense in time, money, and energy. These costs include those for investigation and expert witnesses as well as counsel fees. This is inherent in the nature of the adversarial system. Professor Alan Stone of Harvard explains when IBM is sued in an antitrust case, IBM's lawyers find an economist who will defend IBM's practices, using the very best economic arguments he or she can muster. The other side will hire an economist to attack, using the very best counterarguments.[21] Experts are used in civil and criminal trials whenever the litigants can afford them.

Those accused of crime must also weigh the costs in money, time, and emotional involvement of even a probably successful defense and compare them with the certain results of a cheap, quick guilty plea. Pride, reputation, and other intangibles may influence these decisions. But importance of the legal issue involved is rarely a significant or controlling consideration. The single most crucial factor is cost.

Even those defendants represented by a legal services attorney or public defender must consider the economics of litigation. If an accused proceeds to trial, he must take time off from work to come to court. Usually those defendants who are employed are paid on a daily or hourly basis. If they do not work, they are not paid. All litigants, whether employed or on welfare, have to pay carfare to come to court. Mothers have to find baby-sitters. Women often are caretakers for sick or elderly relatives and have to hire substitutes. A case is rarely heard the first time it is listed. A litigant or an accused may have to come to court four or five times before his case is tried. Although the hearing may take only a half hour, he will probably have to spend the better part of the day in court waiting for the case to be called. For poor people all these small expenses weigh heavily in the decision to embark on the uncertain seas of litigation.

Once the decision has been made to go to trial, regardless of the importance or unimportance of the legal issues involved, the cases will be tried, settled, or disposed of on a one-by-one basis roughly in the order in which the suits are filed or the accused are arrested.

Court administrators and administrative judges who assign cases for trial do not make a conscious decision as to the allocation of court time according to any scale of values or principles of law. They do not know the issues involved. They simply know the amount of time counsel estimates for the case. Like highway engineers, they direct the flow of traffic. The number of cars on the highway is determined by decisions beyond the control of the traffic engineers. The length of trial time is likewise beyond the control of court administrators.

Anglo-American legal practice, developed over hundreds of years, has left to the discretion of the parties and their attorneys major decisions affecting the use of court time. These include the choice of jury or bench trial, the number of witnesses called, the extent of examination and cross-examination, and the presentation of evidence. The lawyer's choices in these matters are in large part dictated by his client's ability to pay for these services.

Some long trials that consume a substantial amount of trial time involve issues that are important to the development of the law and to large numbers of people with similar problems. But many do not. The judge has little, if any, control over these decisions. A judge may urge, coerce, or shame parties into settling cases that involve small sums and trivial problems. But a judge cannot compel litigants and their lawyers to try cases they wish to settle or withdraw. Nor, except for patently frivolous claims or abusive tactics, can a judge limit trial time. So long as the litigant can afford to pay for expert witnesses who present reasonably germane evidence, the trial court must permit them to testify and be cross-examined.

Conversely, trial judges cannot compel litigants to present evidence. Judges can and sometimes do raise legal issues ignored by counsel. But the practice is frowned upon. Implicit in many brief trials are significant unresolved legal issues that are not elucidated or brought before appellate courts.

The decision to appeal, like the decision to proceed to trial, is in large measure controlled by the client's ability to pay. Unless an organization such as the Sierra Club, Ralph Nader's group, the American Civil Liberties Union, or some local organization is willing to finance an appeal, many important legal and social issues simply are not brought to appellate courts, even though an authoritative decision would clarify the rights of countless people with similar problems and avoid much repetitive litigation. If the law is clear, few litigants or attorneys will waste time and money bringing lawsuits that cannot succeed or present defenses that have been held to be without merit.

On a few notable occasions the United States Supreme Court has agreed to hear a case raising a significant issue that had not previously been considered and has appointed a distinguished attorney to represent the litigant.[22] In this way development of important legal principles has been achieved. But in most instances, the growth and development of the law is dependent upon the economic ability of the litigants to obtain skilled and diligent counsel and to pursue the time-consuming, expensive investigation, pretrial procedures, trial, posttrial arguments, and briefs and appeals.

A distinguished, successful lawyer commented, "In our system of justice there are advantages that the one with greater resources is going to have—more lawyers, better lawyers, a larger staff."[23] Obviously, courts cannot control the selection of attorneys, the counsel fees charged, the number and choice of expert witnesses, the amount and quality of research, and all the elements that litigants pay for in order to win a case. But courts can and should control the allocation of court time, which is paid for by the public, to enforce the guarantee of equal protection of the laws.

Equal protection of the laws does not mean that every litigant is entitled to the same amount of trial time. Equality cannot be measured in minutes nor can it be measured by the reputation of counsel or the amount of the fee paid to counsel. Famous lawyers have ignominiously lost cases for which they were paid enormous fees. Patty Hearst was represented by F. Lee Bailey, one of the best-known trial lawyers. She went to prison. The *Washington Post*, represented by Irving Younger, a highly paid lawyer, former judge, and professor of trial techniques, lost a most important libel case. Under the adversary method of trial some parties will win and others will lose even though they have highly skilled, well-paid counsel and adequate support services. There can be no fool-proof guarantee that under any human system of law a just result will be obtained.[24] What can be ensured is that every party with a claim or defense receives an adequate due-process hearing in a court of law.

# CHAPTER II

---

# THE VALUES OF LITIGATION

> We have, we should be aware, 34 million members of
> minority groups whose civil rights have not been and
> must be fully respected. That calls for a combination of
> effective law and good will. In the absence of both of
> these elements, we can only expect chaos.
>
> —Chief Justice Earl Warren

Not even the harshest critics of the legal system have suggested doing away with all courts and all lawyers. Rather they seek to substitute other mechanisms, such as medication, conciliation, and arbitration, in which lawyers would not be needed, as means of saving money and reducing the volume of cases in the courts, which they believe will soon become unmanageable. By extrapolating from recent increases in litigation, incredible numbers of cases are presented as inevitably occurring in the near future. One professor predicts that federal appellate courts alone will decide a million cases a year in the twenty-first century.[1] Such a figure is unthinkable. It would mean, judging by present rates of appeal, that more than five million cases would be tried and decided in the federal courts and at least fifty million cases in the state courts.

If even a quarter this number of cases were heard, the cost of courthouses, judges, and supporting personnel would rival the budget of the Pentagon. Instead of 600,000 lawyers, we would need several million. Lawyers and judges could not possibly read such quantities of opinions. Each judge would be ignorant of the decisions of fellow judges and thus unable to follow precedent. Each judge would be a law unto himself. Such a multiplicity of judges and opinions would lead to legal anarchy. If America did, in fact, face such a problem, drastic means to limit access to the courts would be necessary.

Before adopting or even seriously considering proposals to limit access to the courts and create substitute forums for resolving disputes, caution is needed. The predictions may be false. A careful reading of court statistics discloses that the increase in the volume of litigation over the past decade has leveled off. Since 1980, the number of cases has in fact declined. The percentage change in the number of civil filings in all federal district courts from 1960 to 1981 was an increase of 204.6 percent.[2] Extrapolating from that gross figure could suggest an exponential increase in the volume of cases. However, the increase from 1980 to 1981 was only 7 percent in overall case filings. Only 1.4 percent more civil cases were pending at the end of 1981 than at the end of 1980. Criminal cases in 1981 were 28 percent below the number filed in 1975. This does not look like a litigation explosion. When one removes from that figure prisoner petitions and bankruptcies the picture is markedly different. In 1981, prisoner petitions were 1,172.7 percent over the figure in 1960. Bankruptcies increased from 182,869 in 1970 to 519,063 in 1981. Bankruptcies, of course, are not the result of litigiousness but of economic conditions beyond the control of the courts. Prisoner petitions will undoubtedly decline as prisons are compelled to obey court orders ending unconstitutional conditions of confinement.

Civil cases comprise only about half the court case load. Criminal cases are probably as time-consuming as civil cases. Until someone discovers a way to prevent or prohibit crime, there is nothing courts can do to reduce the number of criminal cases. However, the crime wave of the 1970s appears to have peaked. The number of reported crimes in 1982 was less than that in 1981. If demographic factors are significant, as many believe, the decrease in the number of males between eighteen and twenty-five will result in a substantial decline in the crime rate.

Both police and prosecutors have some discretion in the prosecution of crimes. Sensible police officers often ignore technical and minor violations of law. In some cities half the juveniles apprehended are given a stern lecture and released to their parents at the police station. Many times drunks and vagrants are locked up for the night, given a shower and breakfast, and released. Wise prosecutors also drop charges when no harm has been done and the offense is not serious. If this rule of reason did not prevail in most jurisdictions, court congestion would be far greater. Sometimes, however, an ambitious prosecutor eager for headlines and political advancement insists on prosecuting every case and demanding maximum penalties. Occasionally a prosecutor maintains that he is required to prosecute every complaint, no matter how trivial. When that happens the fragile system collapses. Serious cases are delayed; the prisons bulge with untried defendants; important cases are lost because of inadequate preparation. Finally, the image of a tough prosecutor having been projected, the old practices are quietly resumed.

A recent trivial case illustrates the folly and expense of rigid adherence to the concept that every reported offense must be prosecuted. The alleged theft of $2 worth of bologna from a Fort Knox, Kentucky, army kitchen was given a full-scale jury trial with experts on both sides testifying as to the value of the bologna. The defendant was acquitted after a one-day trial. Court records showed that the government paid at least $750 in jury fees for the trial. There were also the cost of the salaries of the United States magistrate and the assistant United States attorney who tried the case, the court reporter, an army lieutenant colonel, a sergeant, a military police investigator, a food service processor who testified, and a probation officer who prepared a presentence report to be used if the defendant was convicted.[3]

Although the legislatures can decriminalize certain offenses such as possession of marijuana, prostitution, and vagrancy, it is clear that homicide, arson, rape, aggravated assault, and other dangerous acts must be outlawed. When such crimes are committed, they must be prosecuted. Although prosecutors can reduce the flow of cases to some extent by refusing to prosecute trivial cases, the bulk of the criminal court load involves charges that cannot be ignored. Even with the maximum responsible exercise of prosecutorial discretion, the number of criminal cases cannot be significantly reduced by the legal system. The criminal calendar is dependent upon the crime rate and the efficacy of the police in making arrests.

The number of civil cases in the courts is, however, within the control of litigants and their lawyers. It is also affected by statutes and court decisions. The volume of litigation that may be generated is seldom a conscious or determining factor in the enactment of statutes. Legislators perceive a problem and seek to provide a remedy. Courts are presented with cases involving the rights of parties that must be decided without reference to the probable increase or decrease in litigation, although occasionally in enunciating new doctrine the courts will provide that it shall be applied only prospectively in order to avoid retrial of many cases.

Constitutional requirements and the needs of justice properly take precedence over the problems of court calendars. Prisoner filings, the category of cases showing the greatest increase in the federal courts, resulted from a series of Supreme Court decisions. These cases illustrate important social benefits of litigation that transcend the problems and rights of the individual litigants. For two centuries American courts had paid little attention to conditions in state jails and prisons. When in 1969 the Supreme Court held that state prisoners were entitled to assistance in preparing petitions,[4] they began to assert rights to decent conditions of confinement. These cases revealed that prisoners were often denied medical attention,[5] given inadequate diet, and subjected to barbaric disciplinary measures, including long periods of solitary confinement. The forcible use of drugs on children in custody[6] and the use of permanently disabling drugs on adults in mental institutions[7] have been restricted as a result of litigation on behalf of inmates.

Effective litigation resulting in court decisions prohibiting widespread illegal practices may actually reduce litigation in the long run by eliminating grievances giving rise to lawsuits.

Prisoner petitions have unquestionably benefited all prisoners. In 1983, there were at least a half million incarcerated adults and children either serving sentences or awaiting trial. If the trends and practices continue, there will be even more prisoners in the years to come. The rights of these people are important to them and their families. The maintenance of decent, humane institutions is also important to society as a whole. Americans are rightly appalled by reports of conditions in Soviet gulags. We reject the thought that we, too, may have barbaric prisons. But they existed until the conditions were exposed through litigation and abolished by court order. A federal judge described conditions in 1972 in the women's unit of a state prison where seven or eight women gave birth each year. He wrote: "The delivery table has no restraints, paint is peeling from the ceiling above it, and large segments of the linoleum floor around the table are missing. There are no facilities to resuscitate the newborn or otherwise provide adequate care should such complications arise during delivery."[8] Only energetic litigation and forthright judicial decisions brought about changes in prisons and other institutions.

Civil litigation has also been instrumental in improving the environment, promoting safety, and protecting consumers from a wide variety of daily hazards. It was a lawsuit that compelled the Reserve Mining Company to stop dumping asbestos waste into Lake Superior and to pay for filtering the water used by the residents of Duluth, Minnesota.[9] The flood of suits against the asbestos mining and manufacturing companies, by workmen injured and dying from exposure to asbestos and by the relatives of those already dead, has forced the discontinuance of the use of asbestos in ships, school buildings, office buildings, and many other places. Litigation or the fear of litigation has compelled auto manufacturers to recall thousands of defective machines that could have caused injury or death to the drivers and passengers, other motorists, and pedestrians. Had these cars not been recalled, the ensuing accidents would have given rise to many cases brought by car owners and victims of accidents. Experience has shown that when litigation becomes sufficiently costly, industry revises its practices and improves its products. Litigation is the spur to an enlightened corporate conscience.

Similarly, malpractice suits against doctors, lawyers, architects, and other professionals have brought about improvements in their practices and ethical standards. Doctors no longer quietly bury their mistakes. Despite the outraged cries of the medical profession and the filing of some patently unwarranted lawsuits, it is clear that the cause of most medical malpractice suits is medical malpractice. Since self-discipline within the profession failed to halt outrageous incompetence and carelessness, litigation was the only alternative. The ineffectiveness of self-discipline is revealed by a report of the New York State Department of Health and the Board of Regents in 1983 that described a number of cases of abuse by doctors in medical fraud, illegal drug prescriptions, unnecessary operations, and plain incompetence. Among the actions taken by the board was this license revocation:

In recommending that he lose his license last year, the board cited at least 22 cases in which a doctor had recommended surgery to patients whose only symptoms were an earache, a runny nose, or a sore throat.

The case against the doctor dragged on for more than five years, required 16 hearings, and generated a stenographic record of 3,183 pages.

On May 25, 1982, the Board of Regents revoked the license of the physician on charges that the useless and unnecessary surgery constituted gross negligence and incompetence as well as professional misconduct.[10]

One can only wonder at the fate of patients on whom unnecessary surgery was performed while the board conducted hearings for five years.

A simple unreported routine medical malpractice case tried before me illustrates the necessity of such lawsuits to protect the public and the reputation of the profession as well as to compensate injured and often maimed patients.

The plaintiff in this case was a fifty-five-year-old black factory worker who had cataracts. He was operated on by an ophthalmologist who had been practicing for more than twenty-five years and was a member of the state and county medical societies. The operation was performed with the patient lying in the same bed and on the same sheets on which he had slept the previous night. The doctor and nurse scrubbed in the bathroom used by all the patients. Three cataract operations were performed in the same room that morning. The plaintiff developed an infection and lost the sight of that eye. He later had the other cataract removed by another doctor without incident. When the jury returned a verdict of over $100,000 in favor of the plaintiff, the doctor's insurance company canceled his policy. Only then did the doctor stop practicing medicine.

The expert medical witness for the plaintiff was a young doctor brought in from a city more than 100 miles away. He was the nearest doctor willing to testify for the plaintiff. A leading local ophthalmologist testified on behalf of the defendant. After the verdict, several local doctors told me how happy they were that the defendant had finally been put out of practice, that he was a disgrace to the profession.

Legal malpractice cases present similar problems. Most lawyers are reluctant to sue or testify against fellow members of the bar, although a few do it with malicious glee. When a reputable, competent lawyer makes a mistake, he and his insurer usually settle the claim. The plaintiff is compensated for the harm done. The lawyer is more cautious in the future. When there is a pattern of gross incompetence, litigation is necessary.

In another routine case tried before me, a young lawyer represented an elderly widow whose sole asset was a thriving restaurant. When she was no longer able to supervise the restaurant on a daily basis, she decided to sell it. She retained a leading law firm to represent her. One of the partners assigned a young associate to handle what he considered a small matter. When the widow expressed concern over the inexperience of the associate, the partner assured her he would supervise the case. The purchaser was an automobile salesman who had no restaurant experience. His only asset was a house owned jointly with his wife. The young lawyer for the widow drew up an agreement of sale in which the purchaser paid $10,000 cash and gave a series of promissory notes for the balance of the $150,000. He failed to require a lien on the fixtures and stock of the restaurant or to require the wife of the purchaser to cosign the notes. Within three months the business failed and the purchaser defaulted on the notes. At the trial it was revealed that the young lawyer had never opened a file but had simply billed for time on the computer. He had never consulted anyone in the firm at any time about the sale. This young man is now selling cars and the widow, who would otherwise have been on welfare, has been properly compensated.

Architects and builders have also been held accountable for use of defective materials and incompetent design. In one case, a factory was built over an old cesspool without adequate supports. Neither the architect nor the builder tested the soil. The plaintiff who owned the building had to have it torn down before it collapsed.

Psychiatrists and mental institutions have been sued successfully for releasing patients known to be dangerous who subsequently maimed and killed the known object of their hostility and madness.[11] This is a new and salutary development in the law. No one knows how many mental patients known to be dangerous have been released and committed forseeable and preventable crimes. In 1966, I represented a youth who stabbed a man to death in the course of a robbery. My client had a long history of mental illness. At the time of the killing he was under the care of a well-known, wealthy psychiatrist. The doctor had noted in his file the week before the incident: "This man is homicidal." Although the youth's parents had brought him to the psychiatrist and were paying for his treatment, the psychiatrist did not inform them of the severity of their son's condition or recommend commitment. The victim of the stabbing left a wife and children who had no means of support. But at that time no one considered suing the psychiatrist.

The entire field of education, from nursery school through professional schools, has been forced by litigation to become open and accessible to all segments of the community. Schools have been held to reasonable standards of performance. Institutions serving the public, such as hospitals, youth shelters, and old-age homes, have also been opened to judicial scrutiny and been required to establish and maintain standards of sanitation, nutrition, and decency of treatment and to afford proper hearings before disrupting families.

Although these individuals and institutions were subject to ethical codes, professional standards, licensing, and government inspection, lax and dangerous practices and conditions were permitted. Only litigation and the threat of financial loss brought about reform.

Among the significant and essential uses of court cases is testing the propriety of governmental actions. Former Supreme Court Justice William O. Douglas remarked that the purpose of the Constitution is to keep government off the backs of the people. President Reagan has also expressed concern over the reach and scope of government. One need not subscribe to the view that the government governs best that governs least, to be concerned about pervasive and unrestrained interference with the lives of individuals by government agencies. Cases involving conflict between individual autonomy and governmental action occur in a wide range of subjects, many that have never previously been considered by Anglo-American courts.

The right to sue the government is of relatively recent origin. Sovereign immunity, a legal descendant of the divine right of kings, has been a part of American law since colonial times. For decades the courts were closed to individuals harmed by action of government agents. Few of these prohibited actions involved policy-making officials or national security or welfare. When, for example, the driver of a postal truck went through a red light and injured a pedestrian, the unfortunate victim had no redress. Similar doctrines prevailed in the states with respect to state agencies and employees. This absolute bar to the individual's right to claim redress from his government has been abrogated by statute.

The Federal Tort Claims Act of 1976 opened the federal courts to suits by persons injured or denied property by action of the federal government. This legislation was a reasoned act of Congress, a recognition that government in its manifold activities must be accountable to people it harms whether such claims arise from automobile accidents, operations of mental institutions, prisons, the military, or swine flu inoculations.

The swine flu cases illustrate the wisdom and fairness of the abrogation of governmental immunity. In 1976, the United States government, anticipating an epidemic of influenza that never occurred, undertook a massive immunization program. Almost immediately a large number of people contracted a painful, disabling, and sometimes fatal illness known as Guillain-Barre syndrome as a result of the vaccination. Those who were properly diagnosed and informed that the vaccine was the probable cause of their illness sued the government. After lengthy trials which became battles of experts testifying as to the causal relation of the vaccine to the illness, some victims of the disease were awarded damages.[12] This litigation has undoubtedly added to the case load of the federal courts. But one of the principal functions of a legal system is to provide redress for wrongs done.

Other actions are brought against government to compel public officials to obey the law, to refrain from arbitrary and ill-considered actions, and to demand accountability to the public of those who should be the public's servants, not its masters. Individuals who bring suits under the Freedom of Information Act and the Occupational Safety and Health Act perform a public service. Congress has recognized the public benefit this litigation confers by enacting the Equal Access to Justice Act, enabling such plaintiffs to recover costs, counsel fees, and other expenses of litigation in successful suits against the government.

Today the government cannot reduce or impair people's rights to welfare, social security, and pensions without affording the aggrieved individual a hearing and, if necessary, an appeal. Under the Freedom of Information Act, the citizen can obtain information about his government. Minorities, women, the handicapped, and all who are victims of government misconduct and discrimination can obtain the facts and redress. Not only the aggrieved individual but also the entire public benefit from litigation testing the actions of the government with respect to public property and natural resources, pollution, and secret government deals in domestic and foreign affairs.

Much of this litigation has been instituted by antipoverty lawyers representing classes of indigent people affected by illegal and high-handed actions of government officials. The public as a whole has benefited from court decisions establishing standards of conduct for the management of the public business. To curtail or prohibit such lawsuits in a quest for speed, efficiency, and a current court calendar would violate the express will of Congress and the state legislatures, leaving the citizenry with no peaceful, licit means of holding government accountable.

The financial benefits of litigation brought on behalf of people heretofore excluded from the legal system are dramatically revealed in the numbers of allegedly mentally ill persons who are institutionalized. Prior to a series of lawsuits raising the right of the mentally ill to be treated in the least restrictive environment, there were approximately 600,000 people in state institutions. In 1983, this number had been reduced to 150,000. The freedom, dignity, and happiness of those released cannot be measured. The savings to the public can. At a minimum, it costs about $10,000 a year to confine one patient. A savings of $4½ billion per year more than compensates for the cost in time and money of this litigation.

The dollars and cents savings to the public from litigation was recognized by the New York state legislature which appropriated up to $1 million for legal representation of disabled New Yorkers whose social security disability or supplemental security income benefits have been denied. It is estimated that this measure could save state and local governments $7 million to $10 million a year.[13] Of course this not only saves money but also provides justice for those whose benefits were improperly denied.

Some litigation does not directly save public money but effectively reduces the volume of cases by clarifying the law. Statutes, of necessity, establish only broad outlines. It is impossible and, indeed, undesirable for busy legislators to attempt to anticipate every possible permutation and combination of events that may occur. This function, called interstitial legislation, is wisely left to the courts. Many decisions have no social significance but simply clarify and make certain a latent ambiguity. If a statute gives a party twenty days in which to file a pleading, does one count the first and the last day? Is an offer accepted when the answer is mailed or when it is received? In a no-fault auto liability statute limiting court jurisdiction to cases of personal injury involving medical expenditures of more than $750, must the expenditures have been made before filing suit or will the $750 include expenditures reasonably anticipated? These matters sound like trivia. It will not make a significant difference which way they are decided. But the litigants and lawyers must have a definite answer or the same question will be raised again and again. A clear and certain court decision on an issue that applies to all others similarly situated obviates the need to relitigate the same question.

Courts in the United States fulfill another very important but often ignored function: the development and modernization of the law. Unlike judges in civil-law countries where courts have the more limited role of enforcing statutes, American judges have a long tradition of interpreting law in the light of changed needs and conditions. Good judges must continually be pouring new wine in old bottles. While some argue that courts have exceeded their role of adjudication and have become a superlegislature, others complain of the powerlessness of the judiciary. Despite this ongoing conceptual argument among jurisprudentialists,[14] American courts have for years developed and undoubtedly will continue to develop the law and legal doctrine because there is no other agent to do so. Legislatures operate by consensus and through coalitions. Legislators are supposed to be responsive to the will of their constituents. They find it difficult to reconcile public opinion with the limitations and strictures of the Constitution and the preservation of fundamental liberties. This is a function that courts are uniquely able to perform.

The Congress is burdened with problems of international affairs, national defense, the budget, raising taxes, and countless other difficult and complicated matters. There is little time to consider and enact domestic legislation. For a decade, Congress has attempted to pass a much-needed new Federal Crimes Code but the members have been unable to agree on its many complex and controversial provisions. It is a physical impossibility for the Congress to legislate minutely, carefully, and specifically on the multitude of questions that the federal courts decide.

State legislatures are similarly overwhelmed by budgetary problems, financing schools, building prisons, attracting industry, and, of course, levying taxes. Although some state legislatures have long sessions and adequate staffs, many do not. It is unrealistic to expect part-time legislators to deal with the diverse and complicated problems that are decided by the courts.

In an age of rapidly changing social and economic conditions, many judicial doctrines become outmoded. Often these are judge-made rules designed to accommodate the needs of other times and parties. If courts refuse to act while waiting for the legislatures to pass laws repealing judge-made decisional law, injustice is judicially sanctioned. The doctrine of charitable immunity illustrates the need for judicial revision or abrogation of outmoded doctrine. In the nineteenth century, when hospitals, orphanages, and old-age homes depended upon small private gifts for their maintenance, an action for damages would probably have compelled them to cease operations, thus causing hardship to many who relied on their free services. Today these institutions receive payments from patients and residents. Some of those payments come from the individual, others from Medicare, Blue Cross, or welfare. In addition, insurance coverage is now widely available. There is no reason to shield hospitals from liability to patients injured by the hospital when they are legally liable to employees injured in the course of their hospital duties. The doctrine created by courts was abolished by courts through litigation when the legislatures failed to act.

Other significant developments in the law were brought about through litigation. The entire law of personal injuries has developed through the slow accretion of cases. The common law of England did not protect the person with the same care as it did property. Only through a long series of cases did injured individuals obtain the right to recover damages for loss of limbs, eyesight, and other disabilities. The right to recover for nonmonetary losses—for pain and suffering, for loss of the pleasures of life, and the lessened ability to earn a livelihood—were engrafted onto the law through litigation.

The law of products liability providing that a manufacturer of dangerous products is liable to the reasonably foreseeable users of those products was developed through litigation. Automobiles, airplanes, and many other products have been made safer and countless lives and limbs saved as a result of vigorous litigation.

Litigation also has an educational value. It makes the public and the legislators dramatically aware of many problems and thus leads to reform. Recent developments in tort law illustrate this incidental benefit of litigation. For years, under the common law, a party injured through the negligence of another could not recover if he had been even the slightest bit negligent himself. This was known as contributory negligence and was an absolute bar to recovery. The doctrine was a relic of eighteenth-century English law when in the dawning years of the Industrial Revolution the courts protected employers lest the burden of claims put them out of business. After evidence of a sufficient number of outrageous cases became public knowledge, the legislatures in state after state enacted laws requiring that fault be apportioned among the parties and damages be awarded proportionate to fault.

Legislatures also became aware of the mounting carnage on the streets due to motor vehicle accidents. In order to provide more prompt and less expensive recovery of small accident claims, twenty-three states have adopted some form of compulsory no-fault auto accident insurance scheme. This wholesale revision of the law could not have been accomplished by the courts. However, litigation of a multitude of claims brought the problem to the attention of the legislatures. Such prudent laws relieve the courts of enormous numbers of cases. There is a lag of several years from the effective date of a statute to the time when it substantially affects the case load of the courts. Cases arising prior to the statute must be tried in the courts. Until this backlog is cleared the case load is not reduced. Thus any extrapolation of projected volume of cases from unevaluated statistics is bound to be erroneous.

Not all litigation serves a public purpose. Many cases simply decide the rights and obligations of the parties involved. Suing and defending cases in court is expensive. The public pays for courthouses, judges, and supporting personnel. The public also pays for lawyers for the indigent. It is estimated that nonindigent Americans pay $30 billion in legal fees annually. These are not inconsiderable sums. But only courts can develop legal doctrine, establish precedents, make the law consonant with the needs of society, enforce orders on recalcitrant litigants, and limit the powers of government. Other dispute-resolution mechanisms are simply a means of resolving private disputes outside the protections and safeguards of the legal system. Justice Oliver Wendell Holmes remarked, "Taxes are what we pay for a civilized society." The cost of courts is what Americans pay for a free and lawful society.

# CHAPTER III

---

# THE PRICE OF JUSTICE

We will sell to no man, we will not deny or defer to any
man either justice or right.

—Magna Carta

T his chapter examines an underlying problem rarely discussed by
courts and legal scholars: the imposition of fees for the use of
courts. For centuries Anglo-American lawyers have paid lip service to
the principle that justice should be freely available to everyone. But, in
fact, access to the courts has never been free. It is not now. The English
practice of imposing fees for filing civil suits was instituted in America
in colonial times and has been continued with little thought or discussion.

Until the 1960s most litigants in civil court were represented by
private counsel. Since court fees constituted only an insignificant item
in the total costs of litigation paid by the parties, neither lawyers nor
clients had much incentive to protest the payment of these small sums.
Court budgets, while never excessive, were adequate to deal with the
actual costs of operating the courts and processing the cases filed. Therefore, court administrators rarely questioned the adequacy of the fee
schedule.

In the 1980s this equilibrium has been destabilized by sharply increased costs of operating court systems. The rise in expenses of the courts is due not only to the volume of cases and inflation but also to sophisticated management techniques. A new profession, court management, has evolved. Formerly there was a court clerk who, with the help of a few assistants, docketed by hand in large bound volumes each case that was filed. Today records are computerized, requiring machines and high-priced staff to operate them. Formerly cases were listed for trial when counsel was ready and chose to bring the case to trial. Today there is case management in which the courts set schedules and monitor the cases and the lawyers. All this requires more personnel that are paid higher salaries and, of course, more money. Although there has been some attempt to raise filing fees to a more compensatory level, in most jurisdictions the fees have not been raised substantially. The issue of court fees has become critical because many poor people are seeking to claim their rights and to obtain redress for wrongs done them. Even small fees often pose an insuperable barrier to access to justice for them.

The terms *fees* and *costs* are often used in tandem but they refer to different charges paid to different recipients and under different circumstances. Costs are usually paid by the losing party to the winner. They are, in most jurisdictions, awarded in the discretion of the court. Although in theory costs are imposed to make whole the winner who had to undergo expenses in bringing or defending the action, costs do not cover the actual expenses of litigation. The largest item of expense to a litigant is usually the lawyer's fee. Except in class actions or suits brought under special statutes such as the Equal Access to Justice Act, counsel fees are not recoverable as part of costs. The award of costs reimburses the litigant. It does not pay the court system for any part of the expense to the taxpayers of processing the case.

Court fees are a fixed set of charges for filing papers in court in civil litigation. In some jurisdictions fees are paid to the governing body— state, county or municipality—and become part of the general revenues. In others, fees are used to defray in part the expenses of the judicial system. Fees are established by statute or rule of court. They are imposed uniformly on all litigants. Except for indigents, judges have no authority to waive the imposition of fees. Courts are required to waive court costs to permit indigents to sue in only a very few limited circumstances.

In order to institute a civil suit, a plaintiff must pay a filing fee. If he wishes to assert his constitutional right to a jury trial, he must pay a jury demand fee. In order to compel the attendance of witnesses at the trial, he must pay for witness fees and subpoenas. In 1495 England provided by statute for free subpoenas for the poor,[1] but today indigents must, in most jurisdictions, pay for subpoenas to compel witnesses to come to court. A plaintiff is permitted to make service on the defendant and the witnesses himself; but if he is unable to do so, he must pay charges, which may be several hundred dollars, for the service of these papers. There are also fees for filing motions and other pleadings.

Most filing fees are modest and do not defray any substantial portion of the actual cost to the court of handling the papers. They bear no relationship to the actual cost of the trial. In New York City, the fees are twenty-five dollars for filing suit, fifty dollars to place the cause on the trial calendar, and thirty-five dollars for a jury demand.[2] Fees in most jurisdictions are also small. Once having paid these fees and obtained service on the defendant or defendants, the parties can litigate for an almost limitless period of time so long as they can afford to pay their attorneys or until the other party either succumbs, outwaits, or outlitigates his opponent.

Fees are not based on the actual cost of processing papers. In New York in 1982, it cost ten to fifteen dollars in salaries alone each time a judicial action was taken in the city criminal court.[3] Such action could be as simple as granting a continuance.

Fees are uniform. They are the same for filing a claim whether it involves $10,000 or $10,000,000. They bear no relationship to the public expenses involved in the trial of a case. The cost to the public of any trial is in large measure based on the length of the trial. A two-day trial costs the public approximately twice as much as a one-day trial.

There are no national statistics with respect to the public expenses of litigation. One can, however, gather some notion of the dimensions of the problem from isolated studies of particular courts in certain types of cases. New York City paid more than $10 million in 1968 just to process misdemeanor and minor offenses and arrests and preliminary hearings in felony cases.[4] In thirty-two counties in California, the average annual total expenditure for the superior courts in the mid-seventies was in excess of $2 million. The average cost of a jury trial at that time was $1,772 and that of a bench trial was $844.[5] The costs have risen substantially in succeeding years. In 1982, the average jury trial expenditure for a tort case (a civil case involving personal injury or property damage or libel or slander) ranged from $2,790 to $8,649, depending on the state.[6] In federal courts, the average expenditures ranged from $5,843 to $12,035. Nonjury cases cost about half as much as jury trials.

These figures represent average costs. They are based on the average trial time. They were compiled from cases that lasted only an hour and those that lasted for months. As we have seen, a very small number of litigants use a very large percentage of court time. But all litigants pay the same fees. And all the taxpayers pay for the major part of the costs of the courts.

There are three interrelated questions that must be considered in any discussion of equal access to justice. Should the civil courts be open without charge to all who wish to litigate? If fees are imposed, should access to the courts be denied to those who cannot afford to pay? If user fees are imposed, should they be flat fees or based on the actual cost to the public of each case?

The answer to the first question depends upon one's philosophy. If courts are considered an essential part of government, then the answer is clear. There should be no charge for justice. On the other hand, if one views courts as fulfilling a private or only quasi-public function, then user fees may be a reasonable means of reducing the burden on the taxpayers. This is particularly appropriate when those who use the most court time are, on the whole, able to pay for the costs of their litigation. A journalist phrased this point of view crudely but trenchantly: He asks; "Since more than 90 percent of us never use the courts in our entire lives, why are we paying for the treasure hunters and prosperous computer companies to solve their private disputes?"[7] It is not only treasure hunters and computer companies who utilize a large portion of court time but also insurance companies, manufacturers of allegedly unsafe products, polluters, antitrust violators, rich persons accused of crime, and wealthy corporations.

Criminal cases constitute about half the case load of the courts, and account for at least half the expenses of the courts. In criminal cases the public bears not only the entire costs of the courts involved in trials and appeals but also the expenses of the prosecution, including salaries of the prosecutors, witness fees, investigation costs, and fees for experts. If the defendant is indigent, the public also pays for defense counsel and, in some cases, small sums for investigation and related expenses. Serious constitutional and practical problems are involved in charging the costs of prosecution to criminal defendants who are acquitted. For years, it was customary in minor cases to charge costs of $7.50 or $10.00 to persons acquitted of motor vehicle and misdemeanor charges. Justices of the peace and magistrates, who were often compensated from these fees, routinely assessed costs against all defendants, guilty and innocent. Those who were acquitted paid without protest, since the costs were less than the fines that could have been imposed if they had been found guilty. In recent years the practice of paying the minor judiciary from the charges assessed against criminal defendants has been abolished in most jurisdictions. Several courts have held that costs may not be assessed against acquitted defendants.[8]

There are no national statistics with respect to the economic status of persons accused of crime. One indicium of indigence is the appearance of a public defender, legal services lawyer, or court-appointed counsel to represent a defendant. In many metropolitan areas, at least three-fourths of all defendants are represented by counsel paid by public funds or charitable organizations. A number of jurisdictions do require the assessment of the costs of prosecution and also mandate the payment of costs as part of a plea bargain.[9] Those who can afford to pay costs can plead guilty to a lesser charge. In some jurisdictions suspension of sentence is conditioned upon payment of costs.[10] Those who can pay do not go to prison, while those who cannot must serve their sentences. Such unfair practices are prevalent even though the United States Supreme Court has held that individuals cannot be jailed for failure to pay fines when they are financially unable to do so.[11]

Little attention has been given to the question of taxing convicted defendants who are not indigent the actual costs of their prosecution. Obviously a $25 per diem charge taxed as costs to defendants in some jurisdictions is only a token charge when the actual costs of a jury trial exceed $1,000 a day. Taxation of actual costs of prosecution against a nonindigent defendant is not a fee for access to justice. It may be analogized to the imposition of a fine as a penalty for crime. However, for defendants of moderate means, this may be a form of economic coercion to compel a guilty plea rather than risk the costs of trial.

A person accused of crime is haled into court by the government. He does not seek access to the use of the courts. His sole concern is to be able to present an adequate defense. In the past few decades the Supreme Court has issued a series of landmark decisions holding that those accused of crime, even though indigent, have the right to counsel and supporting services.[12] These decisions were intended to ensure that justice in criminal cases not be dependent upon the defendant's ability to pay. However, the Court has not manifested a like concern for the rights of poor litigants in civil cases. It is in civil cases that the imposition of court fees is crucial. The absolute declaration that due process of law requires "all the means a defendant or petitioner might require to get a fair hearing from the judiciary on all charges brought against him or grievances alleged by him"[13] has been ignored all too often in denying indigents access to civil courts and denying them the right to counsel. Although the Court made this statement in the context of a criminal case, it is carefully worded to include petitioners with grievances. Plaintiffs in civil cases are petitioners who have—or at least allege—grievances. Unless they have a court hearing to decide the merits of their allegations they are unquestionably denied due process of law.

It may be argued that civil claims do not rise to the status of constitutional rights comparable to the defense against criminal charges. A person accused of crime, if convicted, may lose his liberty and even his life. A person denied access to civil courts may lose much that makes life worth living: his family, his means of subsistence, his good name, and the ability to begin a new economic life.

Traditionally Americans have not been charged for the use of public facilities. It has been assumed that society as a whole benefits from parks and museums even though some members of the community choose not to visit them. The entire community benefits from public schools because society needs a literate, educated population. Thus, for more than a century it has been the practice in the United States to pay for public schools from general revenues even though many taxpayers are either childless or do not send their children to public schools. Most highways are built with public funds even though many people do not drive cars. The nation as a whole benefits from a good highway system. Toll roads are built and maintained by user fees. Gasoline taxes to support these roads provide a reasonably fair and proportionate system of user fees.

Charges for use of public facilities and, conversely, public support for institutions that charge entrance fees raise ethical questions that have been ignored by lawmakers and judges for too long. Other public officials have shown some sensitivity to the problem but have found perhaps Pickwickian solutions. The New York City cultural affairs commissioner, when queried about city support for the Metropolitan Museum, which charges admission fees, salved his conscience in this way. "No one is happy about this," he said, "but we realize that some user fee—provided it's strictly voluntary—is appropriate. Hence the so-called pay-what-you-want agreement."[14]

Courts cannot function on a pay-what-you-want basis. If fees are to be charged, it should be done on a rational basis. Courts are qualitatively different from museums, parks, and highways. Administration of justice is an essential government function. Although some private disputes can be and often are settled pursuant to private agreements for arbitration, conciliation, and mediation, many cannot be resolved without the force of government sanctions. Many cases involve the rights of the individual vis-à-vis government. Unless agreements can be legally enforced, unless disputes can be resolved peaceably and lawfully, unless law violators are lawfully accused, tried, and punished, no member of the community can feel a sense of assurance in the pursuit of his daily life. Indeed, it is that very lack of assurance that the law will be enforced promptly, fairly, and appropriately that is the cause of much public dissatisfaction. Although an individual may never sue or be sued or be accused of a crime, he derives benefit from the justice system just as every individual benefits from the existence of a competent fire department, although the likelihood that one's own property will catch fire is remote. To date no one has suggested that the hapless victim of a fire be further victimized by having to pay for the use of the fire department that responds to his call, although some proposals are being made to limit the use of the Coast Guard to rescue small boats and require small-boat sailors in distress to use private rescue companies.

If, nonetheless, one concludes that user fees are an appropriate means of fairly distributing the costs of litigation, the second question must be answered. Should access to the civil courts be denied to those who cannot afford to pay fees?

In 1971, the Supreme Court first ruled on the right of indigents to

sue without paying a filing fee.[15] This is another basic question that
should have been decided at least a century ago. The plaintiffs in this
case were indigent women who wanted divorces but were unable to pay
a filing fee of sixty dollars. They were represented by a legal services
organization. Counsel knew how to present the case and pursue the
necessary appeals. Of course, for decades indigent spouses have wanted
divorces. But it was the policy of most legal aid societies not to take such
cases. Divorce was considered a luxury for the rich, not a right available
to all. The Supreme Court held that the litigants were entitled to free
access to the courts because courts monopolized the means for legally
dissolving a marriage.

Two years later the Supreme Court held that the requirement of a
filing fee of fifty dollars in order to petition for voluntary bankruptcy was
constitutional even though it was admitted that the petitioner could not
afford to pay the fee.[16] The lower court had held that the requirement
of a fee in order to obtain a discharge in bankruptcy and be legally
relieved of one's debts violated both the due process and equal protection clauses of the Constitution. The result of the Supreme Court's
decision is that bankruptcy must be deemed a privilege for the rich that
may legally be denied to the poor.

In an even more shocking case, the United States Supreme Court
held that a recipient of old-age assistance whose payments were reduced
could not appeal this decision without paying a twenty-five-dollar filing
fee that admittedly the petitioner could not afford.[17] Mr. Justice Douglas dissented trenchantly, observing that "the Court upholds a scheme
of judicial review whereby justice remains a luxury for the rich." The
Court has also held that an indigent mother whose parental rights were
terminated by the state was not entitled to free counsel to represent her
in asserting her rights as a mother.[18]

Professor Frank I. Michelman of the Harvard Law School, in discussing these cases, comments: "Much recent discussion about this methodology has considered whether the two major dimensions—nature of the
interest, strictness of review—are or ought to be treated as calling for
relativistic evaluation along continuous bipolar scales, or rather as posing
'either-or' questions of assignment to dichotomous categories."[19] The
nature of the interest asserted by the plaintiffs in all these cases, regardless of the factual contexts in which they arose, was access to the means

of justice, i.e., the courts. Either there is access or there is not. A relativistic evaluation is conceptually and factually impossible. The question at issue is neither the interest asserted nor the scope of judicial review but whether justice in the courts is a right available to all or a privilege for the rich subsidized by the public. Due process of law and equal protection of the laws are specifically enunciated constitutional rights that have not heretofore been construed as excepting from their ambits certain classes of people. Whether or not one deems poverty a suspect classification, there should be no exceptions whatsoever. Most access fees were established by acts of the legislatures. They can be abolished by the legislatures regardless of the decisions of the Supreme Court.

If fees are to be imposed at all, they should in a democratic society be based on the actual costs to the public of the litigation. Those who command the major share of court time would then pay for those services if they could afford to do so. But no fee should be imposed as a precondition for seeking justice.

Sound arguments can be made for either abolishing all fees and court costs or for setting fees at a realistic figure to cover the actual expenses of the courts. The present practice is difficult to justify.

Those few scholars who discuss this subject give lip service to three principles: (1) that justice shall not be for sale, (2) that there shall be private payments for private benefits, and, (3) that imposition of fees discourages unnecessary litigation.[20]

That justice shall not be for sale is a self-evident proposition. It begs the question of whether justice is a commodity or a right. If access to justice is a right, then it should not be conditioned upon the payment of a fee. However, if courts are deemed to be a facility, no different from other public facilities, then there is no conceptual barrier to imposing access fees.

The second proposition, that there be private payments for private benefits, would be conducive to imposition of user fees based on actual costs to the system. Some suggest that fees be paid not by the litigants but by those who derive a livelihood from the courts, such as bail bondsmen. This argument has a deceptive appearance of sweet reasonableness. Why should the public pay for a facility that constitutes a money-making institution for a small defined group? However, courts are not gambling casinos that benefit the owners and provide a living for a cadre of croupiers, clerks, and janitors. Nor are they factories producing an intangible commodity known as "justice" for the benefit of a select group of lawyers, judges, clerks, probation officers, and other personnel. It would be as reasonable to suggest that doctors pay for the hospitals where they treat patients and teachers pay for the schools where they teach.

These arguments misconceive the function of government. Courts, like most agencies of government, are not established and maintained to produce revenues or to be self-supporting. They exist to provide services to the entire public. Success is measured by the breadth and effectiveness of the services, not the ability to operate in the black. It costs money to monitor the purity of food, drugs, air, and water. It costs large sums of money to maintain fire departments, police departments, and the armed forces. These agencies are not expected to be self-supporting. They should not be wasteful, corrupt, or extravagant. Neither should they deny services in order to save money. The public pays for the salaries, fringe benefits, offices, and supplies of all government employees and officials, from the trash collector to the president, because government is not only a benefit but a necessity. Thus any charge for justice should be justified by more than monetary considerations.

The third reason asserted for imposing fees is to discourage unnecessary litigation. Frivolous cases may be and usually are summarily dismissed by the courts. The Supreme Court has awarded damages to a defendant subjected to a series of frivolous lawsuits.[21] It is interesting to note that in such cases the litigants had paid their access fees and obviously were not discouraged by those charges.

The notion that filing fees will deter litigants who can afford to pay not only filing fees but also counsel fees and the other costs of litigation is obviously fallacious. It is highly unlikely that filing fees totaling at most $200 for instituting a lawsuit will deter a client who pays his attorney at the rate of $100 or $200 an hour. The only persons who will be deterred from presenting claims will be poor plaintiffs who cannot find a lawyer willing to take their cases on a contingent fee basis and advance fees and costs.

What is unnecessary litigation? Neither the legislatures nor the courts have ever defined necessary litigation. Is the prosecution of a drunk, a vagrant, or a runaway child necessary? Is a claim for injuries arising from an accident necessary? Is an action to collect a debt or assert one's right to be treated in a nondiscriminatory fashion unnecessary?

Some may think that litigation over school prayer, the length of a schoolboy's hair, the right of women to be police officers, the protection of the snail darter, a parent's right to custody of his child, and similar cases that do not involve claims for money are unnecessary. These incidents, perhaps trivial in themselves, involve basic individual and public rights. Most of them are brought reluctantly when all efforts to achieve protection have failed. Courts are uniquely equipped to decide these issues. Unlike litigation for money, they cannot be compromised or conciliated. There is no way to divide a child in half, to pray secularly, to accord only partial, second-class citizenship. To impose a test of "necessity" as a precondition to use of the courts, would further burden courts and litigants by requiring a preliminary trial to determine the right to sue.

The public costs of courts and litigation, when compared with other governmental expenditures, are minimal. The entire federal court system in 1983 cost the taxpayers little more than $5 billion. The price of 1,000 small missiles that same year was $70 billion.[22] How does one weigh the price of justice? Is the collection of a $25 fee more important than access to the courts? These are questions the public must decide.

The price of justice and who shall pay it are leitmotifs of this book. They will be heard again and again as we examine the roles of lawyers, judges, and academics as well as the actual operations of the various courts. Resolution of the problems of assuring equal protection of the laws depends in large measure on the answers to these questions.

# CHAPTER IV

---

# LAWYERS

Only them lawyers big with great cigars and lesser with
brief cases, instead of minds move calmly in and out.

—John Berryman

$$T \times R \times N = F$$

Because lawyers and judges are the principal actors in courts, it is
helpful to know what they do and why they behave as they do. An
understanding of their roles and limitations explains why relatively small
numbers of litigants are able to command such a disproportionate share
of court time and scholarly attention.

Law is a profession; it is also a livelihood. Unless a lawyer is paid by
the government or subsidized by a foundation or agency, he or she must
take in enough in fees to pay the overhead of the office and earn a living.
Society should not expect lawyers to donate their services to the needy,
any more than it expects doctors, teachers, plumbers, police officers, and
garbage collectors to perform their essential services without pay. Although some lawyers devote considerable time to public interest work
and give much service to poor clients, the administration of justice
cannot depend upon such private charity. As economics is the single
most important factor in a client's decision to go to court or to assert
a legal defense, so the arcane laws of economics also govern the decisions
of lawyers.

The basic economic fact of legal practice is that a lawyer's only product is his skill. Although a lawyer is a member of a learned profession, has university degrees (usually at least two), and operates under a code of ethics, he must sell his services for a fee. The lawyer's fee, like a plumber's charge, is based on time plus expenses. If we let $T$ equal the lawyer's time, $R$ equal the rate of hourly charges, $N$ equal the multiplier (calculated on many variables), and $F$ equal the fee, we arrive at the equation $T \times R \times N = F$. The multiplier includes overhead expenses, the cost of doing business. In the 1980s this is a very substantial item. To understand why legal fees are so high, it is necessary to look at lawyers, law firms, and law as it is practiced today, putting aside memories and literature of another generation.

Just as the little red schoolhouse with one spinster teacher who taught youngsters of all ages and abilities, and the family doctor who came in a horse and buggy day or night whenever he was called and who delivered babies, set broken bones, and ministered to the dying, are anachronisms so is, for the most part, the family lawyer. The practice of law has changed dramatically in the past half century. Elderly lawyers can recall a time when a law office consisted of a lawyer, a secretary, and what the English call a "clerk"—a person who filed papers, spoke to clients, and arranged schedules. The only equipment most lawyers had was a telephone, a typewriter, and a small shelf of books. A lawyer represented the clients who came to him for his services no matter whether their problems were a murder charge, a family dispute, or a tax matter.

Today even a small law office has many phones and a switchboard, word processors, calculators, Xerox machines, the ubiquitous computer, and an extensive library. It is staffed by lawyers, paralegals, secretaries, and messengers. Twenty to twenty-five percent of salary is the usual allowance in industry for social security taxes, unemployment compensation, workmen's compensation, Blue Cross, Blue Shield, sick leave, and vacations for ordinary staff of a company. Pensions, of course, are extra. Executive fringe benefits are much higher. All these expenses must be figured into the hourly fee or the multiplier. In addition to this staff, many large and growing law firms also retain public relations firms. Hill and Knowlton, Inc., one of the largest public relations firms, reports that among its clients are many law firms.[1] Other law firms engage in extensive advertising in the press and on the air. The Philadelphia law firm of Rawle and Henderson, which describes itself as the oldest law firm in the nation, advertises daily on radio.

Many large law firms have more than a hundred partners and scores of associates and paralegals. They have clerks, accountants, secretaries, librarians, and office managers who have assistants. It is not uncommon for such firms to employ more than five hundred people. They have branch offices in many cities and in foreign countries. Not only do they have enormous expenses, they earn enormous fees. Partners charge from $100 to $300 an hour or more. Leading Washington law firms earn close to a billion dollars a year. Big law firms are growing bigger, specializing in bankruptcy work, mergers, and acquisitions. Neither bankruptcies nor corporate takeovers are activities that promote economic growth and stability or contribute to the equal administration of justice.

At the other end of the spectrum are lawyers who eke out a precarious livelihood relying on political jobs, court appointments, collection cases, and other small matters. I frequently receive requests for court appointments from lawyers who have been members of the bar for more than a decade. These appointments yield fees of only $300 to $1,000. Between these extremes are lawyers of a wide variety who engage in many kinds of legal practice, and many lawyers who are salaried employees.

Despite the many kinds of legal practice and the wide range of incomes, it is safe to say that there are two major divisions among attorneys. They may be called the fast track and the slow track. The fast track leads to a substantial income, in six figures, prestige at the bar and in the community, membership in clubs and civic organizations, and often a significant behind-the-scenes role in politics. On occasion this influence ripens into high-level government appointments. The slow track leads, at best, to a modest income in private practice, a medium-grade government or quasi-government job, or a position with an agency for the poor.

This bifurcation of the legal profession encompasses not only the practicing bar but also the bench and academia. It is an important factor in the unequal treatment of litigants in the courts. The fast track of lawyers consists predominantly of large firms, although some lawyers in smaller firms have comparable incomes. I stress the income of lawyers because it is derived from fees paid by clients. Not many Americans can afford to pay $300 an hour for a lawyer, no matter how important the problem is to them or how significant the legal issue may be.

A few figures with respect to the economics of legal practice in the 1980s reveal the enormous gulf between the haves and have-nots in seeking justice through the courts. Starting salaries for young associates in the 200 largest law firms in 1982 were over $30,000.[2] In New York the entry-level salary for lawyers in large firms was $43,000.

Joseph A. Califano, former secretary of the Department of Health, Education, and Welfare and now a Washington lawyer, points out that wealthy lawyers don't represent "the little guy."

There is a middle range of private practitioners. The average income of those in a two- to six-person firm was $54,000 in 1982.[3] These lawyers also have to pay rent, plus salaries and fringe benefits for associates, secretaries, clerks, and messengers. In order to earn a livelihood they must charge at least $50 an hour.

Those who cannot afford to pay even these relatively modest fees must seek help from legal services organizations, in places where they exist, or forgo their rights.

According to Ronald F. Pollack, director of the Villers Foundation, in 1982, there was only one legal services lawyer available to represent every 9,585 poor people eligible for legal services.[4] Only $241 million is available to provide civil legal services for the poor. In Washington, D. C., in 99 percent of landlord tenant cases at least one side proceeded to trial without counsel because the party could not afford to retain counsel and no legal services were available.

Lawyers are not evenly distributed. There is approximately one lawyer per 400 people in the United States. But in Palo Alto, California there is one lawyer for every 64 residents.[5] Most of them do very well specializing in high technology clients. This maldistribution of lawyers is conspicuous in the courtrooms in America. In most criminal courts one public defender or legal aid attorney handles fifteen or more cases a day. In another courtroom, there may be twenty or thirty lawyers trying a single case. In the bankruptcy court hearing on the agreement by Braniff International Corporation to sell or lease equipment to PSA, Inc., there were one hundred lawyers.[6] Of course, all of them were being paid at the usual rate by their clients.

I cannot predict the future shape of legal practice. But change may come not only because of protests by clients and critics but as a result of economic factors. Big law firms, like commercial enterprises, face troubled times in the 1980s. In an effort to control costs of legal work many corporations are now retaining top lawyers on a salaried basis for important work, whereas formerly house counsel handled only routine matters.[7] For example, the National Student Marketing Company paid outside counsel $1,950,000 in legal fees.[8] But, in 1983, corporations employed some 66,000 attorneys as in-house counsel. As a result of this trend, increasing competition, and the fact that many of their clients are in financial difficulties, many law firms are following the lead of industry and merging. But they are not lowering their fees.

Another new trend is the establishment of law firms to provide pre-paid legal services on a group basis for unions and other associations. Low-cost legal services are also provided by a number of chains of law offices similar to the H. R. Block accounting firm.[9]

It will probably take more than a generation for any substantial alteration to occur in the availability to the poor of legal services, unless there is some dramatic change in the present division of the legal profession into two tracks: the fast track and the slow track.

The differences between these two tracks have been cogently described as follows: "The corporation lawyer is typically drawn from a private liberal arts college and a prestige law school. In contrast the lawyers who practice solo or metropolitan style are frequently of new American stock, from low status families, and are graduates of the less prestigious law schools. Their clients are both individuals and small business men and the cases they handle are primarily personal injury, criminal cases, workmen's compensation cases and real estate. There is little contact between the two types of lawyers."[10]

Many lawyers on the fast track never go to court. They put out stock issues, write opinions as bond counsel, arrange mergers and acquisitions. Many of those who do litigate limit their practice to federal court. Those who appear in state courts represent clients in time-consuming cases involving a great deal of money. Such lawyers never see felony courts or family courts. They do not participate in small civil cases, which are often settled for inadequate sums because counsel is unprepared or cannot afford to litigate.

A generation ago most big law firms were closed to women and racial and ethnic minorities. Law firms were rigidly segregated by race, religion, and sex. Banks, insurance companies, and big corporate employers of attorneys also excluded women and minorities. Consequently, honor law graduates who were not white Anglo-Saxon Protestant males found

employment in government, legal aid, and public defender offices. Able
young graduates who were not white Anglo Saxon males often clerked
for federal judges and Supreme Court justices and thereafter hung out
their own shingles. Many leading law firms less than forty years old were
founded by these brilliant lawyers who were excluded from the established firms. The innovative alphabetical government agencies of the
Roosevelt New Deal era were staffed by honor law graduates of the
leading law schools, to the great benefit of the government and the
public at large. Although there were great disparities in income then,
there was not the gulf in ability and competence between the top 10
percent and the remainder of the practicing bar.

In the last few decades the membership of the bar has been undergo-
ing a rapid and accelerating change as more nonwhites, women, and sons
and daughters of the poor are attending law school and being admitted
to the bar. This broadened base of the legal profession is also increasingly
apparent in the personnel of the judiciary.

For more than a century the American bar and bench were drawn
primarily from the small, well-to-do, educated segment of society. Even
though neither a college education nor a law school diploma was a
prerequisite for admission to the bar, an aspiring lawyer had to spend
time "reading law" in the offices of a practicing lawyer. Young men who
had to earn a living were, for the most part, excluded from the profession
unless they were exceptionally ambitious and able.

Today almost every leading law firm has at least a few token women
and minority lawyers as associates, if not partners.[11] A young law school
graduate, if he or she was an honor student at a good law school, has
a multitude of choices. Although race, religion, and gender are no longer
impenetrable barriers to the fast track of legal practice, the dichotomy
has not been blurred.

Not all bright, capable graduates of prestigious law schools enter large
law firms. Some prefer a smaller firm because of the greater opportunity
to participate in firm decisions, closer contact with clients, and more
individual responsibility. Other talented young fast-track lawyers opt for
industry, finance, or academia. Good law schools pay good salaries ($40,-
000 to $75,000) for a work week of six or seven hours of classes and a
working year of approximately thirty weeks, with sabbatical leaves and
the opportunity to consult for a fee and to do research supported by
substantial foundation grants.

Among the nation's 600,000 lawyers there is infinite variation not only in income but in type of practice within the two major divisions.

There are also variations in methods for setting fees. In commercial and domestic relations litigation, antitrust cases, and defense of civil cases, fees are calculated on a time basis, also taking into consideration the amount of money in controversy and the potential recovery. Obviously a divorce of millionaires will command a higher fee than a divorce of a couple with an income of $50,000, even though the time required might be the same. In fact, the more money involved, the more legal time is incurred. A variant of the Peter Principle—"Forer's Formula" —may be expressed this way: Legal work multiplies to justify legal fees. A recent antitrust case exemplifies this.[12] Thirty-two law firms filed fee petitions ranging from $16,529 to $4,397,321 and totaling $20,220,962. They claimed compensation for 93,439 hours of work. The court disallowed 19,797 hours of work. I do not doubt that much of this time was actually expended, but, as the trial judge held, this work was not necessary or productive. Fees allowed totaled $4,345,557.63.

Although most lawyers calculate fees on a time basis, there are two notable exceptions: criminal defense lawyers and plaintiffs' negligence lawyers. Private criminal defense counsel charge a fixed retainer based partly on time anticipated, partly on the gravity of the charge, and partly on the client's ability to pay. In the TV panel discussions "The Constitution: That Delicate Balance," Charles Peruto, a successful criminal defense lawyer, was asked by Professor Charles R. Nesson of the Harvard Law School, "Would you take this case [the rape/mutilation of a nun] if the client paid you $10,000 in advance?" Mr. Peruto indignantly replied, "This isn't disorderly conduct." His fee, he indicated, would be about $100,000.

A small group of top private criminal defense lawyers earn substantial fees and have incomes equal to those of senior partners in large law firms. Typically criminal defense firms are small. But the cost of adequately defending a major criminal case is large. In such cases, a substantial amount of investigation and a number expert witnesses are also required. In a not unusual case, it cost Harvey Weisman $75,000 in legal bills to defend himself against the charge of diverting $7,300 in Medicaid funds. Cyril Wecht of Pittsburgh, an unsuccessful candidate for the United States Senate, reported incurring more than $250,000 in legal expenses in a six-week trial to defend himself against charges of misusing his office as coroner.

Criminal defense counsel usually receives half the agreed-upon fee, whether it be $1,000 or $100,000, when he is retained and the other half just before trial commences. In criminal cases, the clients rather than counsel take the risk of losing. Common sense and necessity, as well as the canons of ethics, dictate this form of fee payment. Obviously, if the client is convicted, he may not be inclined to pay his lawyer.

Negligence lawyers representing plaintiffs customarily are retained on a contingent fee basis. The contingent fee, long frowned upon by establishment lawyers as the mark of ambulance chasing, is subject in many courts to strict scrutiny. But it is a remarkably innovative device that has opened the courts to poor persons suffering serious injury. Absent the contingent fee, these people would be effectively barred from asserting their claims. Under a contingent fee, the lawyer advances court costs, investigation expenses, expert witness fees, and all the other pretrial, trial, and posttrial expenses. These items can be considerable. In a routine products liability case, counsel may not only need the usual investigation of an accident—eye witnesses, medical history and treatment of the client, and the actuarial projection of lost earnings—but also engineers and scientists to examine the allegedly defective product in order to determine the cause of the accident, and to testify as to the state of the art with respect to the product and the existence of feasible safe alternatives. In order to recover, an injured plaintiff must prove not only his injuries but also the malfunction of the product causing the injury and the state of the art, including a feasible alternative product or practice. Adequate preparation of such a case may easily cost plaintiff's counsel more than $50,000 before the day of trial. In an ordinary accident case the out-of-pocket expenses are frequently in the range of $5,000 to $10,000.

Few injured plaintiffs can afford to spend this kind of money to obtain their "day in court." Under a contingent fee agreement plaintiff's counsel is paid a percentage of the recovery—usually one-third to 40 percent of the net recovery after payment of expenses. The lawyer, of course, takes the risk of losing or of obtaining an inadequate verdict. Unless the probabilities of a substantial recovery are good, obviously few competent lawyers will take a case on this basis. Thus a person whose injuries have not resulted in substantial medical expenses, loss of earnings, and considerable pain and suffering is remitted to inadequate representation or a coerced settlement. Since such a plaintiff cannot afford to go to trial, he must accept whatever offer his lawyer can obtain from the defendant. The income of a good plaintiff's negligence counsel is on the whole equivalent to the income of a senior partner in a major law firm.

If a plaintiff sues the federal government both he and his counsel are in a favored position. Under the Equal Access to Justice Act, a successful plaintiff can recover not only damages but also counsel fees. This statute is a wise recognition by Congress of the unequal status of an aggrieved individual and the government. Ernest Fitzgerald, described as a "Pentagon whistle-blower," was dismissed from his job after disclosing to Congress cost overruns on an aircraft project. After a twelve-year battle,[13] Fitzgerald was reinstated. His counsel was awarded $200,000 in fees.

All levels of government employ thousands of lawyers for much routine work and some highly specialized matters requiring skilled counsel. They also retain large firms to represent them in lucrative specialized work such as bond counsel. These plums are usually awarded only to qualified attorneys. But, under the old Jacksonian spoils system, those large firms that contribute to the winning party receive fees worth many times the amount of the amount of their political contributions.

Despite the seemingly inexhaustible resources of the federal government, it is often at a disadvantage when salaried civil service lawyers are pitted against leading law firms. It is interesting that the United States Attorney's Office for the Southern District of New York (including New York City) the busiest and largest of these offices, employs only a hundred attorneys, fewer than many law firms in New York City.

State attorneys general, county prosecutors, and city legal departments are at an even greater disadvantage. They do not command the best legal talent and a very large proportion of their staffs are inexperienced.

The other large group of salaried lawyers work for agencies for the poor, such as the public defender, legal services organizations, and special pro bono publico offices and agencies. Although some of these employees receive salaries at the $50,000 level, most do not.

The situation of lawyers for the poor is steadily worsening. Legal aid and defender lawyers are bearing the brunt of the increased number of criminal prosecutions and the new demands of the indigent for justice. At the same time funds for legal services have been sharply reduced. New York City legal aid lawyers struck in December 1982; but their demands were not met. The debate between funding legal services and relying on the pro bono services of the private bar to fill the gap has been a futile exercise. In only very few communities has the bar responded adequately. The salaries of those lawyers who are still employed by legal services organizations are, on the whole, lower than those of government attorneys doing comparable work and much lower than those of neophyte lawyers employed by large firms. When I was in charge of a legal services office, a young attorney there calculated that on his salary and with the size of his family he was eligible for free legal services.

Able young attorneys are under considerable economic, professional, and social pressure to get on the fast track. Tuition at leading law schools in the mid 1980s is $10,000 a year or more. Even night law schools charge a minimum of $1,000 a year. The night course is four years instead of the customary three for day school. A law student, of course, has living expenses. Some students have wealthy families; a few brilliant students are awarded scholarships and fellowships; the majority borrow some or all of their law school expenses.

The slow-track practice does not have the same prestige at the bar as the fast-track. Socializing among lawyers tends to follow the track of their practice. Despite the young graduates' idealism or desire to engage in public service, the economics of debt and future security as well as the natural desire to succeed and to be a part of the legal and social establishment constitute powerful pulls to get on the fast track. The top quarter or third of the class in leading law schools will receive offers from big law firms and most will accept. A few of the bright ones will go into academia or the higher echelons of industry. The less able will pursue low-level careers in government and work in legal aid and public defender offices and public interest law firms.

In 1981, the nation's law schools graduated 36,000 students, but there were only 26,400 law-related job openings, according to the United States Department of Commerce. Twenty-seven percent got jobs in large law firms.[14] With large law firms commanding the best talent, indigent clients and clients of modest means receive not only less time from their counsel but inferior representation.

Many critics assert that the legal profession is draining off the most talented young people, diverting them from engineering, teaching, and other careers in which ability is sorely needed. Attorney William K. Coblentz of San Francisco also deplores the fact that so many bright individuals are lawyers. He writes, "The problem is not too many dumb lawyers, but too many smart ones."[15] These critics are apparently unaware of the vast numbers of mediocre and incompetent attorneys now practicing law.[16] I see lawyers who are unable to speak English correctly, who can repeat legal maxims but do not understand them, and who, despite good intentions, do their clients great harm. Inevitably these lawyers represent poor, ignorant, vulnerable people. Even though there are many able lawyers who work for agencies for the poor, they do not have time to train and educate their inadequate colleagues. On-the-job training cannot compensate for inadequate legal education. As the *Harvard Law Review* pointed out in 1967, "The quality of service provided by legal aid societies has been significantly deficient."[17] Fifteen years later, the situation has materially worsened.

The "rising tide of mediocrity" that the National Commission on Education in its 1983 report finds to be engulfing American education has overwhelmed the legal profession. Law schools have increased their admissions and lowered their standards. New law schools emerge like dandelions after a rain. There is no assessment as to whether more law schools are needed. After a few years most law schools are accredited despite obvious deficiencies in curriculum and faculty. Today American high school students take courses in family life and driver training instead of Latin and calculus. College students take courses in "film" instead of philosophy. And law students take courses in women's rights, juvenile law, and poverty law instead of jurisprudence. These courses are often taught by young people who themselves have had an inferior legal education and no experience in the practice of law. The rights of women, children, minorities, and the poor are certainly issues of great importance. But the legal principles and procedures applicable to the problems of these classes of people should be learned in courses on constitutional law and civil and criminal procedure. Having avoided the tough courses, these graduates are on the whole less able to conduct the uphill battles that representation of disadvantaged clients requires than those who represent more affluent clients whose cases do not involve the development of new theories and procedures.

The amount of time and preparation a lawyer can devote to a problem, as well as the lawyer's ability, often makes the difference between conviction and acquittal, a meagre recovery and an adequate award, or civil liability instead of a favorable verdict. It is simply an economic fact of life that a lawyer who is paid only a $1,000 fee cannot afford to spend ten days of trial time and retain costly witnesses. His client will get the justice he pays for—a $1,000 defense or the $1,000 presentation of a claim. This will amount to perhaps two days of trial and the testimony of three or four witnesses. The lawyer who has been paid a $5,000 retainer will usually give a far more lengthy—and perhaps more effective —representation.

These disparities in representation are often compounded by the assembly-line method under which many law offices for the poor operate. An indigent accused may get a hasty interview by one lawyer, preparation of the file by a paralegal, a ten-minute interview in the cell block the day of trial by the lawyer who actually tries the case, and— if he is lucky and the defender is persistent—an hour of trial time. If there is an appeal, it will be prosecuted by still another lawyer who does not know the client and is unaware of errors of omission in the trial.

The litigant with a small civil claim is usually at a disadvantage. There is a commonsense cost/benefit calculation that sensible counsel and clients make. If the plaintiff's losses are $10,000 or less, he will, if he has good counsel, settle his claim for $6,000 or $7,500. This may not be justice, but if he went to trial and obtained a verdict of $10,000 he would net less than that amount after paying expenses and counsel fees.

Trial is always risky. One may lose even a good case. If the client wins, the other party may appeal. If the plaintiff needs the money, he will forgo his rights and settle for the best deal his lawyer can make. If the plaintiff is not in want and can afford the costs of trial and appeal, he can pursue his remedies for years and claim the full measure of his rights. Similarly, a defendant in a civil suit who has limited means will settle rather than incur further costs, even though he has a good defense. A wealthy defendant who has a weak defense has every incentive to delay, to file pretrial motions, to litigate, and to appeal. Many civil defendants are in fact insurance companies that are in no hurry to pay claimants. Wealthy clients also settle big cases rather than take the risk of trial and its attendant expenses. The cases involving the stock market scandals were finally settled after a decade of discovery and negotiations for $30 million, including $3 million in legal fees.[18] But lawyers who represent wealthy clients have an economic interest in litigating and appealing. They are being paid for their time and efforts.

The lawyer who believes his poor client has a good claim or a good defense faces a moral and practical dilemma. Under the canons of ethics a lawyer is supposed to represent his client vigorously. But he is not required to represent the client at a substantial loss to himself. If the lawyer does this too often, he will soon cease practicing law.

Let us examine the lives and practices of a half-dozen lawyers[19] to see how the two-track system of legal practice functions and the ways in which it limits the lawyer's ability to promote the equal protection of the laws. Peter, Don, Bill, Laura, David, and Dennis were all admitted to the bar twenty years ago and began practicing law in the same city where all of them grew up.

Peter Ingersoll attended a prep school, Princeton, and Yale Law School, where he was an honor student. He clerked for a federal judge for a year, then a coveted honor. He then entered a leading law firm. In 1964, his starting salary was $26,000. The partners in his firm immediately had him appointed to several bar association committees. He lunched with them and the firm's clients at prestigious city clubs. He played golf and tennis at leading country clubs where he met wealthy clients, potential clients, and important political figures. Peter was an idealistic young man imbued with a belief in equality of opportunity and restructuring society through abrasive, innovative litigation. At his request, the firm loaned him to the legal aid society for a month. There he was thrown into small claims and misdemeanor courts. For the past fifteen years Peter has not seen a poor client. Other than the maid, he does not know a poor person. From time to time Peter writes a brief and argues an appeal for the American Civil Liberties Union or a local environmental group. He serves on a bar association committee to help fund legal services for the poor.

Peter earns more than $250,000 a year as his share of the firm's income. He also has substantial investments made on the advice of his clients. Peter is an expert in corporate taxation and has lectured on the subject. Since that long-past month with the legal aid society he has never been in a criminal court or a family court. He does not know how to stop a sheriff's sale, how to lift a detainer (an order holding an accused in jail pending trial), or how to try an accident case.

Peter is a concerned citizen. He worries about prison overcrowding even though he has never visited a prison. He reads about overcrowded court calendars and long delays. But for the past fifteen years, he has not answered the call of the court when client and witnesses are ready and are told, "No courtrooms are available. Come back tomorrow." He does not have to wait day after day to get on trial.

Don Bocino attended parochial school, a local university, and local law school. He was a much better than average student but did not have time to work on the law review because he spent many nights playing in a jazz band to support himself through college and law school. On admission to the bar, Don went into the law firm of Angelo, a neighbor and family friend. Angelo had a general practice. He was active in politics. For the first four or five years Don had a great time representing all the neighbors in their family squabbles, their run-ins with the police, their auto accidents, and their business problems.

Gina, Don's wife, complained bitterly, "You're like an old-fashioned family doctor, on call twenty-four hours a day. Today doctors keep office hours. Plumbers only work from nine to five. Everyone but you. I haven't seen you for two weeks. And you don't even make any money. When you do come home, the kids ask me, 'Who is that man?' Don, I love you but you've got to choose between that half-assed law practice and your family."

Don knew Gina's complaints were justified but he loved his law practice. He had dreams of being a first-rate trial lawyer. He pleaded with Gina.

"Y'know I love you, honey. Don't push me so hard. Just be a little patient. I'll get you that house in the suburbs soon—just another year or two. Angelo's going on the bench next year."

"What!" she exclaimed. "You must be kidding. That fool can't be a judge. You know he doesn't know any law. Without you and Armando he'd be disbarred."

"It's true." Don told her. "The county chairman told me he's slating Angelo. They need an Italian on the ticket."

"I'm glad I'm an honest beautician," Gina declared. "I don't want any part of a system that makes Angelo a judge. Besides, when he's gone you'll just work that much harder."

For two years Gina and Don argued. Angelo went on the bench. And then Don discovered that a client who was the mainstay of the office was a gangster, a man Don suspected of being high in the drug business. Don left the firm and bought into a fast-food franchise. Today he and Gina have their house in the suburbs. Don plays his clarinet more. He says he doesn't miss the law. But the legal profession lost a talented lawyer who understood the system.

Bill Harmon was a classmate of Peter at the university and in law school. Bill was a basketball star, a friendly, likeable chap who went through college and law school with substantial scholarships. He was in the middle of the class. Bill's uncle Norris was a lawyer, a brilliant man who had worked his way through law school shoveling coal in furnaces. He established the largest and most successful black law firm in the city. Norris was an old-fashioned trial lawyer who mesmerized juries. He quoted the Bible, Shakespeare, Milton, and Uncle Remus. He made jurors laugh and cry and agonize over their doubts. They acquitted Norris's clients—the innocent and the guilty. Norris owned three buildings on prime locations where many leading law firms rented office space. But Norris had his office in an old house. His tenants would not have liked a black law firm as a neighbor.

In 1963, young Bill Harmon had his pick of offers from leading law firms and corporations. Every law firm and business wanted to integrate. Bill was personable; his record was fair. Like Peter, Bill accepted an offer from a leading firm. He served on bar association committees and was conspicuous at clubs and civic functions. Bill served on all kinds of committees for the poor and disadvantaged but he had less understanding of the problems of the poor than did Peter. Bill had not even served one day as a volunteer in a legal aid office. Clients liked Bill. His work was adequate. After five years, Bill was bored with pension trusts and corporate board meetings. With the help of his law firm, Bill was appointed to an important federal commission. He then became an ambassador. He will surely become a federal judge. But he has had no experience with the legal system or the problems of the poor and disadvantaged. His children attend the same exclusive schools as Peter's children. Surreptitiously Bill is called an "Oreo" (after the cookie— black on the outside, white on the inside).

Laura Fein was a thirty-four-year-old elementary school teacher when she entered law school. She was a divorcee with a six-year-old son whom she supported. Laura taught third grade in a slum school where almost all the children were on welfare. Few of them could read or tell time. Most had never been more than a mile from their homes. Their only contact with the world was the soap operas they saw on TV. But they all knew about numbers writers, drug pushers, and political bosses. Laura saw battered wives and alcoholic, mentally ill, and dangerous parents. She saw abused children whom she was powerless to protect. She decided to go to law school. For four years she taught during the day and went to law school at night. She also worked as a volunteer in a juvenile law center funded by the Office for Economic Opportunity.

Laura graduated third in a class of 150. She sent applications to thirty large and medium sized law firms. She was interviewed by most but not offered a position. Laura at thirty-eight had graying hair. She was no longer a trim little size eight in a neat Brooks Brothers suit with a foulard tie.

The Juvenile Law Center offered her a job at $18,000 a year. She saw that the center had really done nothing to help the children she cared about. The young lawyers were busy writing grant proposals and bringing landmark lawsuits that might not be heard for years. She wanted to work with skilled lawyers who could train her. Also, she saw no reason to earn less than her classmates. Thanks to a phone call from one of her professors, Laura got a job in a small, first-rate law firm, a spin-off from one of the big law firms. She became an expert in antitrust litigation and class action suits. She now earns more than $150,000 a year.

Despite her law school education, gender, and social background, Laura is on the fast track. She serves on bar association committees involved with juvenile law, rights of women, and legal services. Laura's son is an honor student at an Ivy League college. She has discouraged him from becoming a lawyer. For her there is little satisfaction in her big court victories that take money from bloated corporations and put it in the pockets of people who do not need it. Year after year the committees on which she serves discuss the same intractable problems and pass vehement resolutions. But nothing changes. Laura told me that she wishes she had become a scientist. Perhaps in this field she might have contributed to the resolution of problems or advanced knowledge by some small degree. All she has done is earn a good living by very hard and unsatisfying work.

David Goulden likes the idea of working in a public interest law firm. He is sixty-two years old. He has a genuine concern for protection of the environment. David was a biologist working for a pharmaceutical company before he went to law school. He was bored with his routine job. His wife had a job as an actuary; he had a small inheritance; they had no children. So David quit his job and went to law school. His record was acceptable but undistinguished. He has never tried a case. He is not interested in the problems of the legal system. He seldom attends bar association meetings. His greatest worry is that the public interest law firm that employs him will lose its funding.

Dennis Ryan is the son of a famous criminal trial lawyer who was a champion of civil liberties. Dennis is bright but lazy. He graduated at the bottom of his class. With the help of his father he got a job in the prosecuting attorney's office. He is still there. Dennis was always weak on preparation but effective in cross-examination. He can reduce the most hardened defendant to incoherent, sputtering anger by his sly insinuations. He loathes the petty purse snatchers and muggers he prosecutes. He would prefer trying homicide cases, but that requires more effort.

When Dennis loses a case, it is always the fault of the softheaded judge or the decisions of the Supreme Court. He has been with the prosecutor's office for twenty years. Dennis is not stupid. He knows that many of the defendants who are convicted may well be innocent. He consoles himself with the thought that they have probably committed some other crime and they will all get out in a few years anyway. These cases have nothing to do with the great principles of law his father used to expound. Dennis does not earn the big fees his father used to command. Dennis knows he is doomed to remain on the slow track until he is pensioned off. For the next fifteen or twenty years he will hastily try routine cases simply to keep the faltering justice machine from breaking down. Often he thinks that only his nightly bourbon prevents him from breaking down under the unending, hopeless, routine recycling of misery.

Most middle-aged lawyers were motivated, at least in part, by the vague belief that law is the basis of a civilized democratic society. The sons of farmers, immigrants, and factory workers saw law as a very special American vehicle not only for self-advancement but also for the advancement of democracy. The sons of the privileged were also often imbued with some idealism gleaned from their professors in the New Deal era. Even the least caring recognized the legal profession as an honorable calling. They had a sense of noblesse oblige as well as a good measure of snobbery.

Members of the bar who attended law school in the sixties were fired with the belief that the problems of society would be solved or at least ameliorated by abrasive innovative litigation opening opportunities to minorities and the disadvantaged, forcing government and the private sector to operate fairly and in the public interest. Many of the more able lawyers of this decade became disillusioned with the petty politics and the mediocre level of legal practice in some pro bono offices as well as with the limited results of their brave litigation and with their limited incomes. Within a few years they become associates and partners in successful law firms.

The new lawyers of the seventies and eighties are different from their elder brothers and sisters of the sixties. Each year from 70 to 100 law school seniors apply to me for a position as my law clerk. It is not a coveted job. I know that the better students who wish to be law clerks will apply to the federal judiciary. Most of the top students will accept positions with prestigious big law firms at salaries from $35,000 to $40,000 a year.

The first question I ask each applicant is, "Why do you want to be a lawyer?" Most are amazed by the query. Apparently they never asked themselves this question before investing three or four years of their lives in attending law school and so limiting their choices of other careers. When they recover from the unexpected shock and fumble for a reply, most of the men answer, "To earn a living." Most of the women say, "To fulfill myself."

I suggest to them that the real rewards of a legal career are the intangibles of service to clients and advancement of the substantive and procedural law to achieve more just results. Few law students express much interest in these goals. There is little difference in the attitudes of men and women, whites and blacks and Hispanics. Among the many job applicants I interviewed was an attractive young man, a wealthy scion of a distinguished family, a graduate of an Ivy League college where he had been an art history major. He had a good but not distinguished record in law school. Why did he go to law school? "It's a way to make a living," he replied. He wanted to be my law clerk simply to postpone for another year entering the large, excellent law firm his uncle heads. All too often the new generation of lawyers see the practice of law not as a calling but only as a means of livelihood that they erroneously believe will be easy and lucrative.

I see many lawyers. Most are competent and conscientious. A few are brilliant. But too many are not interested in their clients. Occasionally a young lawyer will protest the scheduling of a case because he will have to work at night or over the weekend to prepare for trial. "I don't get paid overtime," the lawyer declares belligerently.

A judge's contacts with good lawyers, whether young or old, is one of the pleasures of the office. Good lawyers work very hard as they rush from one courtroom to another. Before the jury returns a verdict in one case, they have commenced another trial. Each does the best he can for his client within the restrictions of time and resources. Many are interested in the development of legal doctrine. From time to time a lawyer will tell me in a pretrial conference, "You'll like this case, Judge. There's a new point of law involved." His eyes shine as we discuss the ramifications of the issue. Such development of legal doctrine is also a special pleasure for many judges.

Unfortunately few practicing lawyers have the opportunity to engage in law reform. They rarely see the many different types of courts in the communities in which they practice and what happens to other lawyers' cases. Few have the leisure to examine the justice system of which they are an integral part, to assess its shortcomings and make recommendations for change, although many devote much unpaid time to the improvement of substantive law and practice in their specialties. The trouble with the law is not lawyers, but a system that victimizes them as much as it does their clients.

# CHAPTER V

---

# THE DIVIDED
# JUDICIARY

If you can't take the heat, stay out of the kitchen.

—Harry S Truman

The judge condemns himself when he chooses his
occupation, as surely as the pickpocket or the embezzler,
to long periods of imprisonment.

—John Mortimer

The gulf between rich Americans and the other Americans[1] is reflected not only in a two-track division of the bar but also of the bench. Those who were on the fast track as lawyers generally serve on the federal bench. State court judges are more likely to have been lawyers on the slow track. Inevitably the quality of justice a litigant receives in court is directly affected not only by the competence, diligence, integrity, and sensitivity of the lawyer who represents him but also by the qualities of the judge who hears his case.

Some cases in state courts involve only small sums of money and minor offenses. But many criminal defendants are charged with serious offenses for which the penalties may be years of imprisonment or death. Many civil cases involve millions of dollars. State courts decide very important questions. They determine the guilt or innocence of more than 90 percent of all persons (children and adults) accused of crime. It is these courts that decide, at least initially, some of the most important and sensitive issues of our time: the right to life, the right to die, the right to marry and divorce, to bear children or not to bear children, the right to have custody of one's children, and the right to use one's property as one wishes. State courts decide how many people may share a home and their relationship to one another. They rule on conditions of employment and access to jobs; the safety of food and air; the adequacy of garbage collection; the qualifications of schoolteachers, doctors, lawyers, and countless other professionals and skilled workers; the rights of schoolchildren; the rights of the mentally ill; the legality of strikes that affect an entire community; and the financial obligations of state and local governments. These are issues that control the daily lives of Americans. It does matter who makes these decisions. It depends upon the individual judge whether the ruling is based on the facts and the law or whether it is corrupt or arbitrary.

How competent are the judges who make these decisions? One person in a position to know is Judge Ernst Watts, dean of the National Judicial College. This is a school for state judges who are already on the bench. They attend on a voluntary basis. From observations of the college, I find that the more able, dedicated, and concerned judges attend the courses. The less able and less diligent devote their vacations to leisure rather than judicial training. Judge Watts commented, "Everybody who gets to be a judge for the first time doesn't know how to be a judge."[2] He mentioned in particular the increasing number of judges who because of youth or specialization lack substantial trial experience.

There have been and are many outstanding judges on the state courts. One thinks of Justice Vanderbilt of New Jersey, who reformed the courts of that state. Justices Oliver Wendell Holmes and Benjamin Cardozo served on the state courts of Massachusetts and New York, respectively, before their appointments to the United States Supreme Court. Many judges today are quietly and competently serving on all levels of state courts. But there are also corrupt, incompetent, and arbitrary judges. On occasion attorneys for both sides in a civil case and the prosecuting attorney and defense counsel in a criminal case will present a motion or petition to me. I tell them that the matter should be heard by Judge X, who has been assigned to such matters. The attorneys expostulate, "But

Your Honor knows that Judge X refuses to follow the law." Rulings by such judges cause infinite hardship to the parties and burden the system with appeals and retrials that could have been avoided.

Blatant irregularities, indifference, and politics as usual prevail in state judicial systems. From local magistrates to the highest courts, state judges are wrangling, making accusations against one another, and openly flouting the canons of judicial ethics. Serious charges have been brought against justices in the highest courts of New York, California, Pennsylvania, and Ohio,[3] to name only a few states. It is charged that eleven judges in Chicago are corrupt and that the entire court system of that city is plagued with corruption. Disillusionment and outrage are compounded when judges publicly declare that some of their colleagues are "outright thieves, fakers, failures, and misfits."[4]

Not all federal judges are able, honest, and sensitive. Some have betrayed the public trust and have resigned in disgrace. Others are venal and intemperate, deny litigants a fair hearing, and abuse the lawyers who appear before them. Many federal judges who have been rumored to be venal and known to be incompetent have quietly been persuaded to resign and no charges were brought against them. This internal, unofficial housecleaning has improved the federal judiciary without exposing it to public obloquy.

Just as there are bitter complaints about lawyers, serious charges are made against the judiciary. An American Bar Association poll reveals that 51 percent of those questioned agreed with the statement, "A significant proportion of judges are not qualified to preside over serious court cases."[5] The question did not differentiate between federal and state judges. The respondents consisted of 528 members of the American Bar Association and 78 law students. The study does not indicate whether these lawyers were trial lawyers, how many cases they had tried, before how many different judges, and in which courts. One can only speculate as to the qualifications of the students for assessing the judiciary.

Whether judges are this incompetent cannot be objectively established. Who evaluates the evaluators? Are the lawyers themselves competent and experienced? Are their views slanted by bias or prejudice? Are their opinions colored by social or economic philosophy? Although the vast majority of civil cases are settled, in those that do come to trial usually one party wins and the other loses. Also, one lawyer wins, the other loses. Often the losing attorney is dissatisfied, if not disgruntled. The possibility of bias is inherent in such evaluations. There is no way of knowing whether success or failure before a particular judge affects a given lawyer's opinion. However, in bar association plebiscites on the issue of retention (reelecting sitting judges) there is a remarkable agreement among lawyers as to those judges who are adequate and those who are not.

Although there have been no polls on the relative merits of state and federal judiciaries, lawyers often express the belief that the federal judiciary as a whole is superior to the state judiciaries. Many lawyers admit that they will try every technical ploy possible to get their cases out of the state courts and into the federal courts, where they believe they will get a better hearing before a better judge.[6] They share the public's low regard for most state courts.[7]

Mr. Justice Rehnquist, in discussing the qualities of a good judge, set forth certain attributes which most people would undoubtedly accept as an appropriate minimal standard. He stated: "Perhaps the bare minimum requirement should be that the person be a pretty good lawyer. . . . whether it be denominated 'common sense,' some patchwork of knowledge of the human condition gained from experience, or put some other way, the best judges undoubtedly have some sort of understanding of human nature and how the world works."[8]

The disparity between the federal and state judiciaries did not always prevail. In the late eighteenth and early nineteenth centuries state courts had a status equal to, if not higher, than that of federal courts. Judge Robert Hanson Harrison of Maryland refused an appointment to the United States Supreme Court by George Washington, preferring his seat on the state court. The bulk of litigation then was in the state courts. The United States Supreme Court decided an average of only thirty-five cases a year from 1801 to 1835. The first chief justice, John Jay, complained that the court was an "inauspicious" body characterized by little work and lack of popular esteem and understanding.

With the growth of federal agencies in the Roosevelt era and the rise of national business, federal courts became critically important to the financial interests of the country and the lawyers who represented those clients. Lawyers recognized that in complicated litigation involving

mazes of statutes, regulations, and difficult factual situations it was
essential to have competent judges. The old Jacksonian spoils system
might produce politically acceptable judges but not individuals who
could deal adequately with the wide variety of sophisticated legal issues
coming before the courts.

In 1946, the American Bar Association established a Standing Committee on Federal Judiciary to screen and recommend appointees to the
federal bench. Since that date almost every federal judge has been
screened by the committee. No similar concerted effort by leaders of the
bar has been made to obtain better state judges, although in many
communities there are ad hoc committees and programs ostensibly
designed to improve the quality of the bench.

A serious defect of the American Bar Association committee has been
its restricted membership and class bias. The committee was composed
of lawyers drawn from the fast track. During the period 1946–67, all
members were white males. More than half were associated with large
firms. None specialized in criminal law or domestic relations. All were
active in bar association affairs. They were predominantly Republican
and Protestant.[9] The judges approved by this committee closely reflected its composition.[10] In the entire history of the United States
Supreme Court there have been only five Jewish justices, six Catholic
justices, one black justice, and one woman justice.

For many years, the American Bar Association was a bastion of
wealthy white male Protestants. Blacks were not admitted until 1953.
The elitist character of the association stems from the tradition of
Anglo-American legal practice. In class-conscious eighteenth-century
England, the law, the church, and the army were considered suitable
occupations for the scions of the upper class. Judges were generally
drawn from the gentry. Many were knighted after ascending the bench.
English civil law dealt principally with property rights. The kind of
justice dispensed in criminal court by many of these aristocratic judges
would horrify any contemporary lawyer.

In the mid-1980s membership in the bar has been democratized. The
GI Bill of Rights made legal education available to many poor people.
The civil rights movement in the 1960s and the women's movement in
the 1970s opened the legal profession to many who had previously been
excluded. Socioeconomic status, race, and sex no longer present formida-

ble barriers to the practice of law. These changes are being gradually reflected in the composition of the bench. Until 1977 only eight women had sat on the federal bench. In 1983 women comprise less than 7 percent of the federal district court (trial) judges and 8.5 percent of the federal appellate judges. Blacks account for only 7.6 percent of federal appellate judges and 7 percent of the district court judges. There is only one Hispanic federal appellate judge. Of the district court judges, 3.49 percent are Hispanic.[11]

In the 1980s there are significantly more women judges and judges from minority ethnic groups. But this change in the racial and sexual composition of the bench has not bridged the gulf between the two major divisions of lawyers and legal practices. Indeed, I sense an even greater division and an institutionalization of the two tracks of courts as the practice of law continues to be stratified by income levels. The trend of the legal profession to specialization, certification, and the ever-expanding size and wealth of leading law firms all militate against a cohesive bar. Such bifurcation of the bar will, unless conscious efforts are made to alter membership and judicial selection practices, continue to be reflected in the state and federal judiciaries.

Both court systems include judges who may be described as liberal, moderate, and conservative. Striking differences in attitudes towards the role of the courts, the authority of government, and the rights of different classes of litigants are apparent among the justices of the United States Supreme Court and judges of all other courts. But the similarities in training and backgrounds of members of each court are more pervasive than the differences in their philosophies. It has been noted that there is a common hypothesis that "backgrounds are a major cause of division or variance among the judges; but the contrary assumption, that background experiences contribute to consensus and unanimity has never been carefully examined."[12] I believe that these similarities are more significant. Sandra Day O'Connor, the first woman justice of the Supreme Court, described the sexual discrimination she encountered as a lawyer. She might, therefore, have been expected to be a "liberal." However, she has been characterized by Mr. Justice Blackmun as part of the conservative bloc on the court.[13] Justice O'Connor is a graduate of Stanford Law School. She was a member of a prestigious law firm. She was enthusiastically approved by the American Bar Association committee. In all attributes other than gender she closely resembles the American Bar Association profile of approved judges.

A recent study of judicial candidate ratings by the American Bar Association Standing Committee on Federal Judiciary[14] reveals some very interesting statistical verification of the importance of similarities in background between the committee and the approved candidates for the federal bench. The study concludes: ". . . the strongest possible relationship which emerged in our analysis was that between the American Bar Association rating and the candidate's white male status." The American Bar Association gave higher marks to "those who practiced predominantly before federal and appellate tribunals; those who practiced predominantly in civil litigation and in the traditional subject areas of the law; those who were born in the jurisdiction of their appointment; those who attended elite law schools; those who had at one time achieved a prestigious legal clerkship; and those who earned relatively higher incomes than other candidates." Even as recently as the late 1970s, half the male judges appointed by President Carter were drawn from large law firms.

The study also found that political activity, as measured by speech making and prior service as a public official or as a candidate for office, was not a significant factor in Bar Association approval. However, more subtle but equally political influences, such as substantial financial contributions by the candidate or his sponsors, or the relationship of the candidate's law firm to the members of the committee and/or members of the United States Senate and even the president, were not evaluated. Partners of senators, powerful congressmen, and political leaders frequently are approved by the American Bar Association and appointed to the federal bench without regard to experience and other qualifications.

Another survey[15] published in the same journal reports that 50 percent of male federal judges were active in party politics before appointment to the bench. Some had held high appointive public offices. Others had been advisors to prominent politicians. Almost every appointee had either directly or through his partners made substantial contributions to the political party of his choice. Many were prominently involved in bar association activities. Bar associations, like most organizations, have internal politics.

Other criteria used by the American Bar Association committee are age, legal experience, and publications. No one under the age of forty or with less than sixteen years experience was found by the committee to be exceptionally well qualified. There was a strong correlation between the number of publications and a high rating.

No comparable study of state judges has been published. But it is undoubtedly true that in many jurisdictions judges with less than ten years of legal experience, some with less than five years, are sitting on state courts with the approval of local or state bar associations, screening committees, and ad hoc organizations for "good judges." The vast majority of state judges did not attend elite law schools nor were they honor students. Few have published any scholarly papers. Class standing, experience, and scholarly publications are, I believe, legitimate and desirable criteria in evaluating judicial candidates for any court. These are not factors related to race, gender, or status, but significant measures of competence.

The screening process of the American Bar Association, although improving the quality of the federal bench, has not succeeded in eliminating all mediocre, biased, and tempermentally unfit judges.[16] The reason for such appointments was cogently explained by Albert E. Jenner, Jr., a distinguished lawyer and chairman of the Standing Committee on Federal Judiciary. In 1966, he reported:

Your Committee must regretfully if not dejectedly report that various additional factors other than judicial qualifications have, unfortunately, continued to play a part in the Federal judgeship selection, nomination, confirmation, and appointment process. Without going into detail, these factors embrace personal friendship with one or more of those taking part in the process of preliminary consideration and ultimate appointment by the President, and confirmation by the Senate of the United States; "cronyism"; performance of service to political party organizations or to the United States Senators, or others in high public office, state and federal; ethnic origin; religious faith of the candidate; vigorous personal campaign by the candidate himself; current or prior holding of high public office, state and federal, on the part of the candidate or his personal or political friend or sponsor; and other like considerations wholly irrelevant to the matter of judicial qualification.[17]

Despite the unmistakable bias in the selection process for the federal judiciary, the level of competence of the federal bench since the 1940s has been remarkably high. Its decisions, on the whole, have not exhibited class or race prejudice. Federal trial and appellate judges have met the singular challenges of the times and forced the law to extend protection to children working in factories, labor unions, injured employees, minorities, and women, against the claims of industry. Freedoms of speech and press have been sustained and extended. Criminal procedures have been drastically altered to provide that those accused of crime receive a fair trial. The right to dissent and to demand accountability from government have been given new protections. The entire civil rights movement of the 1960s owes much of its success to courageous, incorruptible federal judges. One might paraphrase Winston Churchill and say that never have the rights of so many Americans been owed to so few: the federal judges.

Unfortunately, most state courts during this same period have not met their challenges. They have frequently refused to enforce the law and permitted delays, backlogs, and hasty procedures that deny litigants any semblance of due process of law. There are, I believe, four principal reasons for the disparity between the federal and state judiciaries: the selection process, working conditions, salaries, and prestige.

Federal judges are appointed for life. Most state judges are elected. Only twelve states do not have some form of election for judges of their highest court.[18] Federal judges are also dissatisfied with their salaries, working conditions, and prestige. Many have left the bench for more lucrative work.[19] But federal courts still attract able, experienced lawyers.

The situation in state courts is critical. Only ten states do not elect trial judges. When a judicial vacancy occurs, a judge is appointed by the governor, usually with the consent of the state senate. The judge must then run for election for a full term, which may be as short as four years. The election may be a partisan political election, a nonpartisan election, or a retention election in which there is no other candidate and the voters simply decide whether or not to retain the judge in office.

But, regardless of the legislative scheme, political considerations play a large role in the selection and election of state judges. An old-fashioned political boss who was responsible for the appointment and election of a generation of judges in a large metropolitan community told me his view of judges. "What's a judgeship to me?" he asked rhetorically. "Just another job. For everyone who gets a judgeship, I have one friend and dozens of enemies—those who didn't get the job. It's a headache." This attitude still prevails.

Judicial aspirants under all these systems must, except in extraordinary situations, have political backing. Political support usually entails contributions to a political party. When I was up for election, the party demanded a contribution of $10,000. At that time the judicial salary was $30,000. One should question why people would pay so much for a job that pays so little. I did not make a "contribution." Many candidates did. The twenty-five judges on the party ticket with me were swept into office along with the heads of the ticket. The public neither knew nor cared who the judicial candidates were. Twenty-five chimpanzees slated on that ticket would have been elected.

A judicial candidate who feels obliged to make the "requested" contribution can either pay it himself or raise it from friends and supporters. There are only two groups of people interested in a judicial candidate: (1) friends and family and (2) members of the bar. Few members of the public are sufficiently concerned to make contributions on behalf of a judicial candidate. Robert E. Woodside, a former judge, testifying before the Pennsylvania state legislature, stated: "Today statewide judges are sold over television like soap, and the selling costs lots and lots of money. . . . That money comes from lawyers and those special interest groups who are involved in frequent litigation. This system puts the judges under direct obligation to lawyers and litigants who consistently appear before them."[20] The knowledge that lawyers who will appear before the judge have contributed to his election campaign is disquieting. So is the knowledge (less publicized) of behind-the-scenes politicking engaged in by or on behalf of federal judges. But, there is difference. United States District Judge David Edelstein of New York points out: "Now, of course, you [on the federal bench] are in politics in the strictest sense. But it's a different sort of politics where the route to the bench is through clubhouse politics and the wards."[21]

A judge who is facing reelection or retention is also under considerable internal pressure to tailor his decisions to meet public approbation or at least not to outrage public sensibilities. Offenders are apt to be sentenced more harshly before elections than after. A candidate for election dares not be deemed "soft on crime." Controversial constitutional issues may be avoided or muted when the judge must write with one eye on the litigants and the other on the press and public.

Despite the problems inherent in election of judges, there is much to be said for election rather than appointment for life. State judiciaries have been more accessible to nonestablishment lawyers, women, and minorities. Arrogant, unfair, and corrupt judges do have to face the public at election. Such judges have on occasion been rejected by the voters. Short of the threat of criminal prosecution or actual prosecution it is very difficult to force a federal judge out of office no matter how corrupt or incompetent he may be. No federal judge has been impeached since 1936. Although public scrutiny and adverse comments by the media may inhibit or influence judicial decisions, judges should not be immune to public exposure and criticism. When a judge acts arbitrarily or illegally, the media should call it to the attention of the public. A Wisconsin judge who considered forcible rape the normal conduct of American males was voted out of office.[22] An outraged public demanded investigation by the Colorado Supreme Court of Denver Judge Alvin Lichtenstein, who sentenced Clarence Burns to two years work release and two years probation for killing his wife.[23] Such criticism and actions are an essential part of the democratic process.

In an effort to retain the benefits of election and improve the judiciary many states have established judicial screening committees. Unlike the federal committee, which is composed of lawyers, these state committees often have nonlawyer members. It is argued that this opens the judiciary to public scrutiny. The Pennsylvania State Bar Association's committee includes an educator, a clergyman, and the president of the League of Women Voters. Would any rational person suggest that these individuals evaluate surgeons, engineers, or scientists? To evaluate legal competence requires more than public spirit and concern. It requires expert knowledge. The committee's criteria for investigative interviewees suggested newspaper personnel, radio station personnel, and civic leaders. Most of these people would have no occasion to know judicial aspirants unless they were personal friends or flamboyant personalities. Even if they were acquainted with the candidates, what value would their opinions have? The conclusions of such a committee are, at best, based on hearsay, gossip, and rumor.

A Bar Association plebiscite represents the opinions of those in the best position to know the aspirant. Yet, frequently, judicial nominating and evaluating committees ignore this one reliable source of information.

There is no foolproof method of selecting judges. No one can know in advance whether a lawyer given the enormous powers of a judge will become arbitrary and autocratic. However, the lawyers who have observed a fellow member of the bar engaged in the practice of law over a period of twenty years know whether that lawyer is competent, hardworking, courteous, and honest. Appointment of judges who have been approved by a bar plebiscite and who then after a period of two or three years are approved by the electorate in a nonpartisan retention election would screen out the egregiously inappropriate aspirants to the bench.

Salaries are an important factor for both federal and state judges. Salaries of federal judges in the 1980s exceed $70,000, which they receive for life. Most state judges earn approximately $50,000. This is far from poverty-level income but it is also far from the income of successful lawyers. When one considers that college tuition is more than $3,000 a year in most public institutions and $10,000 a year in Ivy League and other private universities, a judge who has two or three children and does not have independent means or a working spouse has financial problems.

Some prominent judges, principally on the federal bench, supplement their incomes by making speeches for handsome honoraria and serving as members of corporate boards, foundations, and other organizations that pay substantial stipends.[24] Many state judges eke out a livelihood by teaching in law schools and colleges. Although some judges teach in night schools, others have classes during the day. This practice of moonlighting in the daytime requires the judge to choose whether to adjourn court early to the detriment of the litigants or to postpone classes to the detriment of the students.

Many of the least competent lawyers see the judiciary as a safe sinecure with a guaranteed salary, fringe benefits, and relief from importunate clients and the chancy results of trials. These aspirants rarely consider the time-consuming work of the conscientious judge and the intellectual and emotional burdens of decision making.

Simply increasing judicial salaries will not automatically improve the quality of the judiciary. The higher the salary the more desirable the position becomes to the least desirable candidates. In many rural courts and small towns where the case load is light and the cost of living low, federal and state judges are overpaid. In metropolitan areas, where the case load is extremely heavy and the cost of living high, judges are underpaid.

Working conditions and facilities of state judges are a real deterrent to attracting able attorneys to the bench. Except in remote rural areas, the case load of state judges is substantially greater than that of the federal judiciary, although many federal judges are also overworked and struggling to keep up with the case load. A state judge is under more pressure to decide more cases more quickly. There is seldom sufficient time for adequate research or reflection. In busy courts, a judge must get permission from the administrator or chief judge to take a day off. A sixty-year-old colleague, a quiet, diligent judge, came to me in distress one day because he had been refused a day off to attend his son's college graduation. State judges are often assigned to inconvenient locations without their consent or even the courtesy of discussion.

Although some counties have adequate courthouses, many do not. State and local judges often sit in tiny, uncomfortable, ill-ventilated, unsafe courtrooms. Frequently I preside over trials in a room so small that the witness on the stand—sometimes a defendant accused of violent crime—is within touching distance. There is no place to hold a conference with lawyers. Occasionally a defendant who has just been convicted or sentenced strikes out at a witness or attempts to assault the judge. Outside the courtroom there is no protection for witnesses or judges. The judge, the defendants (if they are on bail), their friends and relatives, and the witnesses use the same elevator and often the same public rest rooms. Many times I have been stopped in the corridors of the courthouse by accomplices and family of a person I have just sentenced to prison.

Federal courthouses are often sumptuous. But even the oldest and least luxurious federal court has the amenities of conference rooms, adequate libraries, and reasonable security for the judges. The cost of providing proper facilities is not beyond the capabilities of even the most hard-pressed state or county. However, neither the organized bar nor the public demands adequate court facilities, although jurors frequently complain of the dirty, crowded conditions under which they serve. The needs of state courts just aren't considered important.

A major difference in working conditions of state and federal judges is the quality of legal representation. Some lawyers appearing before me do not know how to ask a question or present a legal argument. A judge can rephrase a question for an incompetent lawyer. A judge can glean the legal issue, even when it is not argued by counsel. But a judge cannot make an opening address to a jury or a closing argument. Lawyers addressing a jury have said, "This is not a very interesting case, but I'll try not to bore you." Often lawyers have neglected to tell the jury anything about the plaintiff's damages. Prosecutors make inflammatory, impermissable statements that require a mistrial. And defense counsel fail to point out the discrepancies in the testimony. It is my practice to ask counsel how long their closing arguments will be so I know when lunch for the jury should be delivered. One attorney replied, "I don't know. I never know what I'm going to say until I get up and say it." This lawyer's client lost a case that should have been won.

Presiding over such badly mangled trials is frustrating and upsetting. Grossly incompetent and uninterested lawyers seldom appear in federal court. Most briefs in federal court comply with the rules. Words are correctly spelled and sentences are grammatical. A judge can more easily achieve a just result when a case has been properly presented.

Not altogether in jest, I wrote the following description of the physical qualities needed for a state court trial judge. The newspaper headlined it "JUDICIAL ASPIRANT? READ THIS FIRST!"

I find that five physical attributes are desirable for all judges and especially for the trial bench. Unfortunately, few lawyers are so endowed by nature; but by diligent application some judges manage, despite principles of genetics and evolution, to acquire these characteristics.

The ideal anatomy of a judge is derived from attributes of machines and of other creatures that have better adapted to their environments than have human beings.

1. The morphology of a jellyfish so that the corpus judici may sit for hours without undue discomfort. The lack of spine is also a decided benefit to the court system because such a judge will obey without objection orders issued by computers, clerks, and administrators.

2. The judicial epidermis should be the hide of a pachyderm in order to

withstand the criticisms and barbs of the press and politically ambitious prosecutors and fellow judges.

3. The nervous system of a robot is essential so that the judge may be able to work six days a week without fatigue.

4. The mind of a computer is highly desirable to enable a judge to follow sentencing guidelines and mandatory sentencing guidelines without consideration of extraneous factors such as viciousness, remorse, intelligence level, or other human qualities of the defendant, his family, and the crime victim.

5. Most importantly, a trial judge needs two tin ears to enable him or her to listen daily without suffering to repeated waiver colloquies (the warnings to the defendant that he is relinquishing his right to a jury trial) containing the following questions and statements:

"Please listen carefully to he and I."

"Dja know you have the right to seven preemptory challenges?"

"If any one indicates they cannot be fair, they will be removed."

"When I axe you a question, you gotta say yes or no."

"A reasonable doubt is that kind of doubt that would cause a person to restrain themselves in a matter of importance."

The physical ideal of judicial functionalism might not result in a creature that conforms to usual standards of pulchritude. However, such a judge would doubtless admirably fulfill the requirements of the system."

Public esteem is difficult to measure but it is an important factor in the desirability of any job or office. For years teachers, clergy and judges embarked on their careers despite the low pay. Today teachers leave the schools to become computer programmers; ministers, priests, and nuns abandon their callings for secular life; and judges resign to enter lucrative private practice.

The prestige of the federal bench is high, and deservedly so. Most lawyers would feel honored to be considered for or appointed to the federal bench. Many able lawyers refuse to accept nomination or appointment to the state bench despite the need for good judges and the importance of the state judiciary to the administration of justice. These lawyers are not impressed by the robes and honorific titles, which are meaningless relics of a bygone era that probably should be discarded.

The press is critical of the bench, rightly so in many instances. Sometimes the criticism is unwarranted. However, the press is the only institution that can hold judges accountable.

There is a widespread movement to have the organized bar establish committees to respond to criticism of the bench. Fourteen states have such committees and others are contemplating similar action. The *Judges Journal* published an article advising the judiciary to obtain help from the bar in answering these attacks.[25] Many court systems have public relations officers as part of their staffs whose function it is to generate good publicity for judges. Judges are often urged to make speeches to improve the image of the judiciary. All these proposals are only cosmetic devices to mask real blemishes.

Far more serious than overt criticism is the apparently common misperception that judges are subject to influence and manipulation. During my first year or two on the bench, many lawyers and politicians phoned me about cases. I told each caller that I would not discuss the matter and then promptly disqualified myself. I soon learned not to accept phone calls unless I knew the purpose of the call. A congressman I had never met left a message with my secretary stating that he was personally interested in a defendant who was listed to be tried before me the following day. I had the case transferred to another judge. I have not had such calls for many years. Nor have I received Christmas gifts since my first year on the bench, when I returned cases of liquor, boxes of fruit and candy, and theater tickets to the lawyers who had sent them. Their assumption that a judge whom they did not know would accept a gift or respond to a request for a favor indicates a shocking lack of respect for the judiciary.

A change in public attitudes toward the judiciary can, I believe, come only from changed practices by the judges. This is a matter of urgent importance, given the central role of the judiciary in American polity. John Stuart Mill observed:

The worth of a state in the long run, is the worth of the individuals composing it. . . . A state which dwarfs its men in order that they may be more docile instruments in its hands even for beneficial purposes will find that with small men no great thing can really be accomplished. . . ."

So long as the state judiciary is dwarfed in the public estimation, it is unlikely that the courts will accomplish their important tasks.

Most judges, despite low salaries, difficult working conditions, and dubious prestige, remain on the bench—some because they have no other options and some by choice. Those who do serve have very special satisfactions. The rewards of a judgeship, whether state or federal, do not meet the usual American criteria for success. An honest judge will not get rich. A good judge is not likely to achieve public fame or social acclaim. A conscientious judge will not have leisure to pursue hobbies and relax. But the intangible satisfactions are great. To achieve a just result or to write an opinion clarifying or advancing the law is immeasurably satisfying. On occasion one receives that rarest of tributes, appreciation.

A jury, after returning a verdict, sent me a card with this legend:

> With our warmest thanks
> for thinking of us,
> we're thinking of you
> with thanks.

Written on the card was this note:

Dear Judge Forer,

Arriving, at last, at the end of the tunnel, that is, the conclusion of our trial, we your jurors would like to take this opportunity to extend to you and your staff our heartfelt thanks for making our jury duty experience a pleasant and comfortable one.

For most of us, it was a "first," one which we were perhaps a little more reluctant to perform. . . . we have all truly enjoyed a wonderful learning experience that has allowed us to see our system of justice work in a most complimentary manner. . . .

The experience has been a rewarding one and we are sincerely proud to have served. . . .

The card was signed by all twelve jurors. Although I never spoke to them or they to me, the smiles, the nods, and the gleam of understanding were significant. As they found their experience rewarding, so I found mine.

The persons with whom a judge has the most contact are lawyers. The relationship between judge and attorneys trying a case, especially when they are competent and well prepared, is very pleasant and often intellectually stimulating. Few people other than artists, writers, and academics, in their day-to-day labors at earning a living, discuss intellectual problems. Even fewer people have the opportunity to make decisions that directly affect the lives of others. This is both a challenge and a burden.

The most onerous, perplexing, and painful duty of any trial judge is to impose sentence on an offender. The judge is asked by the government, in the name of justice and to protect society, to deprive a person of his liberty. Those who have visited prisons know the ominous clank of the metal door closing behind. The visitor is locked in, if only briefly. One's heart pounds a little faster. Hostile eyes stare blankly down the antiseptic corridors. There is no privacy or dignity. Fear is the constant companion of every prisoner.

What does the judge know of the person on whom he is compelled to impose a sentence? We have exchanged only a few cautious guarded words during the course of the trial. A judge is rightly reticent about asking questions that may elicit inculpatory statements. The defendant is rightfully wary that his answers may hang him. There is little verbal contact and almost no eye contact between judge and accused.

Despite the impediments and barriers to understanding between judge and offender, from time to time we are able to see each other as companions on the difficult journey of life. We can smile together, express concern for each other, and cherish hope for a better day.

An eighteen-year-old, whom I convicted of a minor offense and placed on probation with the condition that he attend school, sent me a card with a carefully crayoned picture of flowers. It read:

TO: Lois Forer
FROM: Vincent
Lois,
You are a wonderful
Woman, and i want to
thank you again for what
you did for me.

Sincerely yours,

P.S. May god bless you.

Members of a communal organization that had been burglarized testified before me. After I convicted the offender and ordered restitution, the secretary of the organization sent me the following letter.

Dear Judge Forer,
I am writing to you on behalf of the decission [sic] you had made in regard

to the case involving Ronald ———. The board members and myself could not have been more pleased with the verdict. The members of ——— have trust in the system, but because of you Judge Forer, we have even more. Thanks again for justice. May good health and happiness always be with you.

                                                            Sincerely yours,

My files are filled with similar notes.

Often on their release from prison, offenders whom I have sentenced and their families come to visit me. Sometimes I perform their marriages. There is joy, humor, and pathos in these meetings. Many persons I have convicted write to me from prison. Sometimes they telephone. One day I received a call from "Sonny." I seized the phone with trepidation. I had convicted Sonny of murder and sentenced him to life imprisonment. Had he escaped? What did he want? Why was he calling? "Sonny, where are you?" I asked.

"Oh, I'm in prison."

"What's the matter?"

"Nothing, I'm fine. They said I could make a phone call and I just thought I'd say hello and see how you are."

Almost every week I hear from someone whose life I have touched in the course of my work. Though often I fear that I preside over injustice, these artless expressions from one human being to another convince me that every person should receive equal justice.

Many of the people whose lives a state judge affects, for good or ill, are poor, ill-educated, and underprivileged. To hear adequately their claims and defenses requires more, not less, time than the claims and defenses of educated people represented by able and well-prepared counsel. But all too often the judges in both segments of our divided judiciary accept the system without question. They become inured to prevailing practices and procedures. State judges accustomed to hasty trials often permit the introduction of hearsay evidence, ignore the accused's right to remain silent, and do not adhere to the appropriate standard of proofs. If the accused is not going to jail, what difference does it make? If the claim is for only a small sum of money, why not compromise it? Federal judges, accustomed to lengthy trials, feel no compulsion to shorten the proceedings. They accept as routine the presence of eighteen or twenty lawyers sitting in one courtroom for weeks or months to try one case. Neither state nor federal judges ask, "Who owns the courts?"

# CHAPTER VI

---

# THE UNEQUAL DAY
# IN CIVIL COURT

> The very essence of civil liberty certainly consists in the
> right of every individual to claim the protection of the
> laws whenever he receives an injury.
>
> —Chief Justice John Marshall, *Marbury v. Madison*

E very law student used to begin his studies by reading cases involving
Blackacre and Whiteacre, two mythical parcels of land to which
the English courts devoted minute, painstaking attention. Land was
perceived to be the most abiding and valuable property. How it de-
scended from father to eldest son, how it was transferred, leased, and
cultivated, the rights to fell lumber, to graze cattle, to impound waters,
to protect it from four- and two-footed trespassers—these were the sine
qua non of a legal education. Every reader of Dickens knows what
tortuous and lengthy proceedings litigants endured in the hope of attain-
ing a coveted estate. The English law reports are filled, for the most part,
with cases involving property.

Today property takes many forms—stocks, bonds, patents, grain factories, partnerships, insurance policies, claims, percentage interests in
athletes, theatrical productions, and investment trusts, as well as land
and buildings, pieces of building, and rights to the air and sunlight above
the ground and the treasures beneath the ground. Civil judges in the

United States spend the majority of their time determining rights to property and money damages. Aside from injunctions and various forms of protective orders, it is a rare civil case that does not involve a claim for money.

In essence the claims are as simple as this: Does B owe A money and, if so, how much? Or did B injure A or A's property rights and if so how much money in damages should be awarded to A? One is a case in contract, the other in trespass. But around these basic questions the most elaborate, time-consuming and expensive methods of proof have developed. The costs to the clients are sometimes astronomical. In one case a law firm leased space to prepare for trial and entered some 500,000 pieces of evidence on its computer. In part, the courts are to blame for this proliferation of documents and, in part, the Xerox machine that facilitates sending copies of everything, relevant and irrelevant, to everyone. The numbers of attorneys, paralegals, and clerks needed to track these documents can only be imagined. The costs to the public are also considerable—$320 million in fiscal 1980 to process 661,000 tort cases in state courts and 32,315 cases in federal courts.[1]

The average cost per case ranged from $279 to $536, depending upon the jurisdiction. While only 2.6 percent to 8.1 percent of tort cases in the jurisdictions studied were tried by jury, these cases accounted for approximately half the total government expenses for processing all tort cases.

Formerly, a case was commenced by the filing of a complaint, petition, or other paper setting forth a bare allegation of facts and a statement of claim for damages or prayer for relief. The opposing party filed an answer. Months or years thereafter the case would come to trial. The outcome depended in large part on the testimony of live witnesses who told their tales to the judge or jury. Opposing counsel rarely knew what these witnesses were going to say. A skillful lawyer, quick on his feet and with a sharp tongue, could confuse or befuddle a witness. The lawyer was in every sense the Hessian or hired gun who dueled with opposing counsel in the arena of the courtroom, where the judge acted as referee. Cases were won or lost by the wit and personality of the lawyer. This image of a bygone age is perpetuated in fiction and movies. Paul Newman as the lawyer in *The Verdict* and Spencer Tracy playing Clarence Darrow bear as much resemblance to a modern civil trial lawyer as does an abacus to a computer.

Today there are no surprises in civil trials.[2] Every important witness and every party has been deposed before trial, that is, questioned under oath with counsel for all parties present and a transcript made of the testimony. Before testifying, the witness reads the transcript of his own statements and tries desperately to say the same thing on the witness stand. Prior to trial the parties have made written answers under oath to every question opposing counsel can concoct. Every written or printed document possibly pertaining to the issues has been produced under court order by all parties. Copies of all these depositions, answers, and documents are furnished to all parties and the court. All parties are required to file elaborate memoranda with the court setting forth the facts, the witnesses to be called, and a brief on the legal issues. The federal pretrial memoranda are more detailed and consequently more expensive than the pretrial procedures in many state courts.

Entire forests are consumed in preparing documents before trial. My chambers consist of a suite with an office shared by my secretary and the secretary of another judge, a small office for my law clerk, and my own office, a room approximately sixteen by twenty-four feet. In these three rooms we have more than a dozen filing cabinets, each with four drawers, and shelves above the desks on which large paper cartons are stored. My room is piled with scores of cartons containing documents in cases that have not yet come to trial. I often wonder who, if anyone, reads all these papers. A conscientious judge reads the pleadings, the pretrial memoranda and briefs, and also those depositions and documents that are introduced into evidence. But the answers to interrogatories, company records, scientific studies, and thousands of other documents that are produced but not introduced into evidence fill expensive storerooms. When such a case comes to trial, the lawyers and their assistants wheel in carloads of documents. Usually each lawyer has an assistant who simply keeps track of the papers.

The theory was that if pretrial preparation was thorough, the trials would be much shorter because undisputed facts would be agreed upon and stipulated. The trial would then consist of testimony on a few contested issues in which the credibility of the witnesses would be critical. A simple example is an intersectional collision in which each driver claims that he had the green light. Obviously one of them is mistaken or lying. The jurors are instructed to observe the manner and demeanor of the witnesses and to use their collective common sense in deciding their credibility. The result of the case will turn on that crucial question. Often the damages can be stipulated. Many times, after learning the significant testimony the parties reach a settlement because it is obvious what a rational judge or jury would decide. These cases are thus fairly and quickly tried or settled. In fact, the vast majority of all cases—both jury and nonjury—are concluded in this sensible fashion. These cases cost the public relatively little. It is the long trials that consume the time of judges and court personnel and require the use of courtrooms, jury rooms, and ancillary facilities.

A few not atypical cases illustrate the unconscionable time and expense in trying cases that raise what are essentially simple issues. A lawsuit against the New York City Board of Education to require appropriate schooling for handicapped children cost the city at least $200,000 in legal fees for the plaintiffs' lawyers, $60,479 for the special master, plus substantial fees for outside counsel for the Board of Education.[3] The Groucho Marx will contest lasted ten weeks.[4] A libel suit brought against the *Washington Post* by William P. Tavoulareas, president of Mobil Oil Corporation, and his son involved two articles published by the *Post.* After a three-week trial the jury awarded Tavoulareas, Sr. $2.05 million. The *Washington Post* reported that pretrial legal costs alone were roughly $750,000.[5] Southwest Airlines claims it has spent more than $1 million in defending itself, often unsuccessfully, against sex discrimination charges by men.[6] In the California asbestos insurance litigation, interim counsel fees totaling almost $3 million were approved by Judge Lifland White.[7]

The IBM case is certainly not typical but it is not anomalous. After thirteen years of litigation, at a cost to the government of $1 million to $2 million a year, the case was finally dismissed.[8] If the case had not been dismissed, what judge or jury could have intelligently reviewed and assimilated such masses of material and reached a reasoned decision? How much in court time and public funds was expended in this abortive effort? Why did the case drag on so long? IBM perhaps can afford the exorbitant expenses to which it was put. But millions of dollars of the taxpayers' money have been wasted. During this futile procedure thousands of litigants could have had their cases heard.

These lengthy, expensive procedures not only cost the public money but often prevent persons with meritorious claims or defenses from pursuing them. The president of a small corporation sued for patent infringement by a giant corporation described his experience as follows:

... We naturally were finally forced to hire a patent attorney. We had to acquire the services of a Texas attorney, and I think there are some two or three patent attorneys in the State. Well, when I arrived in San Angelo and met them there in the hotel, I can conservatively say there was a half train load of attorneys and equipment. There were motion picture projectors and attorneys all over the place. I don't know anyone of the Hartford [plaintiff] legal staff that was not there. They were prepared to give us a nice battle. Well, I had only one attorney and he was considerably lost in that crowd. I wish you might have seen his face that morning. So I promptly asked for a recess until the afternoon, in order to see if we couldn't settle the case out of court.[9]

Such litigation has aptly been called "ordeal by trial."[10] It effectively deprives the less affluent party of meaningful access to the courts and gives the more affluent party an unconscionable advantage.

Counsel fees are only a part of the costs of lengthy trial. Expert witnesses are expensive. It is reported that typical economists charge $800 to $3,000 for a lost-earning report. Yale economist Morton J. Peck received $100,000 to testify for Eastman Kodak in an antitrust case (which Eastman lost). AT&T paid economist James Rosse and an associate $241,000 for studies and testimony.[11]

In uncelebrated cases involving ordinary people and corporations that are tried before me, doctors customarily receive from $500 to $1,000 or more for testifying in a simple routine accident case. These expenses are paid by the litigants. If the plaintiff is an individual and wins, counsel fees, witness fees, and costs are paid out of the recovery. When a corporation is either plaintiff or defendant, the expenses of litigation are treated as a cost of business and passed on to the consumer.

Several questions must be considered. Is such costly litigation a serious nationwide problem? What effect do these long cases have on the administration of the courts? What effect do these costly procedures have on litigants and potential litigants? It is difficult to find hard factual answers. The federal courts keep accurate detailed records of all litigation in the federal system. From these reports, it is evident that lengthy cases are costing the public enormous sums and are primarily responsible for the backlog and crowded dockets. It is probably also a grave problem

in the state courts, even though many of the most complex and protracted cases are tried in federal courts. Federal court reports disclose
that in 1980, almost half the cases in federal courts were concluded in
one day. These statistics do not account for fractions of a day. Probably
some of these cases did not go to verdict but were settled after the crucial
evidence was introduced. In all these cases trial had at least commenced.
The reports do not indicate how many cases were settled before trial
began. Of all cases tried, 78.7 percent were concluded in three days or
less.

But 504 cases took from ten to nineteen days to try; and 187 cases
took twenty days or more. The records do not reveal how many trial days
were consumed by the 187 cases, what issues were involved, or why they
took so much longer than all the other cases. Simple arithmetic discloses
that if the 187 cases took on an average twenty-five trial days each (a
conservative estimate), these cases alone consumed 4,675 trial days. A
total of 177,975 cases was terminated by settlement, verdict, or with-
drawal. The average number of cases terminated per authorized judgeship in 1981 was 345. (Of course, the figure of terminated cases includes
cases settled before trial.) If one were to take a realistic figure of 215 trial
days per year per judge (allowing five weeks vacation and four weeks for
settlement conferences and opinion writing), the 187 longest cases consumed the full time of more than 21 judges, out of a total of 516 judges.
The 504 cases had on the average forty times as much trial time as the
average trial time of all the other cases. If the 504 trials lasting ten to
nineteen days and the 187 cases taking more than twenty days had each
been tried in three days or less, there probably would not be a crisis in
the federal trial courts. One must ask why this favored handful of
litigants consumed such a disproportionate amount of the courts' time
and the taxpayers' money.[12]

Although comparable figures are not available for the state courts as
a whole, the National Center for State Trial Courts reports that in
Allegheny County, Pennsylvania (Pittsburgh) the average cost per civil
jury trial was $4,815 and for a nonjury trial $1,051, as of 1980.[13] There
are no reported records as to the length of trials.

There are no reported figures showing how many plaintiffs or defendants or both demand jury trials, a much lengthier and more costly
proceeding for the public and the litigants than bench trials. Likewise,

there are no figures or reported studies on the percentage of trial time utilized by plaintiffs and defendants respectively. However, it has been my experience that large corporate defendants and insurance companies routinely demand a jury trial and insist on a jury of twelve. In my jurisdiction, unless a jury of twelve is demanded in civil cases, the jury will consist of eight persons, with no alternates. Many insurance companies also instruct counsel not to offer the face value of claims, even when plaintiffs are clearly entitled to a full award, because "it saves the insurers millions."[14]

Much information available about long trials is derived from articles by good investigative journalists, not government reports or scholarly legal articles. Reports by journalists are useful in describing individual trials and conduct of certain lawyers and judges. While they give illuminating insights, one cannot draw statistically valid conclusions or inferences from them. Nor can one rely on the experience or opinions of a small number of judges. Lacking other data, however, I must rely in some measure on my own experience, which is no different from that of other trial judges in busy courts. In twelve years on the trial bench I have presided over more than a dozen cases lasting twenty trial days or more and scores of cases in the two- to three-week range. As a trial lawyer, I tried many long cases. In my opinion all these cases could have been tried much more quickly without depriving the litigants of due process of law or a fair trial.

No matter how technical the evidence or how many witnesses testify, the issue in every civil case is one of these two basic questions: Does B owe A money, and if so, how much? Has B injured A and if so what is the amount of damages? This is true of land condemnations and products liability, which typically involve protracted litigation that is considered complex, partnership dissolutions, corporate reorganizations, commercial contract disputes, and malpractice litigation, as well as run-of-the-mill accident cases.

To see how these lengthy procedures affect the parties, let us examine a run-of-the-mill case. From 1943 to 1968, Ryan had worked at the Navy Yard, where he was exposed to asbestos. This was not disputed. It was also admitted that all nineteen defendant corporations had supplied the Navy Yard with some asbestos products during these years. Ryan was diagnosed as having severe asbestosis in 1973, when he was forced to retire at age fifty. He died at age fifty-four, leaving a widow and five children. Suit was filed in 1975 against two major suppliers of asbestos, who promptly joined seventeen other companies as additional defendants. All parties filed extensive interrogatories and supplemental interrogatories. Over 100 questions were answered by each party. Four doctors who had treated Ryan were deposed. Ryan, his wife, and three coworkers were also deposed. Officials of the defendant companies were deposed. Lengthy depositions lasting several days were taken of experts on asbestosis for plaintiff and defendants. Elaborate pretrial memoranda were filed by all parties. Some of the small defendant companies settled in an attempt to avoid further costs of litigation. The case was pretried before one judge. There was no settlement by the big suppliers. Ultimately the case came to trial before me and a panel of twelve jurors and two alternates. There were twenty-one lawyers in the courtroom, including counsel for those who had settled. Some defendants had two lawyers. Although Philadelphia has more than 5,000 practicing attorneys, several defendants brought in counsel from other states. Those defendants had to pay the travel time and living expenses of these attorneys as well as fees.

It took four days to select twelve jurors and two alternates, people who claimed they had not read or heard of the perils of asbestos. Either these people were remarkably stupid or they were lying. The trial lasted more than thirteen days. Much of the trial time was spent showing videotape depositions of the doctors. Most people enjoy watching TV, but they are accustomed to doing so at home lounging in an easy chair, perhaps knitting, smoking, writing, or doing something else while the program is on. They expect a break for a commercial at least every fifteen minutes. This is a time to get up, move around a bit, get a beer, and talk to the family, before returning to the show. Jury viewing of a videotape is entirely different. The jurors sit on hard wooden chairs. They are forbidden to take notes or do anything at all while court is in session. They sit in a semidarkened room for an hour at a time peering at a TV screen. What they see most of the time is the top of the witness's head, usually a bald spot, because the expert witness is reviewing his notes, not gazing into the camera. Most people who are not professional actors and who are trying to give accurate answers to difficult questions hesitate and think a minute or two before responding. A videotape is filled with pauses in which the witness thinks and gropes for the right word and the jurors squirm with boredom. The testimony drones on. In a not-too-well-ventilated, dark room, inevitably even the most conscientious juror begins to nod.

I call a recess and summon the lawyers to the robing room. "The jury is sleeping," I tell them. "Didn't you notice? Why don't we put on the lights and just read the testimony?" (All videotape depositions are transcribed.)

Seventeen of the nineteen defense lawyers protest. I point out how much time is being wasted. But that does not concern them. They are paid on a time basis. I also suggest that it is not necessary for all of them to be present during the playing of the videotape. They have all seen it. Most of them were there when it was made. The court officer will phone them when we are about to have live testimony. No one leaves. During the next session of the videotape I watch not only the jury but also the lawyers. I am presiding over a room full of sleeping beauties.

After thirteen days of trial and one day of deliberation, the jury returned a reasonable verdict for the plaintiff. The defendants promptly appealed.

I do not believe, as do some judges, that there isn't a civil case that can't be settled if only the judge will be firm and persistent. When I was in practice I resented arm-twisting judges who forced settlements on reluctant litigants. All too often in such a situation the lawyers, fearing that the judge will be prejudiced against the nonsettling party, relinquish their clients' rights. The plaintiff takes less than a fair sum for his claim. The defendant is coerced into paying money for which he may not be liable. However, the cost of trial and appeals can be more than the settlement. Many settlements are fairer than jury verdicts. There is much to be said in favor of settlements. The plaintiff gets paid at once. Both parties are spared the cost of trial, the uncertainty of the outcome, the cost of appeals, and the delay of two or three years or more in getting an appellate decision. An experienced judge who reviews with counsel the claims, the records, and the pertinent portions of the significant depositions can usually arrive at a more appropriate sum than a jury. The judge also knows the extent of insurance coverage, which the jury does not.

In one difficult negligence case tried before me, the plaintiff, a dock worker, had been seriously and permanently injured. But he was not disabled. At the time of trial he was working at his old job. The jury returned a verdict of $1.5 million in favor of the plaintiff. The defendant corporation (not his employer) had only $500,000 insurance. The case was settled for $500,000. As the plaintiff's lawyer explained, "My client is a stevedore. The recovery, if properly invested, will maintain him and his family. If we tried to collect on the judgment, my man would get a business that he doesn't know how to run. He might well lose everything and dozens of employees would lose their jobs."

Not all cases involve large sums of money. If there is a sufficient financial stake, a litigant can almost always find a lawyer. If a controversial constitutional or social principle is involved, an organization concerned with that issue or a pro bono publico law office may undertake the prosecution or defense of the case. But many times important issues are not litigated because no one will subsidize the case. Public interest organizations have limited budgets and an order of priorities.

A case that should have been tried was withdrawn because the amount of damages the plaintiff sustained would not justify the expenditures necessary for trial. Allan, who walks with an orthopedic cane, was descending a flight of stairs when the cane snapped off at the handle. Fortunately he was able to grab a railing and prevent a possibly serious fall. He took the two parts of the cane to an engineer friend, who examined it and was shocked to discover that the handle was attached to the stem of the cane by only one slender nail. This cane is manufactured by a large company that supplies orthopedic appliances throughout the country. The cane poses a serious hazard to anyone who uses it. Allan wrote to the government, to Ralph Nader, and to a number of other public interest law offices. No one was interested. Had Allan sustained serious injuries, many lawyers would have been willing to sue the manufacturer and the store where he purchased the cane. If the recovery had been substantial, the manufacturer's insurance company would have undoubtedly seen to it that this dangerous item was taken off the market. But, since no one will take Allan's case, this hazardous product will continue to be manufactured and sold until someone is seriously injured and obtains a substantial verdict. Allan is not indigent. If he was sufficiently outraged by the defective cane, he would have spent $50,000 to pursue his rights.

Perhaps a fourth of all Americans are too poor to be able to pay for legal services. Some are so indigent that they are eligible for free legal services. When the Legal Services Corporation was established in 1975, pursuant to an act of Congress, the goal was provision of minimum access to legal services. This was defined as two attorneys for every 10,000 poor people. In 1981, funding cutbacks reduced the staff from 15,539 to 10,906.[15] These lawyers are not equally distributed. Greater Miami has only twenty-two attorneys for 350,000 poor people, or one per 15,909. Eastern Michigan has fifteen attorneys to serve 157,692 poor people, or one per 10,513. El Paso has one per 14,333, and Iowa one per 10,000. These staff cuts have occurred at a time when there is high unemployment and reduction of other social services. A larger population of poor people have more legal problems. In addition to the problems of torts, contracts, civil liberties, and family law for which the nonpoor consult legal counsel, poor people need lawyers for utility rate hikes, mortgage foreclosures, and cutbacks in public benefits and entitlements. Two hundred and fifty thousand claimants for continuing social security disability benefits were terminated in 1981. All these people need lawyers to help them pursue their rights and remedies. Educated people who have typewriters, who have the leisure to go to the public library and do research and go to law libraries, can—with difficulty—represent themselves. The majority of indigents lack the education, the leisure, the facilities, and the familiarity with libraries and bureaucracies that are essential to pursue a legal claim, particularly one against the government. Without lawyers, these people have no access to civil justice.

Persons of moderate means who are not eligible for free legal services frequently forgo pressing small claims, as do most wealthy people. If the amount of the claim is small, it is simply not worth the time and effort and expense to assert one's rights. I do not decry this fact. Toleration and forbearance are as desirable qualities as assertiveness and aggressiveness. Living in crowded urban areas, dealing impersonally with multitudes of salespersons, service personnel, business associates, and strangers requires a willingness to overlook small indignities and small losses. Not every wrong rises to the level of a right that should be redressed by the law.

What is the cutoff between trivial claims that should be ignored and legal rights that should be pursued? A claim for $1,000 may be as important to a poor person as a claim for $100,000 to a wealthy person. No one suggests that courts should not hear cases involving $100,000. Small claims courts exist in many communities so that people can present cases involving small sums quickly and inexpensively without retaining counsel. The popular television show "People's Court" gives the viewer a picture of a fair, reasonable judge who takes time to consider the testimony of the witnesses and arrive at a sensible result that accords with the law. Not all small claims courts operate in this admirable fashion. The litigants rarely present their cases so clearly and cogently as they do in the prepared TV program. The judge must hear and decide more cases in a shorter period of time. Most small claims judges are not so capable and considerate. The results are not so satisfactory in real life as on television. The minor judiciary is not an esteemed or desirable office. The hours are inconvenient—nights and weekends. The cases rarely present an opportunity to consider a question of law. A judge of a small claims court never writes an opinion and rarely has contact with lawyers. The cases are repetitious and, for the most part, boring when one hears them eight hours a day (or night), five days a week, year in and year out. Understandably, not many judges of small claims court are learned, patient, and considerate and the litigants appearing before them often do not receive either equal justice or due process of law.

When a public danger or an important principle is involved, the courts should be available for redress regardless of the amount of recovery. Many negligence cases involve more than the payment of damages to an injured plaintiff, although that is often important. A disabled wage earner who is not adequately compensated for his injuries may become a public charge subsisting on welfare. If the disabled person has dependents, spouse and children, and perhaps elderly parents, the entire family become public charges while the wrongdoer or his insurance carrier avoids paying for the damages caused. Some lawsuits arising out of accidents have been instrumental in compelling defendant corporations to improve their products and working conditions. These cases benefit other employees and the consumers. Ford Motor Company, for example, paid about $20 million as a result of lawsuits charging that defective auto transmissions caused 1,500 reported injuries and almost 100 deaths.[16] If these actions had not been brought, there would have been even more injuries and fatalities.

Other cases that should be tried are settled to avoid expense and unfavorable publicity. After three months of trial the Three Mile Island case, arising out of the malfunction of a nuclear power plant, was settled. A nuclear safety engineer commented: "I find it disheartening that the public has to rely on a trial like this to get the whole truth".[17]

A trial is supposed to be a search for truth. The rules of evidence are designed to further that end by excluding unreliable testimony and requiring verification of documents and statements. Rules of procedure are also formulated to aid in the discovery and production of relevant information. When both parties can afford to pursue their rights and remedies and when both are represented by able counsel, that goal is probably achieved. Counsel present the pertinent evidence and argue appropriate legal issues. The outcome then depends, as it should, on the facts and the law. But when one lawyer is able and the other is not, the system falters.

Under the practice in most states, the judge is not supposed to inject himself into the case. Examination and cross-examination should be conducted by counsel, not the court. If counsel is inexperienced or incompetent, the judge must attempt to balance the scales of justice.

In a case tried before me a plaintiff of modest means had a meritorious claim but her attorney was losing the case. He asked his client: "Now, Mrs. Smith, didn't you tell the defendant that you would pay him if he finished the work?"

Opposing counsel immediately rose: "Objection, Your Honor, leading."

The Court: "Objection sustained. Rephrase the question."

The lawyer stood mute, bewildered. How did he get through law school and pass the bar? I wonder. The silence is embarrassing. The jury look bewildered. What will happen to Mrs. Smith's case?

The Court: "Mrs. Smith, what, if anything, did you say to the defendant?"

With tactful questions and side-bar conferences a judge can attempt to achieve a fair trial.

But when one party, often a poor defendant, is unrepresented and the other party has counsel, the adversary legal system fails abysmally. The stereotype of a slumlord is a rich, heartless man who lives in the suburbs, smokes a big cigar, and drives a Cadillac. To increase his ill-gotten gains he lets his properties deteriorate. The tenants have no heat or water. Rats and roaches infest the apartments. There are such landlords. They are represented by able counsel. But many slum properties are owned by people barely one economic step above the indigent tenants. Many times such a landlord is haled into court by angry tenants represented by a legal services agency.

Such a case proceeds like this:

The Court: "Mr. Grivens, where is your attorney?"

Grivens: "I don't have one, Your Honor."

The Court: "You had five days notice of this hearing. Why didn't you get a lawyer? The notice even gives you the phone number of the Bar Association if you don't know a lawyer."

Grivens: "I called them. The lady said I had to pay ten dollars for an interview and then pay the lawyer to come here. I don't have the money. I was laid off for two months. Now I got my job back. I shouldn't be here. I told the boss I'd be back by two. We'll be done by then, won't we?"

The Court: "I'll try to finish in time."

The plaintiff takes the stand. In response to proper questions by her attorney she tells me that they have not had heat in the building for more than a week. The pipes in her kitchen froze and now she has no water. Besides, there are rats and roaches. A clear case of code violation has been established.

Grivens is apoplectic with rage and frustration.

The Court: "Mr. Grivens, you may cross-examine the witness."

Grivens: "What?"

The Court: "Just ask her questions if anything she said is not accurate."

Grivens yells: "Cloette, when's the last time you paid rent?"

Plaintiff's counsel: "Objection."

The Court: "Overruled. Answer the question, Mrs. Coleman."

Plaintiff: " 'Bout three months ago."

Grivens: "More like six months, ain't it?"

Plaintiff: "Mebbe."

Grivens: "If you don't pay the rent how'm I goin' to pay for the oil?"

Grivens sits down.

The Court: "Mr. Grivens, do you admit that the pipes froze and that there are rats and roaches?"

Grivens: "That ain't my fault. Her kid busted the kitchen window an'

I tole her to get it fixed. But she too damn lazy. I bought her a garbage pail but she don't put the garbage in it."

The Court: "What about the garbage, Mrs. Coleman?"

Plaintiff: "That pail's down outside the back door. I gotta walk three flights down and three flights back up. With my blood pressure I can't do that."

The Court: "You have a son who can walk the steps, don't you?"

Grivens: "Cloette, why the hell don't you move out and let me get my property fixed up?"

Grivens is uneasily watching the clock.

The legal services lawyer who is properly pressing for the rights of Mrs. Coleman is all too aware that if Grivens hadn't gotten his job back he, too, would be eligible for legal services. We agree that Mrs. Coleman will give Grivens fifty dollars from her next welfare check, which fortunately is due in two days, and he will immediately buy oil. She will fix the window and he will fix the plumbing.

Thirteen lawyers with their briefcases, wearing neat pin-striped suits, are in the courtroom during this brief trial. Six of them are waiting to go on with the twenty-third day of trial before me in an equity case that involves the dissolution of a group of partnerships having assets of more than $13 million.

Seven lawyers representing two banks and an insurance company are also in court to arrange the scheduling of a case involving the embezzlement of $500,000 of bank assets. At issue is whether the banks or the insurance carrier of the embezzler's employer should bear the loss.

These lawyers are aghast. They have never heard a case like that of Mrs. Coleman against Mr. Grivens. They don't have such clients. They don't know people with such problems.

"Judge, what are you doing with cases like this?" They ask. "Don't they belong in municipal court or small claims court?"

"You mean they shouldn't be cluttering up our courts?" I reply. "Plaintiff's counsel invoked the powers of equity and petitioned for a mandatory injunction, neatly bypassing the landlord/tenant court."

"Pretty clever," the attorneys agree, "but kind of tricky."

"In equity one can get a hearing in five days. In landlord/tenant court they might have to wait a month or two."

"We have waited two years for our hearing," the lawyers for the bank remind me.

"But the bankers aren't cold and the losing party will recover interest. Don't you think," I asked, "that these people are as much entitled to the time of the court as you are?"

No one responded. It is an uncomfortable question that most lawyers and judges avoid, but one that I cannot ignore. Under the rubric of due process and equal protection of the laws, Mrs. Coleman and Mr. Grivens had fifty minutes of court time. Mrs. Smith had less than a day of trial time. Counsel did not file briefs or take exceptions. Mrs. Smith received a very inadequate verdict and settled for even less when the defendant threatened to appeal.

The bank and the insurance company had four days of trial time, many hours of argument, and consideration of briefs. I wrote a lengthy opinion. Exceptions were taken and argued. I wrote another opinion. An appeal was taken. Three appellate judges heard oral argument, read briefs, and filed an opinion.

Before the problems of the quarreling partners were resolved, they had thirty days of trial time plus hours of oral argument, consideration of briefs, and a detailed opinion.

Most lawyers prefer cases involving large sums of money and wealthy litigants. Such clients testify clearly and responsively. They rarely get angry. They understand bureaucracy and delay. They keep records. Documentary evidence can be produced. In such cases the lawyers and clients are at ease, for little risk is involved. The lawyers are well paid on an hourly basis. The clients write off the costs of litigation as a business expense. The problems usually require some ingenuity and skill on the part of counsel. The cases present an intellectual challenge to counsel and the court.

Judges also like these cases, for the lawyers are competent, courteous, and well prepared. The judge has an opportunity to research some obscure points of law, to weave his way through precedent, and perhaps to be a bit innovative. No extraneous emotions such as compassion or outrage sully the pure legal doctrines involved. It is no wonder that commercial, corporate, and probate law are the favorites of the legal profession and receive so much of its tender, loving, lengthy, and costly care.

# CHAPTER VII

---

# APARTHEID
# JUSTICE

There can be no equal justice where the kind of trial a
man gets depends on the amount of money he has.

—United States Supreme Court,
*Griffin v. Illinois*

The United States Supreme Court was hearing argument on the
constitutionality of imposing the death penalty on a youngster
who at the age of sixteen fatally shot a patrolman. The boy, who had
been a severely abused child, was found to have an emotional age of ten
or twelve. Mr. Justice Rehnquist asked Jay C. Baker, defense counsel,
if the defendant should be confined for life under a psychiatrist's care.
Mr. Baker replied yes. This colloquy followed:[1]

JUSTICE REHNQUIST: Why should the taxpayers have to foot the bill?
BAKER: It would be cheaper than executing him.
JUSTICE REHNQUIST: From the taxpayers' point of view?
BAKER: More will have been spent on the defendant's case than would have
been spent had he received some other sentence.
JUSTICE REHNQUIST: Only because of the protracted litigation.
JUSTICE MARSHALL: It would have been cheaper still to have shot the defend-
ant at the time of his arrest.
BAKER: That's correct.

It is startling and dismaying to hear Justices discuss matters of life and death in terms of money. Although probably half the cases in all courts deal with money, this crass subject is rarely mentioned. In criminal cases it is more seemly and dignified to talk about due process of law, the presumption of innocence, or the pursuit of truth. Lawyers and judges like to think that the administration of law is based on high principles of liberty and justice. But the economic status of the accused in criminal cases may be the most significant factor in determining the quality of justice he receives in the courts. Despite lip service to the doctrine of equal protection of the laws, the courts have in effect put a price tag on justice.

The fact that American criminal law provides more safeguards for the accused than the legal system of any other country gives me great pride. But as I preside over the trials of countless routine criminal cases I am painfully aware that these carefully enunciated rights, won after many years of bitterly fought litigation, are a cruel hoax for the majority of accused persons. As a result of a series of landmark cases, every person accused of a felony is entitled to be represented by counsel in every significant step in the proceedings,[2] including counsel on appeal.[3] Every accused person is entitled to apply for release on reasonable bail pending trial.[4] Every accused person must be informed of his right to remain silent and his right to counsel before being questioned by the police.[5] Every person is entitled to a free copy of the transcript of his trial.[6] These are important rights, designed to ensure that all persons charged with an offense shall receive a fair trial according to law. But as one observes the long, complicated operations of the criminal justice system, it is evident that at every stage of the proceedings the poor are seriously disadvantaged. This fact is frequently denied by scholars, lawyers, and judges. It is, however, glaringly apparent to all who observe the criminal courts in any American city, county, or state.

Let us examine two ordinary cases that illustrate the differences in the way the rich and the poor are treated, even when both are represented by counsel and the requirements of the law are meticulously observed. This is not a tale of two cities. These cases were tried in the same courthouse, before the same judge, under the same laws. There are no heroes or villains, only decent people attempting to do their jobs and to keep the legal system operating.

Robert Carnes is a young black high school dropout. Had he been a poor, white, unemployed, uneducated youth the system would have treated him exactly the same. Wilbur Quackenbush is a white, middle-aged banker. It is somewhat unusual to find well-to-do defendants standing trial in state courts, even rarer in municipal and magistrate courts. Perhaps 75 percent of all persons accused of state crimes are poor enough to qualify for free legal services. Both Robert Carnes and Wilbur Quackenbush went through the same carefully prescribed legal procedures. But at every step of the way they were treated differently. The only criterion for the difference in treatment was money.

After a crime is reported, the police begin an investigation. Quackenbush was suspected of embezzling several hundred thousand dollars from the bank where he was employed as an officer. Discreet inquiries were made. Detectives examined the books and records. They talked to other employees. Quackenbush was asked to come to police headquarters for questioning. He came with his attorney and refused to answer any questions. The second time he was called, he refused to come. No one can be compelled to talk to the police if he doesn't choose to.

Robert was suspected of committing a robbery, a common street crime. The victim of the robbery was not harmed. The robber took his wallet, containing about twenty dollars. The victim gave a fairly good description of the robber and the time and place of the robbery. The police searched their files for people in that neighborhood who fit the description, went out on the street, picked them up, and brought them in for questioning. This is standard operating procedure. Robert was one of these potential suspects. He was twenty-two, unemployed, had been arrested twice but never convicted. Neither Robert nor the others were technically under arrest. Under such circumstances most people talk to the police in order to clear themselves. They seldom get up and leave or refuse to talk because they know that if they do not satisfy the police of their innocence they will continue to be investigated. Robert did not have a lawyer on retainer. People like him usually do not even know a lawyer. Until a person is arrested he does not have a right to free counsel.

Possible suspects are often detained by the police for questioning for an hour or two or overnight. If no further incriminating evidence is found, they are released. No charges are preferred. Spending a night in police headquarters is not pleasant. But few of the thousands who are detained for questioning ever litigate the legality of such detentions. Robert was picked up by the police as he left a bar on the block where he lives. He was questioned, held overnight, and then released. This happened six times. Robert never confessed. He thought his statements were exculpatory. In the course of these interviews he mentioned various people he had been with. Some of these people were interrogated by the police. Through them enough evidence was compiled to get a warrant for Robert's arrest. It was late at night when Robert was brought before a judge, given a preliminary arraignment, and was advised of his rights, and bail was set. Robert could not make bail. He had just begun a new job. A few days later Robert had a preliminary hearing at which he was represented by a public defender who attempted unsuccessfully to get the $3,000 bail ($300 cash) reduced. Robert stayed in jail.

In 1982, over 118,000 people were in jail awaiting trial or arraignment because they were too poor to make bail.[7] When these people finally do get to trial they have already been seriously handicapped in their efforts to prepare a defense, as was Robert.

When he was arrested Robert had with him a pocket knife, a note book, nine dollars in cash, and a transistor radio. These items were taken from him. This is also standard procedure. The defender filed a form motion to suppress physical evidence and statements. None of the items had anything to do with the robbery. Robert had not given a statement. The motion was denied. A careful investigation of the people who implicated Robert might have led to a successful suppression of their testimony on the ground that it was the "fruit of the poison tree," that is, that the police were led to them through illegal detention of Robert and questioning him without a lawyer's being present.

Quackenbush was arrested under different circumstances. When the police had sufficient evidence and had obtained a warrant, they called Wilbur's lawyer, who arranged to have him surrender. There was a prompt preliminary arraignment. Bail was set at $3,000. Quackenbush immediately posted $300. He did not spend one minute in jail. He had a preliminary hearing at which his lawyer engaged in sharp cross-examination of the state's principal witnesses and managed to get some useful information.

At a preliminary hearing, the state is required to present enough evidence to show that there is probable cause to believe that a crime was committed and that the accused did it. These hearings are held before a lower-court judge. Usually they are routine. Many defendants waive preliminary hearings. For a clever lawyer they can be extremely useful in revealing the extent of the prosecution's evidence.

Quackenbush's lawyer immediately perceived that Smithers, an elderly bookkeeper in the bank, was the only person who could give eyewitness testimony as to Quackenbush's actions in juggling the books. All the other evidence consisted of painstaking reconstruction of the records by accountants and computer experts. The evidence was difficult to follow but once it was understood the proof of guilt was overwhelming. Quackenbush needed a jury.

Quackenbush's lawyer also filed a motion to suppress various documents. Some items that had been obtained from Quackenbush's secretary without his knowledge were suppressed because the police did not have a search warrant.

Weeks and months passed. Quackenbush was in no hurry for a trial. If trial could be delayed until Smithers was bedridden or died, Wilbur might be in the clear. Quackenbush's lawyer filed a number of pretrial motions. Each time they were listed for argument, he got the matter continued. He used every delaying tactic he could think of.

A poor defendant who is not charged with homicide rarely has a jury trial. If all poor defendants had jury trials, the public defender's staff could not possibly handle the cases and the system would grind to a halt. The defender routinely listed Robert's case as a nonjury matter. Quackenbush's lawyer demanded a jury trial. Quackenbush was treated no differently than any other defendant who has able private counsel.

Robert, who was in custody, kept pressing the defender to get him an early trial date. Robert had two alibi witnesses, friends who could testify that they had been together the night of the robbery. One friend was known to him only as "Fats." Robert knew that if he hung around the local bar he would be able to locate "Fats," get his real name and address, and subpoena him to testify at the trial. The investigator for the public defender made a few inquiries but was unable to find "Fats." The investigator had a heavy case load and could not devote a couple weeks to looking for one witness for one defendant. Robert's other witness, Sam Cannaray, was planning to join the navy. Once he was in the service, Robert would have little chance of bringing him back to testify.

Robert's case was listed for trial five and a half months after his arrest. The law in this state, as in many others, requires that a defendant be brought to trial within six months of his arrest. Although opposed by prosecutors, this has been a salutary measure. No longer do untried accused persons languish in jail for years awaiting trial. On the trial date, Robert's friend, Sam, was present but the arresting officer was sick. The case was continued for another month. The defender protested to no avail. However, he persuaded the court to note on the record the presence of this alibi witness.

Robert's case was called for trial again the following month but was not reached because the preceding nine cases listed for that day had taken too long. By this time Sam was already in the navy. The defender then moved to have the charges dismissed because Robert had not been brought to trial within six months. This motion was denied because the court found the delay was unavoidable. Finally nine months after his arrest Robert's case came to trial. This time he had a different defender, a different prosecutor, and a different judge.

The victim of the robbery positively identified Robert at trial. Unaccountably, there had never been a lineup. A lineup is a procedure in which the victim and eye witnesses to a crime are shown a half dozen people, including the defendant, all of whom are the same race and approximately the same size, age, and description. The defendant has a right to have his lawyer present to make sure that the lineup is fair. If the defendant is young, has a moustache, and is tall and thin, the other five men in the lineup are all supposed to be tall, thin, young, and moustached. An identification in a lineup of fat, clean-shaven, middle-aged men will not be admissable.

At trial the defender cross-examined the victim closely.

Q. "How long did the robbery take?"

A. "This fellow here had a knife at my throat. I said, 'Don't hurt me. Here's my money.' He took my wallet and ran."

Q. "Just like that. Less than a minute?"

A. "I don't know. He just came up to me like I said and the next thing he was running down the street. But this is the one. I'd know him anywhere. He has mean eyes."

Q. "Did you ever see him before the incident?"

A. "Before the robbery? No."

Q. "And how many times have you seen him since then?"
A. "Every time we been in court."
Q. "Six or seven times?"
A. "Yea, I seen him every time. That's the fella."
Q. "This robbery took place at night?"
A. "Yeah, about midnight. I just come out of a bar."
Q. "You'd had something to drink?"
A. "Only a couple of beers. I was sober. I seen him, I tell you."
Q. "It was raining, wasn't it?"
A. "Not that hard that I couldn't see him."

The defendant insisted on taking the stand. He testified that he had been at Sam's house all evening, that he, "Fats," and Sam had watched the late show together. Robert had not left Sam's house until after one-thirty in the morning.

Q. (by the prosecutor) "Where is this friend Sam? Why isn't he here?"
A. "He was here the first time. Now he's in the navy, up in Rhode Island."
Q. "Doesn't he know this is important? That's not so far away."
A. "He don't have the money and I don't have money to pay for no bus ticket."
Q. "Where's Fats?"
A. "I dunno. My lawyer can't find him."

At closing argument, the prosecutor referred to the "mythical alibi witnesses." Robert was enraged and shouted, "Don't you believe me? He was here, I tell you. The judge wrote it in the record."

The defender tried to quiet Robert. This defender had been handed Robert's file at 5:00 P.M. the preceding day. He had had no opportunity to speak with the lawyer who had been in court with Robert the first time the case had been called for trial. In a hurried conversation that morning he had questioned Robert about witnesses. Few of Robert's friends and relatives had telephones. They were not letter-writing people. While Robert was in custody awaiting trial, it was virtually impossible for him to get in touch with anyone. Moreover, any character witnesses could only have been neighbors and friends, people as impoverished and marginal as he. Fortunately the court clerk pulled the file. Sometimes the file is missing.

"Your Honor, here it is," she said. "Judge wrote 'S. Canaway, alibi witness, in court.' " The defender and the prosecutor then checked their files and discovered similar notations made by their respective predecessors. I was convinced that there really had been an alibi witness.

After a trial lasting about forty minutes, I found that I had a reasonable doubt that Robert was the robber. Robert was acquitted. He had spent nine months in jail. His job was gone. His girl friend had taken up with someone else. Even his meager possessions, left in his rented room when he was arrested, had disappeared. The defender petitioned for the return of Robert's property taken by the police. The money, the pocketknife, and the notebook were returned but the transistor radio had unaccountably disappeared.

Wilbur Quackenbush also came to trial nine months after arrest. His attorney knew that the only hope of getting his client acquitted was to select a jury who could not understand the accounting evidence and who would be impressed by a banker. Every defendant is allowed to strike seven members from the panel of prospective jurors without giving any reason at all. These are called peremptory challenges. Quackenbush's lawyer knew that he would strike from the jury panel all bankers, accountants, data processors, actuaries, or bookkeepers—anyone used to dealing with figures. Not many people of that type appear on jury panels. Most jury panels have many retired people, housewives, unemployed persons, and postal workers, and some factory workers—people for whom jury service is not a financial loss but a welcome interruption to the boring routine of everyday life.

Would blacks resent Quackenbush, a pillar of the white establishment? Would the elderly feel that he had betrayed the moral standards of their generation? Would the young look on him with that distrust of their elders so prevalent a few years ago? This attorney knew how to pick juries in accident cases. He conferred with lawyers who practiced regularly in criminal court. They all had their hunches and rules about picking juries by sex, age, race, ethnic origin, and neighborhood; but the case of Quackenbush did not fit into the usual pattern. The lawyer knew the types of people he didn't want on the jury but he was uncertain of the types he wanted. Since money was no obstacle, he consulted specialists on jury selection.

This is a new field of expertise known by the pretentious name of psychosocial science.[8] It is a fast-growing field. Sociologists, psychologists, and market researchers—by conducting interviews, using public opinion surveys, and correlating the background of each member of the jury panel with the attitudes people of that description are presumed to hold—derive the characteristics of a jury that will be favorable to the client who has hired them. If the client can afford it, these experts will conduct a mock trial with a mock jury simulating the characteristics of the actual jury, and then question these mock jurors as to their reactions. What did they believe? Which witness did they disbelieve? What facts that were not presented did they want to know? What would have been needed to convince them to decide in favor of this client?

In the trade this is called a shadow jury. Shadow jurors are paid substantially more than real jurors, who usually receive seven to ten dollars per day. The reactions of the shadow jury as reported by the researchers guide and affect the conduct of the real trial. A "litigation scientist," after describing the techniques and the favorable results of using a shadow jury, concludes, "Jurors, when all the grit is scraped away, do come to a sense of equity and fairness. And, that, after all, is what any case is about."[9] A judge can only wonder about these pious statements. The fees of these litigation science firms run from $20,000 to $250,000. The opinion of a psychologist, market analyst, or pollster can, of course, be obtained for less. This is one device of many that dangerously weight the adversary system heavily in favor of the wealthy client. Ronald Olson, an attorney and past chairman of the American Bar Association litigation seciton, is quoted as saying, "In our system of justice there are advantages that the one with greater resources is going to have—more lawyers, better lawyers, a larger staff. Jury research is just one more such advantage."

The theory of the jury is that it represents the conscience of the community. In England in the thirteenth century the courts periodically assembled 100 local people to try all the cases in that vicinity. These juries were known as the Assizes of One Hundred. So far as we know, there was no procedure to exclude from the jury biased or prejudiced people or people who knew the facts of the case. The idea was that because these jurors did know the facts and the reputation of the litigants they were the best people to arrive at the right verdict.

Today we make every effort to exclude from a jury anyone who knows anything about the case, anyone who has an opinion about the issues, anyone who is biased or prejudiced or cannot be fair to both sides. It is expected that both counsel will make every effort to exclude from the jury anyone who couldn't be fair or who was biased against a party. Jury selection was not intended to result in a jury biased in favor of a party.

Quackenbush did not have a shadow jury. But his lawyer had the benefit of professional advice on jury selection. A number of insurance companies and other wealthy litigants appearing before me have also consulted professionals on jury selection. The selection of the jury in the Quackenbush case took more than five days. There were six little old ladies (two black and four white), two young girls, and four retired men (two black and two white). Only one girl had graduated from high school.

At the time of trial the bookkeeper was in the hospital and could not testify. The state presented an array of accountants and computer experts. There was almost no cross-examination except that each witness was asked:

Q. "You were not in the bank at the time of these alleged transactions, were you?"

A. "No, sir."

Q. "You didn't see Mr. Quackenbush touch the computer or make these entries?"

A. "No, sir."

Q. "In fact, did you ever see Mr. Quackenbush before today?"

A. "No, sir."

The prosecutor brought in accountants, handwriting experts, and computer experts who testified as to the complicated way in which Quackenbush had set up bank accounts in the names of nonexistent people and embezzled more than $200,000. The physical evidence consisted of computer printouts. I was convinced beyond a shadow of a doubt that he was guilty. Quackenbush brought in a roomful of character witnesses: the minister of his church, the president of his country club, a boyhood friend who flew in from California at Wilbur's expense, neighbors, and college classmates. No one from the bank testified on Wilbur's behalf, although he had been with the bank for some twenty years. This singular omission was not mentioned in the closing argument by the young prosecuting attorney. After a four-week trial, the jury deliberated an hour and fifteen minutes and brought in a not-guilty verdict.

Quackenbush, his wife and friends joyously walked out of the courtroom discussing where they would go for the celebratory banquet. A wizened little court officer who has been sitting in courtrooms for thirty-five years remarked, "I always say, you gets the justice you pay for."

Quackenbush had almost five weeks of trial time, including jury selection. This was not a long trial when compared to trials of notorious people. However, it cost the taxpayers at least $50,000, not including the costs of investigators and computer experts. The Brink's robbery trial is estimated to have cost the taxpayers $3 million.[10] Using average annual per-day costs of the courts, I calculate that the trial of Robert Carnes cost the taxpayers about $200.

Trials of wealthy but unknown people are also costly and time-consuming because their counsel file numerous motions, make protracted arguments, and present numerous lengthy witnesses at trial. For example, a pretrial motion in the case of Abraham Slochamsky, a Brooklyn landlord, and Bruce Elliott, a Brooklyn lawyer, was heard for seven weeks. Fees for private defense counsel are often substantial. Claus von Bulow, who was found guilty of attempted murder of his wealthy wife, is reported to have paid his attorney, Herald Price Fahringer, a fee of $500,000. Edwin P. Wilson, a former CIA agent, is reported to have paid Mr. Fahringer a fee of $1 million for defending him.[11]

Even the prosecution and defense of a minor charge is costly when the defendant is wealthy. F. Lee Bailey, the prominent criminal defense counsel, was charged with drunk driving. He had a twelve-day jury trial and was found guilty and fined $50.[12] Bailey's defense cost him $100,-000. The trial, based on average per-day costs, probably cost the taxpayers more than $150,000.

Although there are no national figures for trial time of criminal cases or the number of guilty pleas, bench trials, and jury trials, one can gain a fair picture of how the system works by examining federal statistics and the records of a few state courts. In 1981, 30,221 criminal cases were terminated in federal trial courts.[13] Most federal criminal cases are significant. Many defendants in federal court are charged with political offenses and serious white-collar crimes. Of all federal defendants, 64.5

percent were represented by the federal public defenders. In addition, some indigent accused were assigned private counsel who were compensated by the government. The average payment for such representation ranged from a low of $79 in the District of Arizona to a high average of $946 in the Western District of Pennsylvania. The most telling figure is that the average time in court per case for the federal public defender in 1980 was only 1.7 hours. In 1981, the total average time per case, including appeals by the federal public defender, was 1.9 hours. In Pittsburgh the average time is forty minutes.[14] In-court time includes the appearances made when the case was continued and while counsel is waiting for the case to be called. Actual trial time is much shorter. An adequate defense, even to a minor charge, cannot be conducted that quickly.

A proper defense to a serious charge is time-consuming and costly. Chester W. Fairlie, a New London, Connecticut, lawyer, agreed to represent an indigent man accused of murder. After 650 hours of work for which he was paid at the rate of $12.50 an hour, he won a new trial for his client. Fairlie amassed 3,000 pages of documents. He cannot afford to represent him in the second trial because his hourly expenses were $8.00 more than what the state paid him.[15]

Arthur C. Helton of the Lawyers Committee for International Human Rights, which is furnishing volunteer lawyers for Haitian refugees held in detention, estimates that each case will require about fifty hours of legal time.[16]

Robert was one of the more fortunate defendants. Most poor people never have a trial. They are convicted in what officially is called a "nontrial disposition," a guilty plea. One might reasonably assume that if an accused person admits his offense and is really guilty, there is no purpose in giving him a trial. After all, he should know better than anyone else whether or not he actually committed the crime. The criminal justice system has operated on that assumption for years. Indeed, the system could not function at all if every accused person demanded, as is his constitutional right, to have a jury trial or even a bench trial.

Poor defendants are usually represented by a publicly paid attorney employed by a legal services agency. In most cases the trial attorney has never seen his client until the morning of trial. Another attorney has interviewed the accused in prison. A paralegal has prepared the file. After a five- or ten-minute conference, the trial attorney pleads the defendant guilty. The guilty plea colloquy takes perhaps twenty minutes. The accused stands before the bar of the court and is told that he has an absolute right to go to trial and that he may have a jury trial if he wishes. The differences between a jury and bench trial are explained to him, punctuated by the question, "Do you understand?" The defendant, who is usually a semiliterate high school dropout, answers uncertainly, "Yeah." He is told all the rights he is forgoing by pleading guilty, including pretrial rights, trial rights and privileges, and all appellate rights except for three: the right to contest the jurisdiction of the court, the legality of the sentence, and the voluntariness of the plea. After the first five minutes of the colloquy most defendants give up the effort to understand what they are being told. The final question is "Are you satisfied with your attorney?"

Often the defendant looks bewildered. I usually explain, "Mr. X [or Ms. Y] is your attorney. Are you satisfied that he [she] is defending you adequately?" Usually there is a long pause and the defendant, with wrinkled brow, answers uncertainly, "I guess so." At this point counsel may say, "Your Honor, will you indulge me a few moments while I talk with my client?" After a hasty whispered conference, the defendant says, "I'm satisfied with my attorney and I want to plead guilty." The careful requirements of the law have been met. But few persons in the courtroom can feel satisfied that the defendant has entered a knowing, intelligent, and voluntary plea or that he is in fact guilty as charged.

Some lawyers leave criminal practice in despair over these conditions. Some judges resign in dismay. Judge Alan I. Friess resigned from New York City Criminal Court after three and a half years. Judges in that court hear several hundred minor cases a day. Judge Friess commented, "To compare [that court] to a courtroom is like comparing a seventy-five-watt bulb to a star. It was a zoo."[17] Other judges and lawyers are also disturbed by operations of criminal courts. They see, as I do, scores of poor men and women forgo their rights through stupidity, fear, ignorance, and poverty. They question, as I do, the assumption that all who enter guilty pleas are really guilty of the charges. Perhaps some had legal defenses to the charges.

An interesting study[18] sponsored by the American Bar Association and funded by the Ford Foundation examined the guilty plea process in three states in 1965. It was found that many pleas were entered by uncounseled defendants, that the procedures were too informal, that inadequate records were made, and that pleas resulted in lenient sentences, whereas those demanding trials were sentenced more harshly. Obviously the fear of a heavier sentence induces many innocent people to plead guilty and receive a certain light sentence rather than risk a conviction and a heavier sentence. Although the research was limited to personal observations by a nonlawyer who made no attempt at determining the propriety of the results or making a statistical comparison of verdicts with pleas, it did focus attention on a much neglected, significant segment of the criminal justice process.

Almost two decades later, the situation has not materially changed. Those accused of crime now have nominal representation; the procedures are more formal and the records in most courts are adequate. But there is little assurance that poor defendants who enter guilty pleas are, in fact, guilty as charged.[19]

Procedural changes were introduced into the law as a result of vigorous appeals on behalf of poor prisoners by dedicated lawyers and decisions by courageous appellate courts. Prosecutors fulminated that the accused were being given too many rights, that the prosecution was being hampered in its functions, that guilty people would refuse to plead guilty and might go free. Many newspapers and commentators were highly critical of these decisions. None of their fears has been realized —nor have the brave hopes of the lawyers and judges instrumental in bringing about these procedural changes. What has happened is that more lawyers have been employed by public defenders to provide nominal representation. More work is generated for court stenographers, who must now, in most jurisdictions, keep meticulous records of all guilty pleas. The disposition process has been slowed—but only slightly. Instead of the ten-minute guilty plea noted in 1965, most guilty pleas now take approximately twenty minutes.

The substantial wrongs of the guilty plea as described then still obtain. Most guilty pleas are still entered by poor, ignorant, frightened people who have little understanding of the rights they are forfeiting. There is no way that anyone can know how many innocent people enter guilty pleas and are sentenced for crimes they did not commit. Even with full-scale jury trials, there are a disquieting number of miscarriages of justice, but at least the accused knows that he has been afforded not only the form but the substance of a due-process trial.

After sitting on the bench for more than a decade and seeing an unending stream of poor, disproportionately nonwhite defendants enter guilty pleas, I find that our procedural niceties have not provided safeguards for the unwary but only verbal cosmetic changes to placate the appellate courts. Although in most large courts, all defendants are provided with counsel—sometimes just a warm body with a law degree—in many places not even this requirement is observed. Professor Norman Lefstein of the University of North Carolina School of Law conducted a study for the American Bar Association in 1980 and 1981. He found that in Tuskegee, Alabama, no lawyers were appointed to represent poor defendants charged with crimes such as assault and battery, theft, and passing worthless checks. He states, "People being arrested are not having their cases challenged in any rational, systematic kind of way and the result is, innocent people get convicted."[20] This is true if they have inadequate defense counsel or if counsel does not have sufficient time and resources to prepare an adequate defense.

The purpose of providing counsel is to assure that every person accused of crime receives the full measure of due process of law. Most lawyers believe that, at a minimum, counsel must confer with his client, investigate the charges, interview witnesses, and prepare a defense. Counsel is entitled to see the police report and read the notes of testimony of the preliminary hearing to find out the nature of the charges against his client. No lawyer can go into court and adequately defend a client without this basic preparation. The relationship of lawyer to client, like that of doctor to patient and priest to penitent, has been assumed to be a close and trusting one. Lawyers may not reveal the confidences of their clients. Under the Codes of Professional Responsibilities of all the states, lawyers are required to represent their clients zealously within the bounds of the law and to represent their clients competently, to prepare adequately, and give appropriate attention to the work. A lawyer may not represent a client already represented by another attorney. These strictures are observed and enforced when a client retains private counsel.

A United States Supreme Court case[21] reveals the gross differences in lawyer-client relationships between a paying client and his counsel and an indigent client and the lawyers provided for him at public expense. The defendant in that case was convicted of robbery, burglary, false imprisonment, rape, and forcible oral copulation. Attorney Goldfine, a defender, was assigned to the case and represented the defendant at the preliminary hearing and supervised the investigation. Shortly before the scheduled trial date, Goldfine was hospitalized for emergency surgery. Another member of the staff, Hotchkiss, was assigned to the case six days before the trial date. He conferred with the defendant twice and reviewed the file. On the day of trial, the defendant told the court, "I only have this P.D. [public defender] for a day and a half; we have not had time to prepare this case." Hotchkiss told the court that he felt he was prepared and did not need a continuance. Defendant stated that he was "satisfied with the public defender, but it's just no way, no possible way, that he has had enough time to prepare this case." On the second day of trial, the defendant again told the court that Hotchkiss didn't have time to prepare the case. On the third day of trial defendant presented a pro se petition (filed by himself) claiming that he was unrepresented. The petition was denied and the trial continued. Defendant refused to cooperate with Hotchkiss in his defense. He was convicted on four charges and subsequently tried again, with Hotchkiss again representing him, and was convicted on the remaining charges. The Court of Appeals for the Ninth Circuit set aside the conviction and ordered a new trial on the grounds that the Sixth Amendment right to counsel "would be without substance if it did not include the right to a meaningful attorney-client relationship." The Supreme Court reversed and reinstated the convictions.

Both the majority and the concurring justices relied on the fact that this defendant did not specifically claim at the outset that he wanted a continuance for the purpose of having Goldfine represent him. The majority also laid weight on defendant's statement that he was "satisfied" with the defender. Because I have observed time after time a defendant hesitatingly say he is satisfied with a lawyer he does not know and in whom he apparently has little confidence, I could not lay any weight on such an artless statement made in the unfamiliar, intimidating court surroundings. Obviously this defendant and many others represented by lawyers they did not select and whom they have seen only briefly are getting neither due process nor equal protection of the laws.

Nowhere is the difference in treatment between the poor and the nonpoor more apparent than in entering a guilty plea. This is commonly known as a "plea bargain." The phrase conjures up some kind of a back room dirty deal under which a person guilty of heinous offenses gets off with a light penalty. While this does happen from time to time with wealthy white-collar offenders, politicians, and members of organized crime syndicates, poor offenders seldom get a bargain. Most prosecutors very sensibly charge each accused person with every offense they think can possibly be proved, knowing full well that some of the charges may not stand up. Thus an individual suspected of burglary will be charged with burglary, larceny, receiving stolen goods, possession of an instrument of crime, criminal trespass, and criminal mischief. If the state can prove that the accused unlawfully entered the premises with intent to steal, that constitutes burglary. If the state is unable to prove that the accused was in the premises but the stolen property is found on him, a larceny conviction may be obtained. If not, at least he can be convicted of receiving stolen property. If the accused can be found in the premises but without having taken anything, he can be convicted of criminal trespass. If the accused had a weapon at the time of arrest, or even just a screwdriver, he can be convicted of possession of an instrument of crime. What usually happens is that the defendant pleads guilty to burglary, the most serious charge, and the prosecutor drops the other charges. It is unlikely that the defendant would receive more than the maximum sentence for burglary (ten to twenty years in most states) even if convicted on all charges, unless there were particularly outrageous circumstances. When a defendant pleads guilty before a reasonable judge, the number of charges is really irrelevant. The judge, of course, knows what the charges are and is given a summary of the state's evidence. If the defendant had a gun, that figures in the judge's calculation of the sentence, even though that charge has been dropped. If nothing of value was taken, no one was injured, and no weapon used, most judges will not increase the penalty, regardless of the number of counts charged.

Private defense counsel will seldom plead a client guilty before a so-called "hanging judge." The reputation of every judge is well known to all lawyers regularly practicing in that court and also to court administration. The stern "Maximum Johns," who frequently are the darlings of the press and receive the kudos of the prosecutor, handle very few cases. Such judges may serve ten years or more without ever having taken a guilty plea or having heard a case without a jury. More reasonable judges are usually overworked.

In small communities where there is only one judge—or at most two or three judges—litigants and lawyers cannot make these choices. Significantly, some of the harshest sentences are imposed by judges in small rural jurisdictions.

Although a defendant who pleads guilty has received no bargain, the legal system has. A case that might have taken an hour or two to try before a judge has been disposed of in less than a half hour. Had the defendant demanded a jury trial, it would have taken at least two or three days and cost the taxpayers substantially more. With a jury, there is always the possibility of an acquittal. The prosecutor's batting average is improved by guilty pleas, an important consideration in an election year.

If a defendant who pled guilty had gone to trial and could have brought in an array of character witnesses, if defense counsel could have investigated the background of the witnesses called to testify against his client, including their criminal records and their possible reasons for testifying (perhaps a deal with the prosecutor), if the defendant were employed and his employer would testify for him, the result would probably be different. Even if convicted, the sentence might be lighter if the defendant appeared to be a respected member of his community. If the defendant could afford a jury trial—and the delay and the maneuvering—anything might happen, as it did for Wilbur Quackenbush.

Sentencing is a very significant step in the criminal process. For those who plead guilty it may be the most important part of the entire criminal prosecution. Disparity of sentences is a popular subject of a burgeoning literature on criminal penalties. Most writers discuss the differences in severity of sentences imposed by different judges on offenders convicted of or pleading guilty to the same charges. In response to the proposals of a number of writers, the legislatures of many states have passed laws requiring judges to consider or to follow certain guidelines. Every state has adopted mandatory sentences for a few selected crimes. But there has been little study or consideration of the disparities in sentences imposed on the poor and the nonpoor. This I find pervasive. Poor defendants, on the whole, receive much harsher sentences than defendants who are able to pay for private counsel and supporting services. There is some suggestion that nonwhites receive harsher sentences than whites. Certainly there can be little doubt that white-collar offenders, who are usually affluent, receive more lenient sentences than street offenders, who are usually poor. One need only compare the sentences imposed on the Watergate felons with those imposed on street criminals who steal a few dollars.

Sentencing procedures favor the convicted felon who has able counsel with ample resources and provides favorable information to the court at sentencing. Poor defendants must rely on the information, often inaccurate and prejudicial, presented by court investigators and psychiatric staff. Most up-to-date courts employ presentence investigators who prepare reports that are furnished to the judge before sentencing. Copies are furnished to the prosecutor and defense counsel. The typical report gives a summary of the offense (usually taken from the police report); the defendant's version of the offense; information with respect to the defendant's family, schooling, and employment; and a recommendation of sentence. I do not permit such recommendations, although they are often included despite my instructions.

The presentence investigator is not a lawyer. He does not know what the evidence at trial was. Sometimes an ignorant or unwary defendant incriminates himself in giving his version of the offense. The family background information is unverified. A parent or neighbor will often be quoted as saying that the defendant was "always in trouble." The investigator sometimes comments on the unsatisfactory state of the home or reports that he lives in a "high crime area." School reports are usually accurate but rarely helpful. What I want to know is the defendant's level of literacy and the reason he dropped out of school. Was it to go to work? Was he physically attacked in school? Was he a dropout or a pushout? Did he have to cross the dangerous turf of a rival gang to get to school?

If the defendant's crime was bizarre or unreasonable or if he appears to have some mental or emotional problem, most judges request a psychiatric evaluation. All too often these reports are worthless. Very few competent psychiatrists work for criminal courts. They can earn much more in private practice and, it is hoped, do some good for their patients. Frequently a court psychiatric evaluator is not a psychiatrist or a psychologist but just someone on the staff, perhaps a political appointee. The evaluator, whatever his professional qualifications, sees the defendant for forty minutes at most and makes a diagnosis and a prognosis. Many persons without a medical degree diagnose defendants as schizophrenic or paranoid. The evaluator also bases his opinion in part on the police version of the crime and the defendant's version of the crime, neither of which may be accurate, and his impression of the defendant.

Public defenders and court-appointed counsel rarely, if ever, are present at these psychiatric examinations. Conscientious privately retained counsel who are adequately compensated are present at the psychiatric examinations of their clients and prevent them from making incriminating statements. If they are not satisfied with the court psychiatric evaluator's report, they retain a private psychiatrist to examine the client and render a report to the judge at time of sentencing. Counsel for such defendants will offer a plan of disposition to the court. If the offender has a drug or alcohol problem, counsel will arrange that the client be treated at a private clinic. If the offense is serious, counsel will provide long-term inpatient treatment rather than a prison sentence. For a less serious offense, counsel usually suggests outpatient treatment. If the victim of the crime has been injured or property has been stolen or damaged, counsel will offer that his client pay reparation or restitution to the victim.

A poor defendant is rarely aided by a presentence report or a psychiatric evaluation. At best, his counsel can point out errors in the report. Sometimes I insist upon a second psychiatric evaluation, which is usually as unenlightening as the first. The disparity of treatment between rich and poor criminal defendants prevails in the sentencing process as well as at arrest, pretrial, and trial proceedings.

When Hans Singleton pled guilty before me, I could not avoid comparing his treatment with that of John Hinckley. Hans Singleton knowingly and intentionally shot and wounded an eighteen-year-old neighbor. Hans is nineteen, the son of a German mother and a black American GI father. When Hans's mother died six years ago, he was sent to the United States to live with his father and his father's black wife. Hans is light-skinned. He has blue eyes and blond, kinky hair. In the ghetto where he lives with his father, he is known as "Honky." Hans dropped out of high school. Although he is fluent in English, he does not read well. He shot and seriously injured "Mace," a young neighbor who was his most persistent tormentor and constantly subjected him to racial slurs and cast aspersions on his intelligence and his manhood. Hans pled guilty to aggravated assault. Hans's day in court was an hour and a half. This was an especially protracted guilty plea because I insisted that counsel discuss with Hans and his father the possibility of a "not guilty by reason of insanity" plea. Hans's father is a concerned, caring parent. He earns $18,000 a year and supports his wife and three other children as well as Hans. He retained private counsel for Hans. But he could not afford to hire a psychiatrist to examine Hans and review the boy's difficult childhood history, to interview teachers and neighbors, and to build a case, as well as pay at least $500 a day for trial testimony by such a psychiatrist. At the time of the incident, according to the police report, Mace had been publicly taunting Hans. It appeared to me that perhaps Hans been goaded beyond the brief limits of his endurance. A qualified psychiatrist could have shed some light on this boy's reactions. I sentenced Hans to probation. As a condition of probation, he must live in another city, attend night school, work in the daytime, and pay the cost of Mace's medical expenses and lost wages. The father is paying for Hans's support and contributing to the restitution payments. Mace is happy with the result. Hans and his father are delighted that Hans will not be imprisoned. Hans is deprived of the companionship and help of his father. He will be handicapped for life by this felony conviction.

John Hinckley knowingly and intentionally shot and wounded President Reagan. John Hinckley went to trial before a jury for thirty-nine days and on the basis of expensive testimony by psychiatrists was found not guilty by reason of insanity.

Juan Torres pled guilty before me to burglary, after a ten-minute conference with a court-provided lawyer who does not speak Spanish. Torres's English is rudimentary. A court interpreter translated the colloquy into Spanish. Jean Harris, a well-educated, sophisticated woman, was accused of murder of Dr. Tarnower, the Scarsdale diet doctor who was her lover. She was represented by counsel of her choice. Jean Harris and Juan Torres were both entitled to the same constitutional rights, to the same equal justice. Torres's day in court was twenty minutes. Jean Harris's day in court was sixty-three days. Jean Harris took a gun and went to the home of Dr. Tarnower, where he was shot and killed by her with her gun. Was it intentional murder or an accidental shooting or something in between, as the jury found? Torres, through the interpreter, admitted to entering a store at night when it was closed in order to get some clothing. Did he enter with intent to steal or merely to pick up discarded items? Torres could have been found guilty of burglary, not guilty, or guilty only of criminal trespass—a misdemeanor. Although I placed Torres on probation, he has been harmed by the legal system more than he realizes. Before his conviction he had been arrested twice. These charges were dropped when the complainants refused to testify. But now that he has a record, when a crime is committed by someone described as Hispanic male of his age and size, he will be an immediate suspect.

Why, you may wonder, am I worrying about guilty people who have pled guilty? Isn't the legal system supposed to be a search for truth, not a game that lawyers play where anything goes so long as one doesn't break the rules? A guilty plea is not wrong or immoral. If a person has committed an offense and admits it, he should not perjure himself by pleading not guilty, provided that he understands the consequences of the plea and that it is truly voluntary.

Everyone who pleads guilty or gives up his right to trial by jury is supposed to be asked:

Are you doing this of your own free will?

Has anyone threatened or coerced you?

Has anyone promised you anything?

I believe that most judges require that these ritual questions be asked and answered appropriately before accepting a plea. But no one asks whether the accused is coerced economically. Can he afford to wait in jail for trial? Can he afford to track down and subpoena the fact witnesses he needs? Can he afford to retain expert witnesses to examine the physical evidence? How many poor defendants retain a ballistics expert to prove that the bullet didn't come from the defendant's gun? How many poor defendants retain an expert to prove that the alleged blood on the defendant's clothing was not blood, but paint? A conviction of murder based on the state's evidence that stains on the defendant's shorts were blood (presumably that of the victim) was set aside when experts proved that the stains were paint, as the defendant had maintained.[22] How many defendants have been convicted on scientifically false testimony that hairs found on the victim's body or clothing were hairs of the defendant? For years prosecutors used such "evidence." The FBI published a leaflet, "Don't Miss a Hair." It is now conceded that no positive identification can be made on the basis of a few hairs. No one will ever know the number of people who were convicted, sentenced, and even executed in felony cases on the basis of false and unreliable evidence.

In misdemeanor courts defendants do not have even twenty minutes of court time. There are few presentence reports. The defendant is sentenced then and there on the basis of a few words uttered by counsel on behalf of his client. Professor Edward L. Barrett, Jr., of the University of California Law School, urges that more judicial time be allotted to misdemeanor courts and those that handle minor offenses.[23] Those defendants need more court time and better defense counsel, who have sufficient time to prepare the cases. So do defendants in felony courts, who may be sentenced to terms of twenty or more years in prison. To provide thirty minutes of court time instead of ten minutes is some improvement, but only a very small ameliorative gesture. It may prevent some injustices.

Lawyers, judges, and scholars who propose such minor remedies are avoiding basic moral and constitutional questions. Professor David Rothman[24] suggests that many humanitarian measures, such as welfare, protective legislation, workmen's compensation, and unemployment compensation, are not provided as an act of enlightened conscience but of convenience. I must question, too, whether the nominal rights accorded under our criminal justice system are a matter of conscience or convenience. The courts conveniently dispose of 90 percent of criminal cases swiftly, legally, and without challenge because they have complied with the prescribed ritual. But conscience compels one to admit that although the forms of justice have been meticulously followed, the substance of equal protection of the laws is routinely denied to many poor persons accused of crime.

# CHAPTER VIII

---

# FAMILY COURT

The great kings have their pyramids and barrows
                    to break time like a wave,
their cups and helmet plates still shine,
                    but I
have this pain for small deaths.

                    —Loren Eiseley

Plus ça change plus reste la même.

On a scale of one to ten the United States Supreme Court would undoubtedly be scored ten in prestige and importance by lawyers and judges. Family courts would barely rate one. These are the state courts that decide family disputes and try children for a wide variety of criminal and noncriminal behavior. Less court time is allocated to the trials of children than any American legal proceeding except perhaps traffic court. The only national study of the operation of juvenile courts characterized these hearings as the Five-minute Children's Hour.[1] Although this report was written in the 1960s and a number of landmark decisions of the United States Supreme Court since that time have declared that children have some due process rights,[2] little has changed in the day-to-day operations of family courts.[3]

In the 1980s a child's day in court may be only two minutes. The taxpayers are supporting elaborate court systems with large staffs of supporting personnel and paying for lawyers to be present at these brief, hasty court appearances. In Bronx Family Court, for example, one judge hears 238 cases a week, an average of 47.6 cases a day.[4] One must ask why society is going through this charade of due process.

This is not small-claims court where only matters of small sums of money are involved. It is not misdemeanor court, where an adult can at most be sentenced to six months in jail. Family courts decide questions of custody, child support, protection of children from abuse, abandonment, unfit homes, and determination of the guilt or innocence of children. These are matters of enormous importance to the individuals involved and to society. The decisions also have significant fiscal impact on communities. Placement of a child in an institution can cost a city or county from $10,000 to $40,000 a year. Once a child is removed from his home, he may be shifted from one institution to another until he reaches his majority—at a cost that may exceed a half million dollars per child.

The educational and emotional problems of a child who is moved from one place to another, placed under one set of rules and then another, wrenched from one group of people to another, are enormous, and not unsurprisingly lead to much antisocial behavior. The effect of a juvenile court decree may be more long-lasting and pervasive than any other order a judge makes.

But family courts are treated as the nadir of the profession. It is expected that one judge can hear and decide thirty or more cases involving children in one day. The low status of family court is revealed in an offhand remark by Brooklyn, New York, District Attorney Elizabeth Holtzman, who chided President Reagan for appointing so few women to the bench. She noted that state courts also are not commendable with respect to women judges since "most women serve in family courts, traffic courts, or the like. . . ."[5] Society views the courts where men predominate as being prestigious. These courts deal with important matters like murder and corporate mergers, not the rights of children and families. Prosecutors and public defenders usually consider assignment to family court an exile to purgatory, as do many judges. Consequently the least experienced and the least competent attorneys are often given this assignment. Lacking familiarity with the practice in adult courts, they are inclined to accept the careless methods of juvenile court without protest. Accordingly their clients, who are young, igno-

rant, and unaware of legal rights, suffer far more than adults who are
represented by inexperienced counsel. Many law schools assign students
who have not graduated from law school and who are not licensed
members of the bar to represent children.[6] Adults might complain about
such representation. But the children do not know the identity or
qualifications of those assigned to represent them and do not protest.
Nor do most judges.

Although the Justices of the United States Supreme Court loudly
bewail their overcrowded dockets and their enormous burden of work,
juvenile court judges rarely make similar complaints. In fact, attorneys
frequently complain that some juvenile courts close at two or three in
the afternoon. Those judges reply that they have completed their lists
of thirty, forty, or more children per day in four hours. Other juvenile
court judges are patient, caring dedicated people who make extraordinary efforts to help the children who appear before them. But the loose
practices in most juvenile courts, permitting quick hearings without
adherence to rules of evidence or procedure, inevitably promote arbitrary decisions and commitments to unsafe, barbarous institutions and
foster homes.

Many family courts are housed in imposing structures surrounded by
awesome majesty. Many are housed in the same building as the civil and
criminal courts. But family courts are usually operated like welfare
offices. Little objection is voiced because most of the litigants are poor.
Family court is simply another establishment agency that controls their
lives and that they are unable to influence. When the litigants arrive
they are given numbers. They and their families wait outside the courtroom until the case is called. A visitor to any urban family court will see
large numbers of poor, minority women with restless, bored children and
crying babies, waiting resignedly for a hearing which may or may not
take place. If it does, the entire trial will probably last not more than
ten minutes. Decisions are made from the bench. Few opinions are
written. Appeals are rarely taken.

Divorces are also within the jurisdiction of family courts. If the divorce is contested, it usually involves money. The battling spouses are
fighting over loot, not love. Battles over custody of the children, although framed in the context of the best interests of the child, are most
often a power struggle for money or control or revenge. Both parties are

represented by counsel whose standing at the bar and whose fees generally comport with the economic status of the couple. Some attorneys have highly successful divorce practices. Their cases are given ample time and judicial consideration. The seamy divorce and custody problems of the Pulitzers, while unusual, are not anomalous. This trial consumed six weeks of court time, paid for by the public. If counsel fees are sufficient, the cases can go on endlessly.

The vast majority of divorce cases, however, involve people with few assets. Their attorneys work out the best arrangements they can and avoid litigation their clients can ill afford. Many poor people simply ignore the entire business of legal formalities. They marry without a license and separate without divorce. Even if the first marriage was legally recognized, when they come to a parting of the ways they simply separate and thereafter form new relationships without benefit of clergy or courts. In most instances, this avoidance of legal process is not due to the fact that the couple believe in free love or disdain marriage vows. It is a matter of necessity. They simply can not afford the price of a divorce.

The most significant function of family court is not divorce, custody, and the protection of minors, but the prosecution of children. Here the hypocrisy and unfairness of the litigational process is most apparent. Children are the poorest and least powerful group in our society.

Politically minded organizations represent the interests of elderly, the blind, the mentally ill, women, the physically handicapped, welfare recipients, and minorities. All these people, although disadvantaged in fact and before the law, nonetheless have the franchise. They can petition for rights and entitlements. Some organizations, such as the Gray Panthers, NOW, and the NAACP, have considerable influence on legislatures. These adults, either as individuals or as members of their organizations, can sue to obtain redress in the same courts and under the same procedures as all other adults. When they are accused of crime, they are tried in the same courts and under the same procedures as all other adults. They are entitled to all the protections of the Constitution.

Children are in a different category. Before the law they are "nonpersons." With some few exceptions, a child has no access to the courts of general jurisdiction. A child must seek protection in a special court. When a child is accused of wrongdoing (which may or may not be a crime) he is tried in a special court without the procedural and substantive rights of adults. A child is not entitled to a jury trial.[7] In this court he is in a world where words have lost their customary meanings and concepts their logical bases. When a child goes to court he ceases to be a child and becomes a "juvenile," an appellation with pejorative connotations. The word *juvenile* is commonly used as an adjective to modify the noun *delinquent*. A juvenile is not accused of crime but of delinquency. Ergo, he is not entitled to the protections of the criminal court. Nonetheless, he can be removed from his home and family, deprived of the right to attend public school, and compelled to remain in a place he may not leave. This is not called a jail but a juvenile institution.

The law protects the sensibilities of lawyers, judges, and the adult community by these euphemisms. No one is offended by a report that a juvenile was adjudicated delinquent and placed in the Greenacres Farms for rehabilitation. We might be shocked to read that a child was convicted of stealing five dollars and sentenced to prison for seven years. In fact, that may be the effect of a juvenile adjudication and commitment.

Greenacres Farms is a fictitious name. Institutions for children are always given pleasant names, as if the name could conceal or overcome the unpleasantness of the institution. Former United States Senator Birch Bayh describes the history of a young man who had spent most his life in misnamed prisons. "At the age of twelve he was committed to the Industrial Home School . . . which housed neglected children from the District of Columbia." One wonders what heinous crime this child had committed, in what kind of trial he was convicted and whether he was advised of his right to appeal. Senator Bayh continues, "His most memorable experience there was fighting off sexual attacks of older boys. Since that time he has been successively incarcerated in Cedar Knoll (the facility for juvenile delinquents . . .), the now defunct National Training School for Boys, and a series of federal prisons.[8]

The public at large has been misled by nomenclature and ignorance. Few middle-class people have any contact with the juvenile court. When they do, it is brief and peripheral—perhaps a phone call to help the maid's son who has been arrested or to make a complaint about a youngster who has stolen or vandalized. The press frequently reports that a "juvenile" who has been arrested dozens of times has just been released again by a juvenile court judge. The public response is usually outrage at the judge who has released this hardened criminal, age fourteen or fifteen. From time to time there are well-publicized moves to lower the juvenile court age, to treat children who commit crimes as adults, and to punish them severely. Few people not connected with the juvenile court system really know what is going on there despite a plethora of books on the subject.

At the turn of the century, when the juvenile court movement began, persons accused of crime had few legal protections. Poor people were routinely tried without being represented by counsel. Confessions were beaten out of suspects. Accused persons rotted in jail for many months before trial. Prisons were fearsome places. A special court for children where a kindly judge would place an arm around an errant lad and gently lead him into the paths of righteousness was a laudable goal of reformers.

From its inception juvenile courts were the dumping ground for the problem children of the poor. The courts were overcrowded. The hearings were hurried and harried. Juvenile judges saw themselves primarily as social benefactors helping to reform and rehabilitate children. Consequently they saw little need to observe legal procedures. The privilege against self-incrimination, the ban on hearsay evidence, and the right to have formal charges and procedural rules were treated as impediments to the social aim of helping children.

Confession was good for the soul. If a child were permitted to remain silent and "beat the rap," he would lose the chance of rehabilitation in a juvenile jail. Obviously if the child had a lawyer the goals of the juvenile court would be defeated. Many judges were unaware of conditions in the institutions to which they consigned children. I recall a juvenile court judge telling a weeping mother, "Your daughter will have a wonderful time at Sylvan Farms [also a fictional name]. It's just like the B—— Academy [an elite private girl's boarding school]." In fact, Sylvan Farms was a prison where the children had minimal schooling, no medical care except in serious emergencies, no counseling, and essentially no care. Another juvenile court judge, reviewing a psychiatric report on a child, commented from the bench as he committed a child to an institution, "Barry, your IQ is only seventy-six. That's not good. I want to see an improvement when you come back." The child's lawyer remained silent as the youngster was shipped off to a rural jail with no facilities for teaching retarded children.

Most children did not have families that could afford legal counsel; the actions of the courts were seldom challenged. Even those families who could afford counsel were often warned by court personnel that it would be inadvisable to have an attorney. Indeed, some juvenile courts refused to permit counsel to represent children. The press was barred from juvenile courts, either by statute or custom. Juvenile judges acted without the restraints imposed on all other courts by the presence of counsel and the vigilance of the press. Convinced of their good motives and the obvious needs of the children, many juvenile court judges became virtual dictators. Dr. Jonas B. Robitscher, a professor of both law and psychiatry, commented that psychiatrists and juvenile court judges are the only people in America who can lawfully lock up people who have not been accused of any crime.[9] Unchallenged by counsel and operating in secret, the juvenile court bureaucracy coped with an ever growing flood of cases by decreasing the amount of judicial time accorded each child. Nonlegal personnel were used to "dispose" of cases and practices were instituted that had no analogue in legal procedures. In some juvenile courts, if there is no evidence of the child's guilt but the judge and court personnel believe he is guilty of some offense, he is not discharged but "determined," a ruling that gives the court continuing jurisdiction over the child.

Although juvenile courts were overburdened with cases involving alleged crimes, they reached out to encompass social complaints involving conduct not recognized as offenses under the common law or statute. Young girls were incarcerated to prevent them from becoming pregnant. Children were imprisoned for disobedience to parents, playing hookey, and annoying the neighbors. The juvenile court attempted to fill the roles of parent, family, church, and social agency for the children of the poor. In the process, legal limitations and protections were ignored.

In the rare appeals from juvenile decisions brought by counsel curious doctrines developed: A child has no right to freedom, only to custody. Commitment to a juvenile jail is not a punishment. A child has no need for counsel. A juvenile court hearing on a charge of delinquency is not a criminal trial. A child has no right to bail. The court has powers parens patriae. As Mr. Justice Fortas observed, this is a bad law and bad Latin.

What the juvenile courts meant was that the court had the same plenary powers over a child as his parents.

While these hasty, irregular procedures prevailed in juvenile court, a quiet revolution was occurring in criminal law. Commencing in 1938, when the United States Supreme Court held that an adult accused of a federal crime had the right to the assistance of counsel,[10] a series of landmark cases delineated the rights of adults accused of both federal and state crimes and the rights of adult prisoners. None of these protections was extended to children because few children were represented by counsel. Appellate courts were, for the most part, unaware of the casual procedures in juvenile courts and the abominable conditions in many institutions to which children were committed by juvenile courts.

It was not until 1966 that the United States Supreme Court first considered a case involving a decision of a juvenile court.[11] The following year the Supreme Court decided *In re Gault,* [12] the landmark case upholding the right of a child to legal counsel in a delinquency case. Since then the United States Supreme Court has decided only a handful of cases involving juvenile court practices.[13] There has been no decision holding that children accused of delinquency are entitled to the same (or equivalent) legal protections as adults. Children are still not included within the definition of persons under the equal protection clause of the Fourteenth Amendment.

In the 1980s, as at the turn of the century, the principal function of juvenile courts is still the prosecution of children. Like adult criminal courts, the juvenile courts are overcrowded, operating with difficulty in the face of ever increasing case loads. In 1982, approximately 40 percent of all crimes were committed by children. Most of these cases were processed in the nation's juvenile courts. Almost 65 percent of youngsters who have been before a juvenile court are rearrested on another charge of delinquency. A very large proportion of these children are poor, undereducated, and deprived of minimal care and affection. What the juvenile courts do to and for these children vitally affects them and their future lives as adults. When one considers that more than half of all adult offenders have had at least one contact with the juvenile court, it is evident that juvenile courts play a significant role in shaping the lives of a large segment of American society.

Although there are no adequate studies of juvenile court practices, it is reasonable to believe that the majority of children accused of delinquency in the 1980s are represented in juvenile court by a defender office or some publicly funded or quasi-public agency. There are many juvenile law centers, organizations for juvenile justice, and organizations to prevent child abuse. Almost every law school teaches courses in "juvenile justice." Twenty years ago there was no such subject in the curriculum.

One would expect that this ferment and public interest, implemented by public funding for legal counsel and concern by the legal profession, would have wrought significant changes. Unfortunately, a few Supreme Court decisions and an infusion of money for defense counsel have not appreciably altered the system. The principal beneficiaries of the interest in juvenile law have not been the children but cadres of lawyers, law professors, psychiatrists, psychologists, social workers, and court personnel. There are more and more people administering the system, but its basic structure has not changed.[14]

The vast majority of children appearing in juvenile court today are still poor, deprived, and undereducated. A large proportion of the boys are functionally illiterate.[15] In the early twentieth century many children appearing in juvenile court were children of immigrants. Today many are from minorities. Many represent the second generation subjected to the ministrations of the juvenile court.

Edward S. is one of these children.[16] His involvement with the juvenile court is a classic example of the failures of a well-intentioned system and the dire need for vigorous, experienced lawyers to compel enforcement of rules so that children do receive equal protection of the laws. One might say of Edward that in his beginning is his end. Edward's mother was well known to the juvenile court both as a juvenile delinquent and later as the subject of child abuse and neglect petitions involving her seven children. Edward first came to the attention of the juvenile court when he ran away from home at the age of eight.[17] Was he attempting to escape from abusive treatment? Was he a bad boy? Or was he just a bored child who failed to come home one night? The court records do not indicate. Apparently he was never given a hearing but was charged with delinquency. At age eight his juvenile record had begun. When middle-class children run away from home, the parents usually notify the police. After the child is found and returned, the matter is dropped. Rarely is a charge of delinquency brought. If such a petition is filed, the parents retain counsel who promptly has the record expunged.

When Edward was ten years old his father was stabbed to death. Shortly thereafter Edward was arrested on a trivial charge. He was seen by a court psychiatrist who reported, "Edward tested as a 'borderline retarded' but that this was more a reflection of Edward's emotional problems." He recommended that Edward needs "sustained interest and supervision" and suggested a sponsor such as Big Brothers.

Edward was examined by another court doctor when he was twelve years old. The report included the following:

... A clue to part of the difficulty lies in his response to the question about how he reacted to his father being stabbed to death two years ago. "Its [sic] a long time ago—I don't want to talk about it." I suspect he is basically unhappy and frustrated.

The doctor recommended that Edward "could use a good maternal influence and improved guidance and supervision."

A year later he was examined by another court doctor.

At least three different juvenile court judges saw Edward briefly, recognized that he was a troubled child, and ordered three different psychiatric evaluations. Three doctors saw Edward. They all reached similar conclusions. An army of court clerks typed and filed the reports. No treatment was ever given Edward. No supervision or help was provided. None of the recommendations was followed. The juvenile courts of Pennsylvania, like those of most states, are mandated by statute to provide treatment, supervision, or rehabilitation for children. Edward was simply summoned to court, brought before a judge for a few moments, seen by a doctor, and returned home.

From the time Edward was eight until he was fifteen he was brought before the juvenile court seventy-five times. Each time he was represented by counsel, usually a different lawyer. Many of the charges were trivial. Three times he was charged with being a "runaway," which is an act of delinquency, but not a crime. He was adjudicated delinquent seven times. The first adjudication, at age eleven, was based on an admission made when he was ten years old. There is no indication in the record that Edward was advised of his right to remain silent or that his mother was present when he gave the statement. Unless both these precautions are taken, the confession of a child is legally inadmissible. Nonetheless, Edward was adjudicated delinquent and returned home.

His file continued to build. At age twelve he was adjudicated delinquent for robbery, theft, receiving stolen property, and criminal conspiracy. Although the record is bare of facts, it appears that a group of boys stole a wallet. At age thirteen he was adjudicated delinquent on his admission of possession of a "starter pistol." (A starter pistol is inoperable.) Again, there is nothing in the record to indicate that he was informed of his rights or that counsel objected to this evidence. His next adjudication, at age thirteen, involved a "robbery, conspiracy, and theft" of thirty cents.

Edward was brought to trial before me in adult court on charges of robbery, conspiracy, and simple assault. The juvenile judge had found that Edward was not "amenable to treatment," the standard under which the juvenile court abdicates its authority over a child charged with delinquency and certifies that the child be treated as an adult. A judge sitting in adult criminal court cannot send the child back to juvenile court but must proceed with the trial. The evidence disclosed that Edward in company with several other boys robbed a man of a wallet containing eight dollars. There was no viciousness or cruelty involved. Despite the juvenile court's finding of nonamenability, the boy I saw and spoke with was a small, quiet youngster, soft-spoken, ignorant, and lonely. He hung out with the corner boys because he had no other options. He was not sufficiently intelligent or educated to seek escape in the library. He was not big enough or strong enough to fight his way through the gyms and playgrounds. He was not musical or artistic. For him there was no escape from the chaos of home or the life of petty crime on the streets where he lived.

Occasionally a slum child can escape the destiny of delinquency and crime through some form of exceptional skill. A champion prizefighter came from a similar background. He had spent most of his childhood in foster homes and juvenile jails. He never learned to read, but he did learn to fight. A kindly warden suggested that if he was going to get in fights he'd better learn to be a good fighter. At age twenty-three he had won an international boxing championship and earned several million dollars. But he was illiterate and the prey of a horde of semiliterate sycophants.

Edward had no skills, no talents, no supportive family. No friends or family member ever came to court with Edward on the six occasions when he appeared before me. I never saw him smile.

I do not believe in using point scores or profiles in deciding cases or in imposing sentences. Each defendant should be treated as an individual. Edward, nonetheless, exemplifies the kind of youngster who becomes enmeshed in the bureaucracy of the juvenile court. Almost all these children are poor. Many are nonwhite. They have been deprived of even the most elementary kind of upbringing. Although the murder of Edward's father is an unusual circumstance, most of these children have been exposed to violence and tragedy. Few have fathers living in the home who assume a paternal role. Few have exceptional skills or abilities. They are, for the most part, ordinary children who have been exposed to extraordinarily stressful and hostile environments.

Edward's involvements with the juvenile court, though lengthy, are not exceptional. Many children are repeatedly brought to court, given a hasty few moments, and returned to the situation that causes their problems without being provided any help or guidance. It is not surprising that their problems recur and they are returned again and again to a court that processes thirty or forty cases a day, and simply goes through the same hasty motions again and again.

The case I heard involved a robbery that occurred on July 6, 1978, when Edward was fifteen years old. He was arrested on July 18, 1978, and tried on June 25, 1979, eleven months after his arrest. The dates are significant because, under the law of this state, every person accused of crime must be brought to trial within 180 days of arrest. Similar rules prevail in the federal courts and most states. The Sixth Amendment to the Constitution provides that all persons accused of crime shall have "a speedy public trial." To date, children are accorded neither a speedy nor a public trial. Most juvenile court hearings are closed to the public and the press. Edward was being tried before me as an adult in adult court. Therefore, I reasoned, he should be entitled to the speedy trial rules applicable to adults. The appellate court held that this rule does not apply to juveniles even when they are tried as adults.[18]

Before the case came to me, Edward, like countless other children appearing in juvenile courts, was deprived of innumerable rights accorded to adults accused of crime. Edward was arrested on July 18, 1978.

There is no record of an arrest warrant. A child can be arrested without a warrant and without probable cause. The case was listed for a pretrial hearing on August 9, 1978. Had he been an adult, a preliminary hearing would have been held within ten days, at which time the prosecutor would have had to make out a prima facie case, a reasonable showing that a crime had been committed and that Edward did it. At this hearing, Edward's counsel should have obtained a pretty good understanding of the evidence against Edward and been able to prepare a defense. He might have asked for a lineup to be sure that the victim really could identify Edward. If the arrest was made without a warrant or without probable cause, the attorney could have moved to quash. None of this was done.

The case was continued to September 5, 1978, when the complainant failed to appear and the case was continued to September 28, 1978, at which time Edward failed to appear. The case was continued to October 23, 1978, when the complainant again failed to come to court. A status listing of October 26, 1978, was given to obtain updated neuropsychiatric reports on Edward. The reports were not ready on the scheduled date. The case was continued for a certification hearing to be held on November 12, 1978, when for the third time the complainant failed to appear. At this point any defense counsel in adult court who was awake would have moved to have the case dismissed for want of prosecution. But few lawyers in juvenile court make such motions and few juvenile courts are willing to hear them.

The juvenile judge found that Edward was not amenable to treatment on the basis of a written report from the juvenile jail in which Edward was imprisoned. The author of the report never appeared in court to testify and be cross-examined. An adult is entitled to confront and cross-examine his accusers. Although Edward was brought to juvenile court seventy-five times in a period of seven years, and was represented by counsel, he was never accorded the bare rudiments of a due process hearing.

When I explained to Edward that he had a right to appeal and a right to free counsel to help him take the appeal, that he had a substantial legal issue, he shook his head and told me, "It won't do no good. I don't want to come back to court." He has no faith in the justice or fairness of the legal system. Nor do most of the youngsters who have been subjected to the juvenile court.

Juvenile court laws were designed by well-meaning reformers to help children and to provide treatment for them. But what sort of treatment do children get in these institutions to which they are consigned? Although federal and state judges have issued detailed orders with the respect to the treatment facilities and care provided adult criminals in prison, there are few decisions mandating standards for institutions to which children are committed. Even those decisions are rarely enforced.

One learns about childrens' institutions from outraged citizens and tenacious reporters. The Citizens' Committee for Children of New York, Inc., examined institutions to which children are committed and found some of them adequate and others decidedly poor.[19] The Jacksonville, Florida, *Times-Union and Journal,* December 5, 1982, reported on conditions at the Dozier School for Boys, a Florida training school (i.e., juvenile jail). Eight of the thirty-two children were held in isolation cells. A twelve-year-old boy was shackled and "hog-tied" by the "house parent." The rooms are stifling in summer, freezing in winter. Four hundred and sixty-seven boys are imprisoned in Okeechobee, Florida. A minimum of fifty children in this jail attempt suicide each year. They suffer from grossly inadequate medical care. The Gainesville, Florida, *Sun* reports, "The typical student among the 800 in the state youth prison system is fifteen years old and has a fourth-grade education. The teen[ager] most probably has been the victim of physical or sexual abuse. . . ."[20]

This description applies to juvenile prisons in all sections of the United Sates, in rural and in urban areas. Seven employees of the Philadelphia juvenile detention center were suspended for physical abuse of children. Significantly, this outrageous situation was not brought to to the attention of the juvenile court by lawyers for the children but by a special investigator appointed by the mayor. The legislative mandate to the juvenile courts to provide treatment, supervision, and care for delinquent children has been overlooked in the speedy disposition of cases.

Although delinquency matters constitute the major case load of juvenile courts, the courts are also charged with protection of children from abuse. In this area, not only the courts but also American society is woefully negligent. In 1974 Congress enacted the Child Abuse Prevention and Treatment Act and allocated $190 million over three years for research and demonstration projects. There is a national Model Child

Abuse and Neglect Reporting Law.[21] Every state has enacted some form of child abuse reporting law requiring teachers, doctors, nurses, and any responsible adults to report suspected cases of child abuse. But child abuse has not been curbed. It appears to be increasing.

As a result of the reporting laws many people do make reports. In Pennsylvania in 1981, 13,703 reports of suspected child abuse were filed. Investigation by the Department of Public Welfare confirmed that in 4,689 cases, almost one-third of the reported cases, children were seriously harmed by those responsible for their care. But only 135 (1 percent) of these cases were actually adjudicated in court proceedings.[22] During the same period 36,341 delinquency petitions were filed. Of these, 20,938 (57.6 percent) were heard and adjudicated in juvenile court. These figures are representative of most states. Delaware reported 3,396 cases of suspected child abuse in 1982, an 18.7 percent rise over 1981. Three children died from abuse. New Jersey reported 23,758 cases in 1981 compared with 22,616 for 1980. In New Jersey seventeen deaths were attributed to child abuse.[23] Protection of children is simply ignored, often with shocking results.

Reporter Howard James asks what protection a child has:

One who ponders the problem only briefly must find it incredible that parents, school officials, or neighbors can have a child picked up like a stray dog and hauled off to a children's jail and to court, and that the child has little protection and almost no recourse. Adults also can subject children to so-called therapeutic treatment, put the child in an institution or foster home, or administer painful punishment (within limits) and the child can do little about it. If he runs away, he is returned, and if he refuses to return, he is further punished. The child must endure all, short of extreme physical abuse or neglect and without protest.

What can a child do when he is poorly taught, scapegoated, ridiculed, ignored, or flunked by an incompetent, unstable, or vengeful teacher? What can he do when thrown out of his own home, and placed with foster parents he hates, or in an institution where few of his needs are met, or where he is brutally treated by sadistic adults? In the name of therapeutic treatment he may be manipulated by behaviorists, worked over in group therapy, studied and tested by psychiatrists and psychologists, subjected to electric shocks, locked in solitary confinement, or have drugs injected into his body. I have seen all of these things and more. Adult society—and our justice system—assumes that adults have the right to do these things simply because he is a child.

Instead of protecting the innocent, our society subjects the innocent to treatment that would not be tolerated for an adult prisoner of war under the Geneva Convention rules. That is because in the eyes of the law an American child is property—not a person.[24]

Some facts are undeniable. Over half the reported cases of child abuse involve children under the age of four. Half the deaths occur in children under the age of two. Those who survive often have serious brain and neurological disorders. They also suffer severe emotional problems and frequently become abusive parents. We now have hot lines, organizations to prevent child abuse, and organizations for abusive parents such as "Parents Anonymous." We have laws and agencies and groups collecting money from the public. Despite these hopeful signs, child abuse is rising. Naomi Fiegelson Chase reports, "What little we know about child abuse and neglect, we do know that the most common factor in all child-abuse cases is the joblessness of the father or his absence from home."[25] In times of high unemployment and family stress, the victims of frustration, hostility, and despair are the most vulnerable—the children.

The well-meaning reformers of the 1970s and 1980s, like their predecessors at the turn of the century, would impose utopian standards of omnipotent and omniscient care for all children appearing in court. A law professor and two child therapists who have examined children of broken and inadequate families are rightly critical of many court decisions affecting these children. They have drafted a "Model Child Placement Statute" premised on the right of every child to be a "wanted child." A wanted child is defined as "one who receives affection and nourishment on a continuing basis from at least one adult and who feels that he or she is and continues to be valued by those who take care of him or her."[26] All judges and lawyers who have been involved with children in court know that most of these children are unwanted by anyone. Sometimes the most ostentatiously loving parent is a secret abuser. The same may be true of a foster parent. Yet this model act provides that all placements of a child shall be unconditional and final and that the court shall not retain jurisdiction. Under such a law, once a child was placed, he would not even have the right to protection.

Similarly, the Model Child Abuse Reporting Act, in its laudable effort to protect children from every kind of mental and emotional abuse as well as physical abuse, has mandated reporting not only abuse but also neglect. A neglected child is defined as "a person under eighteen years of age whose physical or mental condition is seriously impaired as a result of the failure of those responsible for his care or others exercising temporary or permanent control over the child to provide adequate food, shelter, clothing, physical protection, or medical care necessary to sustain the life or health of the child."

Courts have difficulty protecting children from overt, manifest physical abuse resulting in verifiable injuries or death. It is beyond the ability of court to provide adequate food, shelter, clothing, and medical care for children. It is certainly beyond the capacity of any government to ensure that a child receive "affection and nourishment on a continuing basis."

Courts cannot provide jobs for parents; courts cannot provide adequate housing; courts cannot transform alienated adults into caring parents. What courts can and must do is give a fair and full hearing to every case. The responsibility must not be delegated to clerks, political bureaucrats, social workers, or court aides. Each report of child abuse must be treated as a capital case and given the time and attention that is devoted to each defendant who faces the death penalty, for indeed a child abuse case does involve the life or death of a small human being.

It is not an acceptable answer to say the calendars of the juvenile court are crowded, that there is no time for a full due-process judicial hearing and careful reasoned decision. Dr. Marvin Roth, a physician in private practice who sees patients in an Atlantic City, New Jersey, medical center where the infant mortality rate is very high explains: "We're tremendously overworked. . . . It's impossible when we see hundreds of patients to do adequate justice to them. We try to have continuity of care, but there isn't [any]."[27] Lawyers and judges dealing with children are also overworked. There is no continuity of representation by lawyers or continuing supervision by judges. And there is no adequate justice.

The United States Supreme Court in another context declared:

. . . the Constitution recognizes higher values than speed and efficiency. Indeed, one might fairly say of the Bill of Rights in general, and the due process clause in particular, that they were designed to protect the fragile values of a vulnerable citizenry from the overbearing concern for efficiency and efficacy that may characterize praiseworthy government officials no less, and perhaps more, than mediocre ones."[28]

No court has more socially and morally important responsibilities than the juvenile court. But it is denigrated by the bench and bar. Its hasty proceedings cause immeasurable harm to countless children and their families. The public must ask, as I do, why we do not accord this court the dignity, prestige, and time to give every child a meticulously fair hearing. Why are not the most learned judges assigned to this court? Why do the best lawyers devote their finely honed minds to working out corporate mergers and acquisitions, stock issues, and tax shelters instead of to the protection of children?

There are many obvious answers. There is little money to be earned in representing children. It may also be a measure of the importance Americans attach to children that pediatricians earn substantially less than other doctors.[29] Judges drawn from the fast track of lawyers have no experience in this area of the law and little interest in it, primarily because it is seen as an inferior branch of the law.

So long as the juvenile court is treated as a turnstile operation where the aim is to dispose of the maximum number of cases in the minimum amount of time, most competent lawyers and judges will avoid appearing in these courts. Only insistent and persistent demand by the public that due process of law be extended to children can change a court that has been ignored by the bench and bar for eight decades.

CHAPTER IX

# THE APPELLATE PROCESS

The appellate process recognizes that there exists an
inherent risk of error, even when cases are decided by
enlightened jurists.

—Judge Thomas Meskill

Appeals from trial court decisions have two major purposes: (1)
correction of error by the trial court and (2) development of the
law. The first goal serves the needs of the litigants; the second the needs
of the public. In the 1980s, American appellate courts fail to fulfill either
function adequately. Moreover, the cost of appeals and the delays inherent in the process present additional formidable obstacles to providing
equal protection of the laws for poor litigants.

The federal government and most American states have established
a judicial system consisting of three tiers of courts of record: trial courts,[1]
an intermediate appellate court or courts, and a Supreme Court.[2] From
the decisions of the trial court, there is an appeal of right to the intermediate court. The highest court in most jurisdictions has some discretion
in choosing the cases it will hear.[3]

Although the right to appeal a decision of a trial court or other
tribunal[4] is one of the congeries of procedural and substantive rights
subsumed under the rubric "due process of law," is it really necessary

to have an appeal or is appellate review simply a traditional nicety that is expensive and cumbersome? The increased volume of litigation in the trial courts engenders vastly more appeals in both the intermediary and highest courts. In every jurisdiction appellate courts are hard-pressed to deal with the enormous quantity of cases.

There are many proposals to limit appeals to save the time of appellate courts. Some fair, sensible means of shortening the appellate process is necessary. But the right to seek review of trial court decisions, I believe, is essential.

Decisions at the trial level are made by a single judge. An appellate court decision is made by either a panel of judges (usually three) or by the entire court. Idiosyncratic decisions, rulings based on corruption, bias, prejudice or simply incompetence of the court and/or counsel, are likely to be corrected by a panel of three or more judges removed from the passion and heat of the trial. Litigants deserve this second look, this impartial review, to correct manifest injustice.

Development of legal doctrine also demands appellate review. The number of trial decisions, most of which are unreported, makes it virtually impossible for anyone to know the state of the law without having rulings on important issues from the appellate courts.

There are no national statistics on trial court errors. No one knows how many state trial court decisions are reversed on appeal. No one knows how many erroneous decisions are not appealed because the litigants cannot afford the time or money to appeal. Federal court records are not compiled or maintained for this purpose. However, the Third Circuit (Pennsylvania, New Jersey, Delaware, and the Virgin Islands) does keep records of reversals of district court decisions.[5] From 1979 through 1983 the reversal rate ranged from a low of 11.6 percent in 1982 to a high of 20.9 percent in 1980. The average for these five years is 16.34 percent. There is no reason to believe that these figures are not representative of the federal courts as a whole. If anything, the reversal rate may be lower than the national average because the trial judges in this circuit are exceptionally well qualified.

Since Federal trial judges are, on the whole, more experienced and better qualified than state trial judges, it is reasonable to assume that the percentage of error in state trials is at least as high as that in the federal court system. This is partially confirmed by the only national survey of the state jury system.[6] That study found that in the opinion of the judges juries decide cases right approximately 75 percent of the time. In other words, 25 percent of jury verdicts are wrong. No one knows how much error there is in bench trials. But even a casual review of reported appellate court opinions in any jurisdiction discloses an enormous number of trial court decisions that are reversed for manifest error. One must conclude that appeals are essential to prevent wholesale miscarriages of justice.

Litigants who cannot pay substantial expenses for investigation and witnesses and counsel fees for competent attorneys who devote time to preparation and trial are less likely to have their claims and defenses presented as ably as those who can afford these services. There is, therefore, a greater probability of error and unjust results for poor clients. The denial of equal protection of the laws at the trial level is compounded when these litigants are denied the right to appeal because they cannot afford to exercise that right.

The long-distance runner, the party who can afford to litigate endlessly and appeal and relitigate and appeal again, usually succeeds in using the appellate courts either to obtain his just due or to defeat the claims of his opponents. Those who cannot afford these tactics are sadly disadvantaged. Life and liberty are not at stake in civil trials. But the decisions in many civil cases profoundly affect the quality of life and the rights of litigants. Many cases also raise issues of public importance. Because the right to free counsel in civil cases is severely limited, a poor claimant or defendant must often represent himself at trial. With the help of the court, he may obtain a just result. For a nonlawyer to represent himself on appeal is far more difficult. Simply to find out what papers must be filed, and where and when, presents almost insurmountable problems. Documents must be typed or printed; they must follow precise and finicky rules as to statement of jurisdiction, grounds for appeal, recitation of facts, and legal argument. College graduates and holders of advanced degrees are often bewildered by legal proceedings. The vast majority of civil claimants and defendants who cannot afford counsel fees are not only economically disadvantaged but also educationally deprived. It is unrealistic to expect them to be able to proceed effectively in the appellate courts without counsel.

Delay in obtaining a decision from an appellate court is another deterrent to poor litigants. Many poor people cannot afford to wait several years to recover damages. They must settle for whatever they can get, no matter how inadequate the sum, whereas more affluent claimants can pursue their rights through the appellate courts. In criminal cases, delay in the appellate process can be devastating to a poor defendant. If the convicted person cannot post bail pending appeal, he must go to prison. By the time his appeal is decided, he may have served a sentence for a conviction that is set aside as illegal or based on insufficient evidence. More affluent defendants post bail and continue their usual life-style while awaiting the decision of the appellate court.

There are no national statistics on the length of time from the filing of an appeal to decision. Many studies measure the time from filing a case to verdict.[7] However, this is only a part of the time span and often a misleading figure. Proper investigation of a case takes time. Often the plaintiff in a personal injury case does not want a trial until time has revealed the full nature and extent of his injuries. Will he recover completely or will he be permanently disabled? If he will be unable to work, his damages will be much greater. An early trial may severely prejudice his case. Civil defendants also need time to investigate claims and prepare their defenses. Judges who force cases to an early trial can show impressive statistics of effective case management. Whether a just result is achieved is more difficult to ascertain. The critical measure of time for both civil litigants and criminal defendants is the period commencing with the incident giving rise to the litigation and ending with the final decision by an appellate court. Until that time, a plaintiff who has won in the trial court cannot collect his award. While a losing defendant appeals, he retains his funds. Ultimately a successful plaintiff will collect damages with interest from the date of the verdict. Similarly, a defendant in a criminal prosecution does not know whether he is a felon or a free man until the ultimate appellate decision. In most states a delay of two, three, or more years in deciding an appeal is not uncommon.

The case of Darryl[8] illustrates the way in which delay and expense in the appellate process operate to deny equal protection of the laws to those who are in need. Darryl, like many Americans, was the victim of an automobile accident. When he was five years old, Darryl was struck by an automobile and suffered permanent brain damage. Although he looked normal and appeared to behave like any other child his age, he was severely learning-disabled. He was eight years old when his case came to trial. At that time, he was unable to read or even recognize letters. A board certified neurologist testified that Darryl's electroencephalogram was abnormal. This was not contested. A psychologist testified that Darryl's intellectual development was uneven, that it was doubtful that he would ever learn to read fluently, that he needed special schooling at once, and that his employment opportunities in our increasingly technological society were drastically limited. Over an average working-life expectancy of forty-five years his lost earning capacity would be at least $10,000 a year, or $450,000. Lost earning capacity was calculated as the difference between minimum wages and what a tradesman such as a carpenter or welder earns today. Twenty years from now the discrepancy in earnings between skilled and unskilled labor may be much greater and there will probably be far fewer jobs for the functional illiterate that Darryl is likely to become.

Darryl's family is on welfare. He has two younger siblings. The attorney who represented Darryl and his mother was far from outstanding. He permitted the mother to come to court each of the six days of jury selection and trial in a different exotic outfit. He did not object to questions asked of her by defense counsel as to her source of income (welfare) and the paternity of her three children, (all have different fathers).

The jury returned a verdict of $50,000, which was patently inadequate. A trial judge has authority to reduce the size of the verdict but not to increase it. The only remedy for an insufficient verdict is a new trial. I assumed that Darryl's attorney would petition me to set aside the verdict and grant a new trial. He came to see me and explained that after discussing the problem with Darryl's mother and the doctor, he concluded it would be better not to ask for a new trial. The jury was racially and economically mixed. It was not clearly biased. The driver of the car claimed that he was not negligent, and that Darryl had darted out in front of him so suddenly that he had no time to avoid striking the child. Skid marks of sixty feet showed that the driver was going fast but also that he had tried to stop. The driver was a young married man with four children, a modest job, and a blameless life. The jury did not know that he had a $100,000 insurance policy and they could not, under the law, be told that fact. It was always possible that at another trial Darryl might not get any award. It would be at least three years until the court would decide whether or not Darryl had a right to a new trial and probably another year thereafter until the second trial. Both the neurologist and the psychologist recommended that Darryl have special schooling at once. Tuition at such a school is more than $3,000 a year.

Darryl's lawyer had advanced the fees for the doctor and the psychologist. It was to everyone's benefit to take the $50,000 rather than pursue an appeal. The insurance company had every incentive to delay. Even if Darryl were to be awarded delay damages (figured at 6 percent to 10 percent of the award) the insurance company could earn far more by investing the money instead of paying Darryl. Despite the plea of the driver, who urged that Darryl be paid at once, an appeal was taken by the insurance company. Six months after the trial, Darryl's case was settled for $45,000. After paying the experts their fees, court costs, and other expenses, as well as the attorney's fee of one-third, Darryl received $25,000. Plaintiffs who are in want often have to compromise their verdicts in order to collect any money without waiting any longer and incurring further expenses. The threat of an appeal usually will induce a verdict winner who is poor to settle for less.

Appeals are used similarly in contract cases. Another typical small case that was tried before me resulted in disaster for the plaintiff, who had a good cause of action. A small textile mill sold $22,000 worth of cloth to a large manufacturing company. Two months passed. No payment was made. The mill owner retained counsel, who promptly filed suit. The manufacturer had a law firm on retainer. He was obligated to pay his lawyer an annual fee whether or not he needed the lawyer's services. He immediately filed an answer and counterclaimed for over $100,000 in consequential damages, alleging that the material was substandard and that the manufacturer's customers had returned suits made from this cloth, causing considerable losses. The manufacturer demanded a jury trial. The manufacturer then served lengthy interrogatories on the mill and demanded to see their books and records. The mill responded with similar demands. Both sides retained textile experts to test the cloth in question. After spending more than $7,000 in counsel fees, expert fees, and costs, the mill owner instructed counsel to withdraw the claim. That was impossible because of the counterclaim. Eighteen months later the mill recovered $22,000, the full amount of the claim, with interest at 6 percent. At that time banks were paying 12 percent interest. But the case was not over. The manufacturer appealed. At this point the beleaguered mill owner surrendered and settled his claim for $15,000, the amount of fees and expenses incurred. Delay always inures to the benefit of the party who can afford to wait for a full recovery or pay for innumerable delaying tactics.

Victor G, a fifty-five-year-old factory worker who was dying of cancer, was also denied his rights because he could not afford the delay involved in an appeal. He sued his family doctor, who had misdiagnosed his condition for years, telling Victor that his complaints were all in his head not in his stomach. By the time Victor went to an internist who recognized his condition and promptly sent him to a surgeon, it was too late. Victor was cut open and sewed up again. There was nothing that could be done for him medically at that time. His life might have been saved if his condition had been properly diagnosed earlier. Victor had a sick wife and three teenage children. His life savings had been consumed by his medical expenses. His $10,000 life insurance policy would not feed four people very long. The only financial provision Victor could make for his survivors was this lawsuit against his family doctor for malpractice. Victor came to court and insisted on testifying, even though he was in great pain. After a jury verdict in his favor, the doctor's insurance company appealed. It was clear from the evidence presented at trial that the doctor was grossly negligent and the award was reasonable. The appeal was taken only for purposes of delay. It was doubtful that Victor would live another two or three years until the appeal was decided. He was destitute; his medical expenses were enormous. On the advice of counsel, Victor settled for two-thirds of the award.

Anita W., who suffered a bad leg injury on the escalator of a department store, also recovered an adequate jury verdict. She was a housewife. Her husband was a successful stockbroker. When the insurer for the store appealed the verdict in her case she refused to settle. Three years later the appellate court affirmed the decision. Shortly thereafter she recovered the full amount of the verdict with interest. Anita had a swimming pool installed in her garden, took a trip to the Orient, and redecorated her house.

Garretty was much more seriously injured than Anita. But he lost in a case tried before me with a jury. Garretty is not an attractive man. He drinks; he has acne; his wife had left him, taking the children; he does not go to church or engage in any civic activities. His only recreation is "drinking with the boys" and hunting. The jury was composed of eight women and four men. Garretty was driving a cement-mixer truck that toppled over when he made a sharp right-hand turn. The truck did not contact any other vehicle. It was filled with tons of cement that sloshed around as he was driving. The drum had to keep revolving or the cement would have hardened inside the mixer. Common sense indicated that the truck was top-heavy, that it was improperly designed. Clever defense counsel brought out all the unsavory aspects of Garretty's life and tried to prove that he was drunk at the time and caused the accident. The jury split ten to two in favor of the defendant. Agreement by five-sixths of a jury is sufficient for a verdict in civil cases in this jurisdiction. The two holdouts were a male accountant and a male factory worker. The other two men on the jury were postal clerks.

I thought that the verdict was against the evidence and that on appeal Garretty would win. In a new trial with a different jury and a better expert witness he could get a substantial verdict. After Garretty filed an appeal, the insurer offered him $10,000. He was then on relief. He had lost his house. He could not bear the thought of another trial where his life would be held up to ridicule and the jurors would look at him with scorn and loathing. He took the $10,000 and withdrew his appeal.

In some cases the persistence of the litigant and the dedication of counsel ultimately bring success. Frederic Lang, an inventor, fought a thirteen-year battle to enforce a patent he had been awarded and finally settled for $4 million.[9] Another protracted battle arose out of a helicopter accident.[10] A wealthy man, piloting his own helicopter, was killed on July 9, 1962. His widow sued the manufacturer, alleging that the aircraft was defective because there was insufficient time when the motor stalled for it to go into autorotation. The jury returned a verdict for the defendant and the plaintiff appealed. The intermediate appellate court remanded the case, holding that the trial court's instructions to the jury were inadequate. The case was tried again and a second jury found for the defendant. Again the plaintiff appealed and again the case was remanded. The Supreme Court accepted an appeal and finally in 1975 issued an opinion clarifying the law.[11] On the third trial, the case was settled before verdict and the widow obtained a substantial recovery, more than sixteen years after the accident. If she had not been affluent and if she had not had a tenacious lawyer, she would not have obtained any recovery. The law as to the duty of manufacturers would have remained in doubt for years until some other litigant could afford to carry an appeal to the state supreme court. The rights and needs of poor civil litigants in utilizing the appellate courts has been ignored by courts and scholars.

The courts have accorded indigent criminal defendants some rights to enable them effectively to appeal from convictions. Probably the most significant is the right of a convicted person to representation by counsel at public expense in taking an appeal. Mr. Justice Douglas explained the importance of this decision:

> . . . the rich man, who appeals as of right, enjoys the benefit of counsel's examination into the record, research of the law, and marshalling of arguments on his behalf, while the indigent, already burdened by a preliminary determination that his case is without merit, is forced to shift for himself.[12]

Indigent defendants are also entitled to a free transcript of the trial proceedings so that an appellate court can intelligently review the record of the trial. In the State of Washington there was no provision for furnishing a transcript to an indigent appellant. The United States Supreme Court reversed the decision of the state court, declaring:

> The conclusion of the trial judge that there was no reversible error in the trial cannot be an adequate substitute for the right to full appellate review available to all defendants in Washington who can afford the expense of a transcript.[13]

Important as these rights are, an indigent criminal defendant is nonetheless severely handicapped in seeking to appeal his conviction. The problems of inferior counsel and lack of preparation time also infect the appellate process. The record in a badly tried case often is not helpful. Inadequate counsel frequently neglect to object to improper questions, dubious trial tactics of the prosecutor, and the presentation of inadmissible evidence. Unless counsel objects, these errors are deemed to be waived and will not be considered by the appellate courts. Often a poor, ignorant defendant, although informed of his right to appeal, considers it hopeless and fails to act within the limited time allowed to take an appeal.

Persons of modest income who wish to appeal must pay for the transcript of the trial and counsel fees. These sums may be substantial. A transcript costs at least $1 per page. The cost of printing portions of the trial record and a short brief may be at least $1,000. If the sentence is probation or only a short jail term, a poor but not indigent defendant will often forgo the right to appeal a conviction even though he has a good chance of getting the decision reversed. To save a few thousand dollars, such a defendant will be prejudiced for the rest of his life by having a criminal record.

Andre, like many other poor, ignorant defendants, found that the appellate rights articulated by the United States Supreme Court were of little benefit to him. He was tried before me and found guilty of burglary, theft, and a weapons offense, principally on the basis of his own statement to the police. Andre was nineteen years old, functionally illiterate and unemployed. This was his second adult offense. After his conviction, when boiler-plate postconviction motions were filed automatically, I learned that Andre had been held in custody almost fifteen hours before making the statement. This was grounds for setting aside the conviction, which I proposed to do. However, when the motion was listed for argument, Andre's attorney said: "Your Honor, we have decided to withdraw our posttrial motions and proceed to sentencing."

The Court: "Who decided to withdraw the motion?"

The attorney: "I beg your pardon, my client has decided to withdraw the motion."

I questioned Andre. I told him he had a good chance to have his conviction reversed. He had nothing to lose and everything to gain by pursuing the motion. I asked him to consult with his attorney again and to talk to his mother, who was in the courtroom.

Fifteen minutes later he again stood before me and carefully repeated the words his lawyer had instructed him to say: "I wish to withdraw my motion." The lawyer explained that Andre had already been in custody more than a year because he could not post $500 bail. Under our system, a defendant may post 10 percent of the bail in cash or put up as security property equal to the amount of the bail. During the entire year Andre had been unable to raise $50. His mother had no property. Neither did his girl friend, who was in court with their child.

Andre's crime was stealing an auto battery worth about thirty dollars from a repair shop. The gate was open. The owner was out. He had left the place unattended a few moments while getting a stalled car started. As he returned to his shop he saw a young man walking away down the street carrying a battery he thought belonged to him. The owner got in his car and flagged down a policeman to whom he gave a description of the young man with the battery. Fifteen minutes later the policeman saw Andre strolling down the street carrying a battery and arrested him. Andre did not fit the description of the thief the repair shop owner had given. Nonetheless, when the police displayed Andre in handcuffs to the shop owner, saying "Is this the man?" the shop owner said "Yes." Andre was held in custody and questioned intermittently for fifteen hours until he gave the police a statement admitting the offense. Two weeks later at a proper lineup the repair shop owner was unable to identify Andre. The battery Andre was carrying was like hundreds of other batteries. No weapon was found on Andre although the shop owner testified he had seen the handle of a gun in the thief's pocket.

If I were to sentence Andre to one year in jail (the time he had already served), he could be released immediately. He had the promise of a job in a fast-food place. If I set aside the conviction, he could be held in jail for years while the prosecutor appealed my decision. If I were sustained on appeal, Andre could be tried over again without using his statement. If I were reversed, his conviction would stand. Andre would come back to me for sentencing a year or two later. If I reduced bail or permitted Andre to sign his own bail, he would be released but would still face a possible retrial in a year or two, after the appellate court decided his case.

I sentenced Andrew to the one year he had already served. He was released immediately. But Andre now has a record of two convictions. Under the mandatory sentencing law, if he is again convicted of a felony (burglary of any amount is a felony) he will have to serve a minimum of five years in prison.

Compare the case of Philadelphia Councilman Isadore Bellis, who was convicted in 1974 of accepting $42,000 in bribes. He posted bail when he was arrested and did not spend one day in jail. After conviction, he appealed. For five years he enjoyed the Florida sunshine until his conviction was affirmed in 1979. During this time, of course, he had not paid the fine imposed and had the use of his ill-gotten gains.

Larry, an illiterate eighteen-year-old, was tried before me for attempted burglary and conspiracy. He and two friends tried to steal a TV set from a home. An alarm went off and the other boys fled. Larry was still standing on the steps when the police arrived. After conviction, I learned that he had previously been convicted of robbery and conspiracy. In company with another agile friend who had eluded the police, Larry approached a twelve-year-old in a shopping mall and demanded money. The child gave him a dollar and promptly notified the mall security guard, who arrested Larry. Unlike the councilman, whose sentence was a fine and probation, Larry was sentenced to three years in prison. He was convicted and sentenced in the United States in 1982, not in the France of Voltaire.

Why didn't Larry appeal? Larry was informed that he had a right to appeal and that if he could not afford to retain counsel one would be appointed for him. It is doubtful that Larry understood the importance of an appeal. His attorney, an earnest but inept young man who had been appointed to represent Larry, was horrified by the sentence. He researched the law and learned that the sentence, though shocking, was not illegal. Larry was clearly guilty. The trial was without error. There was no ground for appeal.

A more experienced lawyer would have immediately petitioned for a reconsideration of sentence and brought in dozens of witnesses, including a child psychologist and a psychiatrist. Of course, someone would have to pay these experts unless the lawyer could prevail upon them to give their services without charge. Many times when I represented indigents, I called upon psychiatrist friends to examine my clients and testify without fee. In return, I did free legal work for them or their patients or institutions. Obviously no legal system can operate on such an informal basis of friendship. The rights of litigants should not turn on the ability of counsel to beg or barter essential services for his client. Larry's lawyer simply didn't have these resources of friends and legal skills. If Larry's lawyer had brought in witnesses and the sentencing judge had refused to hear them or if he had heard them and not altered his sentence, there would arguably have been grounds for appeal. But Larry was indigent. It was unlikely that the trial judge would grant a petition for funds to retain expert witnesses to attack his sentence. Meanwhile the time for appeal expired.

Another poor defendant, "Treetop Turner," was fortunate to have an extraordinarily able and dedicated lawyer. Turner spent seven years in jail seeking justice. He was accused of murder in an incident that occurred on December 15, 1945. After being held in custody by the police from June 3, 1946, to June 8, 1946, during which time he was continuously questioned, he gave a statement that led to his conviction and a death sentence. He appealed to the Pennsylvania Supreme Court. The conviction was sustained in 1948. Turner appealed to the United States Supreme Court, which reversed the conviction, holding that Turner's confession was coerced. Turner was retried, convicted, and again sentenced to death. This conviction was set aside by the United States Supreme Court in 1949.[14] In 1951, he was again convicted and sentenced to death. On appeal the Pennsylvania Supreme Court remanded the case because improper testimony of an alleged accomplice was admitted. Turner was tried again and sentenced to death again. This conviction was reversed because the jury was improperly told of the prior convictions. On the fifth trial Turner was convicted and given a life sentence. This time the conviction was reversed because the district attorney introduced the testimony of an alleged codefendant who had recanted. The prosecutor, of course, knew that this testimony was unreliable and inadmissible. In 1952, this conviction was set aside by the Pennsylvania Supreme Court[15] and remanded for a new trial. At this point the prosecutor decided not to pursue the matter. Turner would have been executed if he had not been represented by a brilliant lawyer who devoted countless hours and years of unpaid time seeking justice.

The cases of Treetop Turner and the helicopter accident are exceptional only in the number of appeals and retrials involved. They are not anomalous in the sense that serious errors were committed by trial courts that could be corrected only on appeal. In reviewing the tortuous courses of these two cases, one becomes numbed and ambivalent. Lawyers and judges may be tempted to laud the American system of justice. It is easy to say, "Only in America would justice have finally triumphed." It is undoubtedly true that in no other country could a civil litigant or a criminal defendant pursue the quest for justice to these lengths. Nor could such litigants have prevailed under any other legal system. On the other hand, it is chilling to contemplate what happens to those who do not have the means to pursue justice and the good fortune to have such able and persistent counsel.

The appellate decisions in both these cases were significant not only to the people involved but also to the public at large, for the cases established important legal principles and clarified areas of the law that had been uncertain for years. Countless criminal defendants have benefited from the decisions of the state supreme court and the United States Supreme Court in the Turner case. The opinions in the helicopter case set forth the duties and liability of manufacturers of dangerous products for one state. These rulings have also influenced decisions in other states.

Development of the law to conform to changing technology, newly acknowledged rights, and unprecedented problems is the second major function of appellate courts. For more than two centuries both federal and state appellate court opinions have shaped the history and ethos of the United States. Depending upon one's point of view, the actions of the appellate courts can be seen as a bulwark of liberty, a protection of the rights of the individual and the maintenance of a democratic society, or as a transgression on liberty, a destruction of the economy, and an impediment to the development of a free society. Whether one lauds or excoriates particular decisions, the opinions of the appellate courts have, on the whole, been thoughtful, scholarly disquisitions on various aspects of the law. These opinions, not statutes, have formed the corpus of American law and the texts of law school education.

Judges ruefully acknowledge that in the 1980s many appellate opinions are hasty, superficial formulations resolving only the specific dispute at hand. Quantity has taken its toll of quality.

In 1981, 5,311 cases were filed in the United States Supreme Court. One hundred and forty-one signed opinions and ten per curiam (by the court) opinions were issued. Chief Justice Warren Burger has urged that the Court limit itself to 100 opinions "if the quality and depth of treatment is to be maintained at a proper level."[16] Reasonable minds may differ as to whether three opinions per week constitute an excessive burden. But there can be no doubt that more than 5,000 cases are too many for nine justices to review and consider. Although the Supreme Court heard fewer than 2 percent of the cases filed, the refusal to hear a case was a critical decision. Among the thousands of cases filed, there may be a few frivolous petitions[17] but it is unlikely that there are many cases that do not raise at least an arguable question. Not many lawyers will spend the time needed to draft petitions and briefs and advise their clients to spend the money to take a case to the Supreme Court unless a substantial legal question or manifest injustice is involved. However, decisions to deny review are often so fast that one must doubt that these cases have received even a cursory consideration.[18]

Other than a proposal to create a new court to hear cases involving conflicting decisions among the different circuits,[19] no serious consideration has been given to means of alleviating the problems of appellate courts by statute or rule. There are few reported studies of the practices of the Supreme Court or any other appellate courts in dealing with the multitudes of cases they pass upon each year.

The case loads of other appellate courts are almost as burdensome as those of the Supreme Court. The United States Courts of Appeals are the intermediate courts between the trial courts and the United States Supreme Court. Unlike the Supreme Court, they do not have discretion to refuse appeals but must decide every case in which an appeal is taken.

In 1977, 19,118 appeals were filed. In 1982, the number had risen to 27,946. During this period the number of judges on the courts was substantially increased. The average number of signed opinions by each judge has remained constant at thirty-eight per year. The number of unsigned opinions has risen only slightly, from thirty-nine to forty-five. But at least one-third more cases are being decided without opinions.

The United States Court of Appeals for the Second Circuit, covering New York and Connecticut, is probably the most important and one of the most respected appellate courts in the country. It has restricted the use of its decisions by refusing to publish them. In 1982, 66 percent of the 1,063 decisions handed down by this court were unpublished.[20] Under the court's rules, these decisions may not be cited by counsel in other cases. Similar rules prevail in the other federal circuits. Fifty-five percent of federal criminal appeals and 63 percent of civil appeals are decided with unpublished opinions. Most state appellate courts achieve the same result by simply deciding cases without an opinion. What this means is that the appellate courts are deciding more than half the cases on an ad hoc basis. Each of these decisions pertains to that case only and does not affect the law as it applies to similarly situated litigants. This practice defeats one of the significant purposes of an appellate court in that it is not enunciating law for the benefit of the public at large but simply passing upon the rights and remedies of the individuals who have the means and sufficiently dedicated counsel to exercise their appellate rights. Meanwhile the trial courts, the litigants, and their lawyers are left in ignorance of the law as it has been interpreted and decided by the appellate courts. This abdication of responsibility is in itself provocative of more litigation.

The thousands of cases arising out of exposure to asbestos illustrate the proliferation of litigation that occurs when appellate courts fail to issue definitive opinions on questions of widespread application. In the early 1970s, countless persons who had been exposed to asbestos during World War II and thereafter began to manifest serious symptoms of asbestos-related illnesses. Many have already died. Thousands of such individuals and their survivors sued the manufacturers of asbestos products to which they had been exposed. By 1983, at least 26,000 suits had been instituted. There will undoubtedly be many more. Johns-Manville and other manufacturers have filed voluntary bankruptcy petitions to avoid paying verdicts already rendered and to avoid responsibility in untried cases. Many serious legal questions are common to all these cases. What is the standard of proof of exposure? Are all defendants equally responsible or is each responsible on the basis of the percentage of its product on the job site? Is the industry as a whole culpable? Is a manufacturer absolved of liability because it produced a product to meet government specifications? If the workers who were exposed to asbestos knew or should have known the dangers, did they assume the risk and are they thus barred from recovery? Are the manufacturers of asbestos products liable for punitive damages because they knew or should have known that their products were injurious? After a decade and a half of litigation, there have been no definitive appellate court decisions on these issues. Why shouldn't these questions be decided before thousands of cases are tried? It is conservatively estimated that the overhead costs to the defendants of paying some $38 billion in asbestos claims may amount to $25 to $30 billion over the next three decades.[21] The public costs of trying these cases, most of which are lengthy jury trials, is enormous. What sense does it make to try 26,000 cases when the law governing the parties is unclear? If the plaintiffs and defendants and their lawyers knew what the law was they could make sensible settlements.

Many legal issues affect the rights of countless litigants. These questions should also be decided by the appellate courts before hundreds of cases are tried and appealed. Lacking definitive rulings, the affected parties must file suit and proceed to trial or lose their rights to make claims for injuries, losses, and benefits. The defendants must answer these claims and litigate them or judgments will be entered against them by default. The system grinds on as cases are tried and appealed on a one-by-one basis. There has been no considered proposal to change the customary practice of hearing cases on an individual basis and deciding each individually on the often anomalous facts of the particular case.

Appellate courts have, however, adopted a number of devices to reduce their burdens. In Louisiana, litigants in cases involving less than $1,000 have a right to appeal only to the district court. This raises a serious question as to whether one's appellate rights may be limited by the amount of money at issue. The Supreme Court, however, refused to hear a case raising this question.[22] Florida has established territorially separate final appellate courts. Each appellate court makes its own decisions. There is no law for the entire state binding on all courts. Is such Balkanization of a state permissible? The United States Supreme Court has declined to decide this question.[23] The Supreme Court also refused to rule on this issue: "Is an appellate court required to render an opinion when said opinion would have precedential value?"[24] Decisions on all these questions would be of inestimable assistance to other jurisdictions that are also attempting to cope with crowded dockets. But the refusal to decide leaves courts and legislators in a state of ignorance.

The Second Circuit limits oral argument on appeals to five minutes for each side. Obviously no lawyer can adequately set forth the pertinent facts, state the issue and its significance, analyze conflicting precedents, and present a rationale for the ruling requested in five minutes. Such limited arguments are a waste of time for court and counsel. The Supreme Court has also refused to rule on the propriety of this practice.[25] The Court has also left in limbo the status of the bankruptcy courts. The entire nation is uncertain as to the right of these courts to continue to function and the validity of their orders. Countless avoidable appeals will be generated by this refusal to decide a question of great importance to the financial community as well as thousands of insolvent or bankrupt individuals and corporations and their creditors. At other times the actions of the Court are unfathomable. A petition for certiorari arising out of a month-long trial with a 4,000-page transcript was granted and then later dismissed without explanation as having been improvidently granted.[26] Other cases are several times remanded to the lower courts with little guidance.[27]

No great perspicacity is needed to criticize decisions of any court. The law journals are filled with lengthy comments by students and professors analyzing opinions. Learned discussions are devoted to faultfinding.[28] These critiques are written in leisure. The authors are not under pressures of time and volume. They have no responsibility to litigants or the public. Appellate judges, however, often feel the need to reach agreement and thus must limit or restrict an opinion to the least common denominator. My purpose in making these observations is not to pass judgment on much harried and overworked courts but to elucidate some of their problems so that feasible remedies may be considered.

In addition to the increased number of cases, the courts must deal with many novel issues. The sensitive nature of these questions and the absence of controlling precedents present exceptional difficulties. Abortion, surrogate parenting, the right to die, a host of environmental problems, and questions of race, gender, and age discrimination require broad social and economic research, deep discussion, and very precise formulation of rights and rules. Such cases demand more time and consideration than traditional legal issues involving property rights, taxation, and administrative law, for which there are well-developed legal doctrines and precedents with which judges are familiar.

The most common shortcut adopted by appellate courts, and in my view the most dangerous and undesirable, is the delegation of decision making to law clerks. Such delegation of judicial power has quietly and surreptitiously occurred over the past decade or two. When a rule or practice is openly adopted, when a decision is made or a petition for review is denied, the public and the legal community can debate the wisdom, utility, and legality of these acts. The courts have an opportunity to reconsider, revise, or reverse their previous rulings. But when a practice develops without acknowledgment or discussion, searching questions should be raised.

For many years each Supreme Court justice and each judge was allotted court funds to hire one law clerk. Today many appellate judges have three or four clerks. Many courts also have permanent staffs to assist the judges and to coordinate conflicting decisions made by different panels of judges sitting on similar cases. It was never contemplated by the legislatures that fund court budgets that clerks and staff would be decision makers. Most readers dismissed the claims of the anonymous law clerks quoted in *The Brethren* [29] that they made important decisions for the Justices as an arrogation of importance by ambitious, loose-lipped young lawyers.

Lawyers assume that every judge, no matter how lazy or incompetent, actually decides the cases assigned to him. Judge Richard Neely of the West Virginia Supreme Court of Appeals describes the traditional, accepted responsibilities of judges as follows: "The judiciary is the only branch of government which absolutely requires that the person making a decision do his own work; the decision maker must personally sit on the bench, hear oral arguments, listen to the testimony of witnesses, make his own findings of fact, and ultimately sign his own name to the order rendering a decision.[30]

It is, therefore, astonishing to read in a learned journal an admission by a well-respected appellate judge that he routinely sloughs off on his law clerks many of his important judicial duties. He writes:

I rarely read the entire record of the trial testimony and documents, usually reading only those parts that seem from the briefs or my clerk's draft opinion likely to be critical. In reviewing a draft opinion, I often accept the clerk's exposition, so that my revisions are mostly stylistic. Sometimes I do not read the record at all. In deciding whether to join the opinion of another judge, I often accept the judge's statement of the record, on my clerk's assurance that the statement is accurate. In ruling on motions, I usually rely on summaries and recommendations prepared by the staff attorney and my clerks.[31]

Before the reader can gasp with amazement and dismay, the good judge disarms his critics by continuing:

I assent to every criticism that may be made of this breakneck way of doing things. I am sure that I should have decided some cases differently had I proceeded in a more deliberate and thorough way. But what else can I, or any judge like me, do? The cases keep piling up. They must be decided.

Unfortunately, this description of appellate decision making is unusual only in its frankness. Many judges and justices do not read briefs. Few of them read the entire record. Many appellate judges come to court without having read the briefs. They are unable to follow the lawyer's argument because they haven't the faintest idea what the case is about. One appellate judge explained that oral argument was not so boring if he had not read the briefs.

Of course, not all appellate judges perform their duties in this fashion. Years ago, I was a law clerk to John Biggs, Jr., a most distinguished, able judge of the United States Court of Appeals at a time when each judge had only one law clerk and wrote some fifty majority opinions each year and at least twenty dissenting opinions. Before oral argument, I read the briefs and the record in every case. I marked the briefs, indicating cases that were not in point, cited other cases, referred the judge to critical parts of the record, and wrote an analysis of both arguments and a list of questions to be asked at argument. The judge read the briefs and my notes and analyses before going to court. Oral argument was an intellectually exciting debate between court and counsel that clarified and sharpened the issues.

My years as a law clerk were an extraordinary learning experience. I did research; I drafted opinions; I reviewed other judges' opinions. But I did not decide cases. When I urged an extreme or unprecedented position, the judge would gently remind me that his name, not mine, would be on the opinion. When his dissenting opinion was adopted by the United States Supreme Court on appeal, he would generously remark, "We nudged the law a little this time." That was the highest accolade. Today I still believe that nudging the law is one of the most satisfying rewards a judge can have.

The judge who candidly admits delegating authority to his law clerks makes several recommendations for dealing with the problem of over-crowded appellate dockets.

He suggests (1) enlarging the court staff, (2) delegating more decision making, and (3) limiting appeals. These proposals I find wholly unacceptable and a perversion of the appellate function.

I believe that the role of law clerks and staff should be very limited and subordinate. These judicial assistants, if they are intelligent and diligent, can save a busy judge considerable time in finding and assembling materials, in writing summaries and drafts. But they should not substitute their judgments and their opinions for those of the judge. Most law clerks have never tried a case, written a brief, or argued an appeal. Their grasp of law is tenuous at best. Their understanding of the social and economic matrix from which litigation arises is minimal. It must be remembered that not only are law clerks young and inexperienced but, for the most part, they are not the most able students. Except for the United States Supreme Court and especially distinguished United States Court of Appeals judges, a clerkship is no longer a prized position. Good law firms pay better salaries than the courts and offer advancement. Students who apply for state judge clerkships are, on the whole, mediocre. Those who seek positions as permanent court staff are even less able, for there is only limited advancement and no opportunity to learn and practice the skills of advocacy. Delegation of more authority is not a satisfactory solution to crowded appellate dockets.

Limitation of the number of appeals would certainly give the courts more time to consider each case. But on what basis should the right to appeal be denied? It is reasonable to assume that the United States Supreme Court and the state high courts that have discretion to decide which cases to hear try to select for review cases presenting the most significant issues. This winnowing process has not been wholly successful. Although there is no indication from the Supreme Court Justices themselves that they delegate this power to their clerks and staff, it is self-evident that no individual can possibly read and review 5,000 petitions in addition to hearing oral arguments, conferring with fellow judges, deciding cases, and writing opinions. Young, inexperienced law clerks, no matter how bright they may be, lack the judgment and knowledge of legal practice necessary to make this difficult selection of the favored 2 percent of cases to be granted review. More than a hundred years ago the United States Supreme Court held that the essence of due process is that a litigant be granted a hearing.[32] I submit that the appellate courts deny that essential due process to many litigants and that the majority of those denied a hearing before the appellate courts are poor people.

# CHAPTER X

---

# THE SIREN SONGS
# OF RESEARCH

Meditation on Statistical Method

Plato despair!
We prove by norms
How numbers bear
Empiric forms,

How random wrong
Will average right
If time be long
And error slight,

But in our hearts
Hyperbole
Curves and departs
To infinity.

Error is boundless.
Nor hope nor doubt
Though both be groundless
Will average out.

—J. V. Cunningham

In the seventeenth century Sir Thomas Browne mused over the elusive question, "Who knows what song the sirens sang?" (to Ulysses). In the late twentieth century, one does not have to ask what songs seduce American judges.[1] They acknowledge in their opinions that they have been persuaded by reports of social science research. These songs are not sung by alluring water maidens but by ubiquitous computers. With increasing frequency judges lay heavy weight on the findings of sociologists, political scientists, and statisticians. Legal conclusions are no longer derived solely from evidence presented at trial and from analysis of the law but from data characterized as scientific research.

It is understandable that judges look for scientific facts to buttress their opinions. In an age that rejects authoritarianism—whether it be the dictates of the church, parents, or the law—there is perhaps subconsciously the belief that "scientific facts" will give legal decisions, particularly in new and troubled areas, a patina of greater authority than will the law. This need for an extralegal imprimatur may be the legacy of legal realists who preached that the law is only what the judges say it is. For whatever reasons, judges often seek information beyond the confines of the record in a case. The quest by courts for "scientific" data is, in many instances, desirable. Some court decisions affect not only the parties involved but also the rights of many individuals and corporations, the economy, and the entire community. In a highly technological, interrelated society, judicial error can have far-reaching consequences. If scientific findings are subjected to accepted standards of proof and are made part of the record, courts should consider such evidence, provided that these facts are appropriate elements in the determination of the rights of the parties. When scientific reports do not meet these requirements courts become entangled in webs of dubious assumptions.

In every aspect of the questions of equal justice considered in this book, the absence of hard, reliable data has been noted. Ignorance of the actual operations of laws and their effects on litigants and society is epidemic. That ignorance is reflected in legal decisions that are, on occasion, admittedly based on no more than "hunch."[2] No judge can be comfortable with decisions that are not grounded on credible evidence.

Traditionally judges based their decisions on the facts of the case and the law. Facts in a legal case are presented by testimonial and documentary evidence. Witnesses are subjected to sharp cross-examination. The authors and keepers of documents and records must also testify and be subject to cross-examination. Lawyers and judges are trained to hear testimony and to evaluate the credibility and sense of the witnesses and to accept or reject evidence. Judges frequently evaluate the testimony of expert witnesses—doctors, engineers, and scientists engaged in many specialties—even though the judge may have no scientific background or expertise. As a result of searching questions by counsel for all the parties and often by the judge himself, the judge is able to make an intelligent assessment of the validity of the scientist's opinion and the information on which it is based.

Parties cannot introduce into evidence books from the library or scholarly monographs without having a witness present these documents. Except for generally accepted information like the census and weather reports, of which courts can take judicial notice, and documents that all the parties agree may be introduced without an authenticating witness, courts do not permit published matter to become part of the court record unless it meets the standards of reliability of all other testimonial and documentary evidence.

In their briefs counsel frequently cite books and articles as authority for the positions they advocate. And courts refer to these publications in their opinions. When these references are to legal and jurisprudential writings, few problems arise, because judges are trained to evaluate and assess the competence and credibility of those documents. But when references are made to "scientific" literature serious difficulties ensue. Judges read the documents referred to. Often the courts themselves seek out scientific literature relevant to the issue at hand. But neither the court nor counsel can subject these documents to the usual legal tests of reliability.

The need for information has been noted by many observers of the legal system. However, the absence of facts has rarely deterred scholars from reaching conclusions and making recommendations that have far-reaching results.

A topic of considerable legal interest is "case management." Should judges exercise active management over the pretrial phases of the case, from the filing of a civil lawsuit until the time of trial? There are good arguments pro and con. Management may speed the discovery process and save litigants time and money. On the other hand, this injection of the judge into the early phases of the case may be obstructive, violate the rights of the parties, and waste court time that could better be spent on hearing those cases that are ready for trial. Typical of the scholarly discussion on this subject is an article by Professor Resnik, who writes, "I believe, *without the benefit of much empirical work*, that judges initiate judicial management during the pretrial phase. . . . Without data, we can only guess how much time judges devote to management."[3] (Emphasis supplied.) Professor Resnik does not cite any data whatsoever to substantiate her belief. A belief, even if it were informed, scarcely provides the kind of information on which decisions affecting the legal system should be predicated. Professor Resnik does not indicate that she has observed the practices of judges or queried a substantial number of judges—or any judges—with respect to the amount of time devoted to management. Moreover, she does not consider the effects of case management on the rights of litigants. Nonetheless, Professor Resnik advocates the appointment of "therapists" to manage cases for judges. These recommendations are being adopted by some courts without further investigation or analysis.

Sentencing of criminals is another subject widely discussed not only by lawyers and judges but also by many people who have no responsibility to the offenders, the courts, or the public for their recommendations. Professor James Q. Wilson of Harvard University is an articulate advocate of severe prison sentences and limiting judicial discretion in sentencing. In proposing long mandatory prison sentences for certain crimes, he wrote in 1977, "No one can know what effect any of these changes in sentencing policy will have on offenders or on society or its institutions."[4] However, ignorance did not deter him from vociferously, enthusiastically, and successfully campaigning for lengthy mandatory prison sentences. Barely six years later, largely as a result of newly enacted mandatory sentencing statutes and sentencing guidelines slavishly followed by many judges, the prison population in the United States had doubled to more than 400,000. United States Attorney General William French Smith, noting the severe overcrowding of all jails and prisons and the cost of constructing new institutions (estimated at $50,000 to $80,000 per inmate), then proposed alternative (nonprison) sentences for nonviolent criminals.[5] No one knows how many nonviolent offenders are now incarcerated, at an annual cost to the taxpayers of from $15,000 to $30,000 or more per offender.[6] No one knows how many offenders have been sentenced to unduly harsh and disproportionate penalties as a result of these laws. Again those most likely to be incarcerated for long and possibly unconstitutional sentences[7] are poor, young, minority street criminals.

A proposal in New York to permit persons charged with crime to use credit cards to make bail was opposed by Manhattan District Attorney Morgenthau, who stated, "This report goes on the fallacious assumption that there are a lot of minor criminals in jail awaiting trial." It should not be too difficult to find out. But, despite a minor industry engaged in research on criminal justice, neither the public nor the legal system has the facts. Those minor criminals unable to post cash bail are, again, the poor.

Why don't the courts have reliable information on which to base decisions? One must ask what the hosts of lawyers, sociologists, statisticians, and academicians have been doing for the past half century. Until the 1980s, when Reaganomics forced cutbacks in education and research, the United States had had decades of research programs well financed by universities, foundations, and government. There was no lack of money or trained personnel. In the mid 1980s, there are some 600,000 American lawyers, most of whom were educated in law schools within the past quarter century. There are some 170 accredited law schools staffed with hierarchies of professors and assistants. There are more than 200 law journals and reviews that regularly publish articles by faculty, students, and lawyers. There is a new academic discipline known as "criminal justice." (Criminal justice is not criminal law.) Schools and institutes of criminal justice publish journals and sponsor research. All universities and most colleges have departments of sociology with faculty and students who are engaged in some form of research that is published in learned journals and books. Most of these publications are funded by ample grants.[8] The business of graduate studies in law, sociology, and other disciplines is research. The product is reports. With hundreds of journals of law, sociology, criminology, and related subjects, why are legislators, court administrators, judges, and lawyers groping in the darkness of ignorance for solutions? Why do so many authorities make proposals without adequate data and without anticipating readily foreseeable disastrous results? The courts, the lawyers, the litigants, and the taxpayers bear the burdens of avoidable mistakes in judgment. The promise of equal justice is betrayed not through malevolence but ignorance.

A brief look at the ways in which legal research is undertaken and funded reveals some reasons for this startling lack of factual information in an age of research, statistics, and computers. Most research is undertaken by professors and their students. Research is an integral part of the academic function. It is fueled by the "publish or perish" system of academic advancement. Few lawyers in private or government practice have the time for research. They are unlikely to receive grants from academic institutions or foundations. Judges and other public officials seldom have time or facilities to engage in research. By default, the study of the administration of justice is confided to academia.

Law is the only profession in the United States that is dichotomized into separate, alien branches consisting of practitioners and academics. Until the early twentieth century, most lawyers "read law" in the office of a practicing lawyer and learned by observing and doing. The rise of law schools and the system of accreditation brought much-needed improvements in education and skills. Unlike the medical profession, in which leading practitioners retain a firm control over the medical schools and teaching faculties, lawyers permitted the development of a new discipline, that of law professor. Comparatively few of the tenured faculty members of law schools are or have been practicing lawyers for any substantial period of time. At most, they have had a year or two of experience as a law clerk to a judge or as a very junior associate in a large law firm. In neither position have they had an opportunity to engage in extensive litigation or negotiations. Rarely have they had much exposure to criminal law, domestic relations, or negligence, or routine commercial cases. These issues constitute the bulk of the work of the courts and of the vast majority of the practicing bar.

The pedagogical methods of American law schools, I believe, influence the choice of subjects for legal research and the approach to those problems. In 1875, Professor Christopher Columbus Langdell initiated at Harvard Law School what has become known as the case method of teaching. Instead of reading textbooks and observing trials, the principal focus of attention and the basic classroom materials of instruction were judicial opinions. The students' view of a law case was obtained from the opinions of appellate courts. Within a short time, the case method of instruction became the dominant pedagogy of American law schools. Analysis of appellate opinions also became the principal subject of legal research.

On occasion, a decision of the Supreme Court radically changes the law. It may directly affect the lives of countless people. It may have far-reaching affects on the national economy and even international relations. Obviously such decisions are worthy of analysis and comment.

Distinguishing one decision or line of decisions from others and pointing out logical flaws in the court's reasoning is a challenging intellectual pursuit that is often helpful to lawyers and judges.

Some court decisions provoke public praise and excoriation. Movements are initiated to enact legislation to implement or to reverse such decisions. The decision in *Miranda* v. *Arizona,* 9 has engendered passionate feelings. The court in that case held that unless specific warnings of his constitutional rights are given to a person accused of crime, any statements he makes while in custody may not be introduced in evidence at his trial. This is known as the exclusionary rule. In the four years immediately following that decision at least seventy-two law review articles and several books were published analyzing the opinion. Most of these articles are repetitious. After all, there are only a limited number of arguments that can be made favoring or opposing any rule of law. It is asserted that the scales of justice are tipped in favor of the defendants and against the prosecution, that the right of the public to be safe from known criminals has been overborne by undue solicitude for the accused, and that the courts have gone into the inappropriate business of policing the police. Advocates of the exclusionary rule point to it as the only effective means of enforcing the Fifth and Fourteenth Amendments and curbing police and prosecutorial misconduct. But there has been little, if any, meaningful research into the actual operation of the exclusionary rule. The public and those involved in the administration of criminal justice should know certain basic facts: (1) the number and percentage of accused persons, possibly guilty of felonies, who have been acquitted because of the rule; (2) the number and percentage of suspects who after being warned of their rights nonetheless make damaging admissions leading to conviction; (3) the demographic, educational, and financial characteristics of those who make admissions and those who remain silent. From this information one could draw reasonably valid conclusions with respect to the desirability of the exclusionary rule. Is it hampering the administration of justice? Is it protecting the ignorant from coercion, or is it a shield for wealthy professional criminals? This is not the kind of research that appeals to law professors or law students who prefer desk-bound studies. Moreover, most law professors and law students are not trained to undertake such research nor do they regard it with the high esteem accorded analysis of legal doctrine.

When I was teaching in law school, the dean asked me to suggest topics of research for a young faculty member who was being groomed for tenure. It was essential that he publish a scholarly article. The young man, who had gone directly from law school to law teaching, had no particular field of interest and little awareness of the needs of the courts, the legislatures, or the legal community. Since I was a part-time lecturer and the only active practitioner on the faculty, the dean turned to me for suggestions. At that time, the federally funded highway construction program was just beginning. Procedures under old condemnation laws, designed for construction of utility lines, were slow and cumbersome. Compensation was erratic, sometimes excessive, and often inadequate. Revision of the condemnation statutes was urgently needed. Direct-mail solicitation for charities was also burgeoning. States had little effective means to prevent excessive charges and outright fraud or to require the prompt expenditure of funds contributed to charity. Research on either project and a proposed model law would have made a significant contribution to the law. The young professor rejected both subjects and wrote an article criticizing a recent Supreme Court decision. It was one of more than a score on the same subject published in law reviews. This research was funded by the law school through his sabbatical leave and also by a foundation grant. It contributed absolutely nothing to the development of the law or the understanding of the decision in question, but it substantially improved the professor's academic standing.

Because legal scholars have largely confined their studies to analyses of legal doctrine, other disciplines have undertaken the examination of the actual operation of courts, the legal profession, and the effects of statutes and decisions. The sociology of law was developed by sociologists, using the methodologies of their discipline. There are fundamental and incompatible differences between sociological and legal methodology and principles. Social science is based on norms and averages. Law is predicated on the individual. For example, it is an undeniable fact that on the average women live longer than men. But not all women live longer than all men. Sociologists make predictions and draw conclusions based upon these average differences. But the law is concerned with the rights of the individual. Consequently, despite these verifiable statistical differences in the life expectancies of men and women, it is unconstitutional to require women government employees to make larger contributions than men in order to obtain the same monthly pension benefits as men.[10]

The differences between social science and law are perhaps most striking in the field of crime. Social scientists compile significant information as to the numbers of the various crimes and offenders who commit each type of crime by race, age, sex, socioeconomic status, and educational level. These findings are extremely useful for informed judgments made by industry and many branches of government. Government needs to know the number of crimes committed and the characteristics of offenders in order to plan sensibly for police protection, prisons, court personnel, and the like. None of these factors is, or should be, relevant in the trial of a criminal case.

Litigation is a one-by-one process. It is not based on averages. Even if 95 percent of all persons accused of larceny of automobiles, for example, were convicted or pled guilty, which would be as high a percentage of guilt as one could find in any crime, such a fact would be irrelevant and inadmissible in the trial, conviction, and sentencing of any particular individual accused of that crime. He might be one of the 5 percent who are innocent. While these statistics are useful for many purposes, they have no place in the litigational process.

Social scientists deal with society as a whole or certain segments of it. They are concerned with percentages, averages, norms. Courts are concerned with individuals. This is a basic, irreconcilable difference between the two disciplines that few social scientists recognize. The social science position was pithily expressed in an article on dispute institutions.[11] Courts are and have been the most visible and formalized dispute-resolution institution in American society. The author attempted to force the litigation process into the structural framework established by Emile Durkheim, one of the founding fathers of sociology, including such factors as social density, functional specialization, and social differentiation. He then explained, ". . . cases, like widgets, can be processed more efficiently if they, or their elements, are treated as being identical." While many cases are similar, few cases are identical. Courts cannot treat individuals as identical widgets.

Because both social scientists and courts deal with problems of people and society, deviant behavior, crime and punishment, there is a tendency for both groups to assume erroneously that they understand each other's approaches, limitations, and goals.

An acclaimed study of juvenile delinquents by the distinguished social scientists, Sheldon and Eleanor Glueck,[12] illustrates the dangers inherent in examination of aspects of the legal system by those unfamiliar with it. In the 1930s, the authors studied juveniles in custody pursuant to court order and constructed a profile of the juvenile delinquent. Not surprisingly, they found that the dominant characteristics were poverty and an uncultured home. I do not doubt that these are the characteristics of children in custody. The study does not, however, present an accurate picture of children who commit acts of delinquency. Apparently the authors were either unaware of or chose to ignore the fact that middle- and upper-class children are seldom arrested except for the most serious offenses and even then they are rarely committed. If their parents make arrangements for psychotherapy, private schooling, or removal from the jurisdiction, these children are not sent to institutions for juvenile delinquents. But two generations of poor children have been subjected to discriminatory treatment by the law as a result of these scientific findings.

Much of the sociological research available to courts does not meet legal standards of reliability. Courts are then faced with the dilemma of deciding a case based on questionable data or deciding without reference to the published literature on the subject. Neither choice is satisfactory.

Decisions as to the size of juries and the unanimity of verdict exemplify the type of social science research that baffles thoughtful judges. The jury is an ancient institution, an integral element of Anglo-American common law, enshrined in the Bill of Rights and codified in the statutes of the fifty states. Depending upon which historian one reads, trial by jury is 500 or 800 years old. Until the 1960s, a jury consisted of twelve members who were required to return a unanimous verdict. Despite its lineage and the reverential awe in which the jury system is held, little is known of its history and practically nothing of its operations. One would think that the jury system—its history, function, operations, and utility—would be a popular subject of legal research. For decades it was ignored by legal scholars, although trial lawyers used and perhaps abused the system. Social scientists rushed in to fill the abhorrent vacuum. Their studies were seized by the courts when faced with deciding the constitutionality of statutes reducing the size of the jury and eliminating the requirement of a unanimous verdict. These statutes were enacted for the express purpose of reducing the cost of jury trials.

In 1970, the Supreme Court sustained the use of a six-member jury in criminal cases.[13] The court held that the limited "empirical" evidence available showed "no discernible difference between the results" reached by six-member and twelve-member juries. Two years later, the court sustained a split-verdict (nonunanimous) jury in a criminal case,[14] again relying on dubious studies that were not introduced into evidence. In 1978, the Supreme Court overturned a conviction by a five-person jury. Although there was no observable difference between a five- and six-person jury, the Court drew the line at six persons. Mr. Justice Powell, in a concurring opinion, observed, "I have reservations as to the wisdom of . . . heavy reliance on numerology derived from statistical studies. Moreover, neither the validity nor the methodology employed by the studies cited was subjected to the traditional testing mechanisms of the adversary process."[15]

The research on which the court relied in more than a half dozen cases involving jury size and unanimity of verdict reveal the difficulties of using sociological studies as a basis of legal decisions. Although a number of those studies were self-styled as empirical, they were not based on observations or experience. They were based on simulated models or questionnaires. No study actually examined the results of real juries in real cases. No study examined and compared the costs in time or money of the jury of twelve and the small jury, or unanimous-verdict and split-verdict juries. Although at least a score of studies have been funded and completed and reports have been published, no one knows the answers to the questions as to the equivalence of large and small juries and unanimous and split verdicts, or whether these devices to save money have in fact done so. The authors of the studies did not testify in court and were not subject to cross-examination. If they had been required to detail their research methodology and the limited amount of data, and if other sociologists had testified as to their studies, it is likely that the Court would not have relied on such information in reaching constitutional decisions affecting the rights of innumerable litigants. In another context Mr. Justice White cautioned the court that constitutionally accepted practices should not be altered "on the basis of surmise and without solid evidence supporting the changes."[16] Based on Supreme Court decisions relying on these studies, at least thirty states have adopted some form of split verdict and the small jury is used in many federal jurisdictions and most states in civil cases.

The best known and most widely cited research project on the American jury is by Professors Kalven and Zeisel.[17] It was conducted in the 1950s and 1960s at the University of Chicago. It was financed in large part by grants from the Ford Foundation totaling $1.4 million.[18] The declared purpose of the study was to find out whether juries in criminal cases decided cases "right." The authors concluded that they did 75 percent of the time. Depending upon whether one believes that a glass is half full or half empty, this conclusion may be heartening or dismaying. Random chance should give a 50 percent right answer. An error of 25 percent or 50 percent, depending upon how one calculates the probabilities of a right answer, seems significant. The authors, however, found that their scientific studies support the popular wisdom that the jury system is fundamentally sound and fair.

It is instructive to detail the methods of this project because it typifies so much research with respect to legal institutions and practices. Questionnaires were sent to a large number of judges, who were asked whether in their opinion juries reached the right decision in the cases over which they presided. The test of correctness of the jury's verdict was determined by the opinion of the trial judge. The report stated: "We study the performance of the jury measured against the performance of the judge as a baseline." The study covered 1,152 criminal cases. The respondents were a self-selected group of 555 judges—those who chose to respond to the questionnaire. Only 205 judges submitted reports on more than five cases. The researchers had no way of knowing whether the judge was right or wrong. Was he a "hanging judge"? Did he have prejudices that affected his view of the case? Some judges who have been prosecutors believe the police almost always tell the truth. Other judges, who have been public defenders, are inclined to take the testimony of the police with more than a grain of salt. There is absolutely no way to verify the correctness of the opinions of these 555 judges. The entire edifice of statistics, suppositions, and conclusions is based on their responses, which, in turn, were not based on an examination of facts but simply upon opinions or impressions.

The ubiquity of the questionnaire in social science research warrants some discussion of the reliability of data derived in this way. Computer

THE SIREN SONGS OF RESEARCH

specialists have a saying: "Garbage in, garbage out." The results can be no more valid than the raw data. Most questionnaires ask not for facts but for opinions. The judges in the jury study were asked their opinions about the decisions of juries. These opinions were treated as facts, carefully collated, quantified, and reduced to percentages. The report, with its statistics and calculations, has all the indicia of scientific study. But its base is an unscientifically selected group of opinions.

Judges' opinions can be as aberrant and baseless as the opinions of any other group of people. Judges' opinions with respect to legal practices are perhaps more likely to reflect the conventional wisdom than a critical view. Lawyers and judges are educated to respect precedent rather than innovation. The study of law is based on past decisions, which are usually extolled as embodying the distilled wisdom of generations. Most judges, like most lawyers, were instructed that trial by jury is a unique and vital element of the American legal system. Few lawyers or judges believe a priori that juries are more often wrong than right. They are, of course, aware of gross miscarriages of justice by juries. But the legal profession is inclined to regard such cases as aberrant. Popular jokes often express folk wisdom that is denied in sophisticated serious discussions. Every lawyer knows the old saw, "If the law is against your client, argue the facts; if the facts are against your client, argue the law; if both the facts and the law are against your client, demand a jury trial." A generation after the Kalven and Zeisel study, no one knows whether juries decide cases right or wrong. Courts still base their decisions on the premise that jury verdicts are inviolable unless gross bias, prejudice, or corruption can be proved.

Several years after a split-verdict law was enacted in my jurisdiction I wondered whether the verdicts of these juries were as fair as those of unanimous juries. I had an impression that the split-verdict juries delibe-rated a much shorter period of time, but I believed that the results were not appreciably different. In order to test this impression, I examined the trial records and verdicts of forty-three consecutive civil jury cases tried before me prior to the split-verdict law and forty-nine consecutive civil cases tried before me immediately thereafter.[19] Other than the split-verdict statute, there were no changes in the law affecting these cases. The juries were drawn from the same pool of registered voters. In the brief period of time covered by these trials there were no demographic or social changes in the community. I found that my impression that split-verdict juries reached their verdicts more quickly was correct. But until I analyzed the cases I did not know that split verdicts were more often wrong (by my judgment) than unanimous verdicts. Wholly unexpected was the discovery that the split-verdict juries decided in favor of defendants more often than unanimous juries. Had I been asked to fill out a questionnaire on the effects of the split verdict before reviewing these cases, I should probably have answered that there was little difference.

A typical sociological study of jury characteristics[20] was based exclusively on questionnaires addressed to jurors. The only characteristics the authors studied were race, sex, age, and education. Although the study does not indicate that fact, apparently it was limited to criminal cases. It does not report the number of cases or the variety of offenses. There was no examination of the characteristics of the offender or the facts of the cases. It has been my experience that occupation, family status (married, parent, etc.), economic status, area of residence, previous crime victimization, and nature of the crime are at least as significant as race, sex, age, and education in affecting jury verdicts. The choice of variables inevitably determines the results of the questionnaire.

During the past few years, I have received scores of questionnaires asking a curious mixture of fact and opinion. Some are directed to court operations and sentencing of offenders. Many are addressed to me because I am a woman judge. All follow the same format. There are multiple choice answers to each questions. Some permit a choice of "other." Most do not. The questioner, in effect, dictates the response.

Apparently most researchers believe that the subjects answer questionnaires truthfully. A judge who hears sworn testimony every day consisting of a mixture of truth, misperceptions, and outright lies can only wonder. A recent questionnaire sponsored by the prestigious American Judicature Society, addressed to women judges, asked the following questions:

Which factors most facilitated your becoming a judge? (Choose all appropriate.)

—— Accepting visible cases as a lawyer
—— Acquaintance with political leaders or their aides
—— Active in bar association work

—— Being a woman
—— Endorsement of interest groups
—— Endorsement of political parties
—— Held party office
—— Held public office
—— High-quality campaign
—— Law school attended
—— Prior professional experience: Please explain ——
—— Well-financed campaign
—— Well-known family name
—— Worked in political campaigns
—— Other: Please specify ——

The authors of the study must be naive or trusting or both. I seriously doubt that any respondent replied "services to the political party," "promise from the political boss," "political contributions," "My partner is a senator," or "My partners wanted to get rid of me."

As most lawyers know, these would be accurate replies for some members of the judiciary. Although this question asks for a factual response, many judges do not really know what particular combination of factors was significant. At best they can only give an opinion.

This questionnaire also illustrates the subconscious biases of the researchers. Apparently they believe that Dr. Johnson's comment about women preachers applies to women judges. The curmudgeonly eighteenth-century Englishman declared: "Sir, a woman preaching is like a dog's walking on his hind legs. It is not done well; but you are surprised to find it done at all." No answers such as "eminence at the bar" or "esteem of fellow members of the bar" were listed. These qualifications should, of course, be the basis of judicial appointments. Similarly, there is no question with respect to the judge's record at law school. Was she a mediocre or a superior student? Nor is there any inquiry as to scholarly publications or contributions to the law. Did the researchers assume that no woman judge had such attainments? The carefully collated answers, with accurately calculated percentiles, will not include significant information about the selection process as applied to women judges. But the conclusions will be presented as "facts."

Some careful researchers have noted the possibility of substantial error resulting from the use of questionnaires. The authors of a cost analysis of court systems attempted to weight the time of judges spent on various tasks, to measure productivity. They candidly reported:

Among problems with the use of a weighting system are the accuracy, dependability, and meaning of the weights. In most case weighting systems, data on how much time judges devote to specific categories of activity have been gathered by distributing questionnaires and asking judges to record their time over a specified period. Substantial error in the results could be caused by the inaccuracies involved in this type of time study.[21]

However, the authors did not utilize a more accurate methodology.

Many reports denominated "studies" are really little more than a journalistic pastiche of opinions of other people, fleshed out with a few personal observations. Journalists often provide perceptive insights into the legal system and its problems. They observe and they report graphically what they see. Such accounts, however, have serious limitations. Are the incidents the reporter sees typical or anomalous? Does he have all the facts or only what he observes over a limited period of time? Does he examine the entire problem or only a portion of it? Does he rely on hearsay information or verifiable facts? Journalists can and do perform invaluable services in alerting the public to problems, prodding delinquent or careless officials, and acting as Socratic gadflies. *Crisis in the Courts,* by journalist Howard James, is such a useful book.[22] I compare it with *Criminal Justice, Criminal Violence,* by sociologist Charles Silberman,[23] because of the identity of subject matter and similarity of style. Both books deal with the criminal justice system. Both rely on secondary sources. Neither presents a systematic statistical study of cases, sentences, judicial conduct, prisons, or any other aspect of the system. James did not claim to have conducted research. He simply reported what he had heard and seen. He described the courts and prisons he visited and the cases he observed. It was not a cheerful picture. He found courts in disarray, defendants inadequately represented, some outright miscarriages of justice, and a system that was not functioning fairly and adequately. Significantly, there were no published denunciations of James's conclusions. Defense lawyers, prosecutors, judges, and court administrators did not leap to defend themselves against his charges.

A few years later Silberman surveyed the same scene and reached contrary conclusions. His book relied extensively on unnamed sources and newspaper accounts of cases. These reports are frequently unreliable and incomplete. There is little firsthand information. Neither book refers extensively to transcripts of trials, court records, or comments by criminals or victims. But the Silberman book, supported by the Ford Foundation, is considered a work of research. The use of journalistic techniques that masquerade as serious research into the legal system is a matter that should be of public concern because judicial and legislative decisions are based upon the conclusions and opinions expressed by such writers in the mistaken belief that they have presented facts.

The ethics of research have been called into question in many fields. Universities are confronting dishonesty in research by members of their faculties and examining their relationships to industry.[24] Many law professors serve as consultants or counsel to industry. A number of legal research projects and legal articles are funded by industry. The American Bar Foundation, the research arm of the American Bar Association, has not addressed the question of ethics with respect to legal research. There may in fact be no conflicts of interest. But without examination of the funding process one cannot know whether or not there is a problem. Courts should be wary of predicating decisions upon studies that may be biased or tainted.

Competence is unquestionably a serious problem in all areas of research. Faith in the unswerving, meticulous quest for truth on the part of academic researchers is insufficient grounds for the use by judges of studies as evidence to support decisions unless these documents are a matter of record and subjected to adversarial testing of validity.[25] A number of law reform projects have been adopted by courts on the basis of research studies indicating that they had achieved great success. After more careful evaluation the studies have been found to be false and misleading. The author of a critical evaluation concludes that ". . . there has not been one scientifically acceptable evaluation of any major pretrial release program. Although enough reports have been written to fill a small library, few meet even elementary research standards. Many of these seemingly impressive data-based reports are little more than promotion pieces that ignore or beg the hard questions."[26] The reader is rightly bewildered by such revelations. He has difficulty in evaluating the criticisms and the studies because there are no standards for legal research. This critic's wholesale denigration of the studies he reviewed is also subject to some caution. His book was a desk-bound research project based on the reports and opinions of others. He states that he wished to make a "critical appraisal of court reform." Therefore, it is not unexpected that he found that the court reforms he studied had not succeeded. Clearly there is a need for factual studies of many aspects of the entire legal system and for standards by which these studies can be evaluated and tested before being utilized as a factor in judicial decisions.

For many problems the findings of social scientists, even if germane and reliable, should have no bearing on a court's decision because matters of individual rights should be decided without regard to the social, economic, or intellectual status of the parties or to popular opinion. In the seminal decision of the United States Supreme Court barring segregated public schools,[27] the Court referred to the opinion of a noted sociologist that integrated schools would improve the educational attainments of black children. Thirty years of experience unfortunately has not confirmed that opinion. But the question is irrelevant. Even if one could prove by reliable and convincing data that there were racial differences in educational ability and that integration hampered rather than promoted learning, those facts should not be considered in deciding whether equality of treatment under law has been denied.

In holding a death penalty statute unconstitutional the Supreme Court referred to the evolving moral standards of the community as being opposed to the death penalty.[28] Two years later, after a number of states had promptly enacted new death penalty statutes to meet the vague requirements adumbrated in the opinion, the Court upheld a death penalty statute.[29] Resolution of constitutional issues should not depend on the temper of the times, whether correctly or incorrectly perceived. When courts yield to public opinion,[30] popular beliefs, or the blandishments of "scientific" research in reaching decisions involving constitutional rights, the law is distorted and belief in the rule of law is eroded.

Before yielding to the seductions of social research, lawyers and judges should bear in mind five principles:

First, human beings are too complex to be reduced to a number of quantifiable variables. A judge who sees hundreds of people who have committed a wide variety of acts—some bizarre, cruel, and evil and others that are only thoughtless or simply venal, and some that are amazingly generous, selfless, and even saintly—should know that astonishing variations in human behavior cannot be accounted for by a limited list of preselected factors or characteristics.

Second, a legal system predicated upon the rights of the individual cannot operate on the basis of averages and norms. It must treat each litigant and each case individually.

Third, predictions of human behavior are inherently unreliable. Judges see countless people who have led apparently law-abiding, rational lives who unexpectedly go beserk or commit calculated crimes or irrational acts. They also see people who have committed one offense but never commit another.

Fourth, every factor on which a legal decision is based, including reports of research studies, should be subjected to rigorous legal standards of proof of credibility and reliability.

Fifth, enforcement of constitutional rights must not be influenced by averages, norms, or popular beliefs.

# CHAPTER XI

---

# POPULAR
# PANACEAS

There is a continual movement in legal history back
and forth between justice without law, as it were, and justice
according to law.

—Roscoe Pound

I do not long for all one sees
That's Japanese.

—W. S. Gilbert

The daily press and popular magazines report that American courts
are in a state of imminent collapse, that the nation is infested with
a plague of lawyers, and that the rights of all are imperiled by these
conditions. Responding to these cries of danger, countless concerned
Americans have offered miracle cures. From humorist Russell Baker to
Chief Justice Warren Burger, each presents a panacea. Russell Baker
suggests that American lawyers be traded for Japanese cars. Under this
scheme the United States could rid itself of superfluous persons and in
return obtain desirable commodities. Justice Burger and Justice O'Connor[1] propose that arbitration be substituted for litigation. Others urge
that law schools revise their curricula and train a new generation of
conciliators instead of litigators.

Critics of the legal system, ignoring history and literature,[2] assume that the courts' delays and the expenses of litigation are recent ills and that in other times all persons, rich or poor, who had legal claims and defenses received prompt, fair, and affordable justice. The fact that these problems of the legal system are of long standing does not militate against the need for reform. It does, however, provide a much-needed perspective.

But instead of examining the past to study both the problems and the very real progress American law has made in bringing justice to large numbers of people, many leaders of the bench, bar, and academia propose radical, untested, instant miracle cures. Many urge abandoning the system of trial developed over centuries in favor of relatively untried, unevaluated substitutes for the resolution of disputes. They look to China, a nation just emerging from an era of brutal lawlessness, for a model people's court. They praise Japan for its scarcity of lawyers, ignoring the fact that the Japanese were for centuries under the absolute rule of shoguns and emperors and only since World War II have adopted a form of government modeled on our own legal system. They disregard the remarkable history of Anglo-American law, under which the powers of the state have been limited and the rights of the individual expanded. They ignore the fact that much of this development was achieved by lawyers through the careful procedures of litigation in courts of law. In the interests of speed and economy, they would sacrifice procedural regularity and due process of law. A few warning voices have been raised. But catchpenny panaceas have taken the public fancy.

This chapter reviews briefly the more popular remedies that have been proposed by responsible members of the legal profession.

It cannot be denied that in the 1980s, there are too many cases for the present number of judges to try properly under present procedures. Logic would indicate that either the capacity of the courts must be increased or the number of cases decreased. If the first route were pursued, either the courts would have to be expanded or trial procedures would have to be revised to permit shorter trials. More rational appellate procedures would have to be devised to facilitate simpler and quicker review of trial decisions.

Expanding the courts by adding more judges would be impractical, costly, and undesirable. More judges will not ease the burden on appellate courts that sit as a body, such as the United States Supreme Court and the highest courts of most states. Every judge or justice would still have to review and rule upon every appeal. To have the highest courts sit in panels, as many intermediate appellate courts do, would fragment those courts and result in conflicting rulings, depending upon the composition of the panels. In essence, there would be no definitive ruling on a particular issue unless the court were convened to sit en banc for special cases. To date, no published recommendations have been made to require or permit the highest courts to sit in panels.

The numbers of trial judges and intermediate appellate court judges have been substantially increased in most jurisdictions. Some trial courts are composed of 100 or more judges. There are serious disadvantages to expanding courts indefinitely. Increasing the number of trial judges involves much more than simply adding another judge. In addition to chambers for the judge, a secretary, and a law clerk, there must be added another courtroom, more court personnel (clerks and criers), and additional prosecutors and defenders to try cases before that judge. The annual cost of adding one judge with a salary of $50,000 is estimated at approximately $300,000. Such expenses are simply not feasible for many states and local communities.

Aside from the expense, there are real disadvantages to expanding the courts. When courts become too large, there is a loss of collegiality. The court becomes atomized. Each judge simply processes the cases as they are assigned to him. There is little effort to deal with common problems in an organized or concerted manner. Law reform is neglected by the judges because responsibility for the court is fragmented.

Increasing the number of judges diminishes the prestige of the office. If the judiciary is to attract lawyers of competence, wisdom, and dedication who are willing to forgot the financial rewards of private practice and the leisure of academia and accept the restrictions, limitations, and responsibilities of public office, then the position must offer intangible rewards. These include a sense of accomplishment, communal respect, and prestige. United States Judge Henry J. Friendly has aptly observed:

There must come a point when an increase in the number of judges makes judging, even at the trial level, less prestigious and less attractive. Prestige is a very important factor in attracting highly qualified men to the federal bench from much more lucrative pursuits. Yet the largest district courts will be in the very metropolitan areas where the discrepancy between uniform federal salaries and the financial rewards of private practice is the greatest, and the difficulty of maintaining an accustomed standard of living on the federal salary the most acute. There is real danger that in such areas, once the prestige factor was removed, lawyers with successful practices, particularly young men, would not be willing to make the sacrifice.[3]

Before further increasing the number of judges, a careful examination of future needs should be undertaken. There are no reliable data indicating that litigation will continue to increase in the immediate future. From the available evidence, it appears to be much more likely that there will be fewer cases. The crime rate in the 1980s is declining. The FBI Uniform Crime Reports reveal that in 1982 the crime rate dropped by 4 percent from 1981, continuing a trend of several years. This has been attributed to the smaller number of young men between the ages of fifteen and twenty-five, the group who commit the greatest number of offenses. Demographics should also reduce the number of cases in family court. Civil litigation may also decline sharply with the spread of no-fault automobile insurance laws and more effective policing of the use of dangerous products. Economic recovery would sharply cut the huge number of bankruptcies. It is also likely to bring more jobs and more housing, thus eliminating much social tension that is provocative of crime and litigation. As the public accepts the implications of the civil rights movement, the women's movement, and the drive to procure equality for many other disadvantaged peoples, the need for hotly contested, lengthy, and bruising litigation to enforce the rights of these persons should be obviated.

Once judgeships are created, they tend to be permanent. Reducing the number of judges requires legislation. Because so many people have a vested interest in all the jobs that each judgeship entails, as well as the judges themselves, there is strong resistance to abolishing these offices. The experience of public schools and public and private universities that have attempted to eliminate unnecessary teaching positions as the school population diminishes indicates the difficulties in abolishing positions.

If the litigational process, both trial and appellate, were less time-consuming, the present number of judges could adequately handle more cases. Shorter, more streamlined pretrial, trial, and posttrial procedures would also drastically reduce the costs to the litigants and the per case cost to the public.

The major impediment to procedural reform is that there is no concerted effort to draft such rules and legislation. Few serious proposals have been made to revise and simplify civil and criminal trial procedures in order to reduce the time and costs of litigation. This is a major, time-consuming task requiring cooperation of a group of experts and adequate funding. The Uniform Commercial Code, a comprehensive statute codifying the law with respect to commercial transactions (sales, bank deposits, commercial paper, etc.) was first proposed in 1940. With an initial contribution of $15,000, the sum of $250,000 was raised from banks and foundations. A group of experts worked diligently from 1945 to 1953 to draft the model code. This was a relatively uncontroversial statute. It was supported by major financial institutions, leading law firms, and the American Law Institute because uniformity and certainty in the law was unquestionably desirable and would eliminate much litigation. Between 1954 and 1968, the act was adopted with minor modifications by forty-eight states.[4] To draft a comprehensive model statute and rules simplifying and expediting court procedures will be a much more difficult task. It will also be more controversial. No cohesive group, such as banks, has a financial interest that will be served by such a statute. Many lawyers and judges may oppose it. The public, which would benefit from such changes in the law, has no organized lobby to promote this law reform or to raise money to fund the necessary work. Little attention to or support for such a program has been evidenced by the legal community or the media.

Unfortunately, attention has focused on the other route: decreasing the number of cases. Most remedies for the problems of the legal system are designed to reduce the number of cases reaching the courts. Litigation arises out of disputes, perceived and actual injustices, and the malfunctioning of technology and of government. These problems will not disappear just because they are not heard by the courts. The problems will persist because they were not created by the courts or the legal system. The law cannot be expected to eliminate crime, accidents, misunderstandings, errors, breaches of contract, bankruptcies, and all the ills that flesh and society are heir to. The law can only provide rules and a forum for the just resolution of disputes and the award of monetary damages to compensate for wrongs done intentionally or unintentionally. This is the traditional function of courts.

The thrust of the popular panaceas is to deny access to the courts for a wide variety of problems. Under the proposals the bulk of the cases that would be diverted from the courts involve poor people. These proposals do not establish means tests. As phrased, they are neutral with respect to wealth, race, sex, and age. But in operation they would institutionalize two separate and unequal systems of justice: courts of law with rights and constitutional safeguards for the rich and speedy extralegal forums for the poor.

The underlying assumption of these alternate dispute-resolution proposals is that lawyers are the principal cause of crowded court calendars. The solution is to omit the lawyers, the judges, and the courts. "A bench, gavel, and black robe are not essential to resolve some types of disagreements," the Christian Science Monitor proclaims.[5] Take the cases out of the courts, the reformers say, get rid of the lawyers, and resolve the problems amicably through conciliation, arbitration, and mediation. The popularity of alternative methods of dispute settlement as a panacea for overcrowded courts is evidenced by "selected bibliography"[6] of alternative means of dispute settlement consisting of more than 1,000 books and articles on the subject, most of them written after 1970. A National Institute for Dispute Resolution was established in 1982. The proponents of these alternatives ignore the fact that the parties involved in litigation are not the lawyers but the litigants. A lawyer can advise, counsel, and recommend. He cannot compel his client to follow his advice. Every day I see reasonable lawyers attempt to persuade their clients to settle disputes. In most cases, the good judgment and goodwill of the lawyers prevail. Thus perhaps 90 percent of all civil cases are settled with a modicum of fairness. It is only when the clients will not listen to reason that the cases go to trial. Without the coercive power of the courts, I seriously doubt that unreasonable litigants can be induced to accept mediation or conciliation.

The proponents of alternative dispute resolution programs believe that these methods are more desirable and cheaper than court litigation. But there is little, if any, evidence to substantiate those claims. Before being beguiled and oversold on this popular panacea, the public should ask searching questions: For whom are these alternatives more desirable? Will civil defendants be assessed damages, even though blameless? Will those accused of crime get a fair hearing? Will the public be adequately protected? Who will save money? The litigants? The public? Who will profit by these alternative mechanisms? Is this another device to clear the court dockets of the problems of the poor? Will our system of justice become fairer and more equal or will it institutionalize the inequalities between rich and poor?

These are not unanswerable questions. There is no need to devise game plans, mock trials, or simulated cases or to conduct opinion polls, to speculate or guess. Alternative dispute resolution programs have been widely used for the better part of this century for many kinds of cases. The statistical techniques, the computers, and the data are available to compare these programs with the traditional system of litigation. What is needed is a rigorous cost/benefit analysis, and a careful examination of the legal, social, and economic effects of these alternatives on the participants and on public attitudes toward the rule of law.

Workmen's compensation is perhaps the most widely used alternative dispute resolution system in the United States. It is an early form of no-fault liability. Every state has a compensation act. Employees injured on the job receive statutory weekly compensation calculated according to the severity of the injury. They do not have to prove fault or negligence on the part of the employer, but they cannot recover beyond the statutory amount of compensation even when the employer is grossly negligent. As originally contemplated, compensation was to be awarded automatically on filing proof of injury. The employee was not supposed to need a lawyer. As the system developed, there were inevitable disputes over the fact of injury, whether it was an accident and whether it occurred "in the course of employment," and the extent and duration of the incapacity of the employee. Employees found that they had to retain counsel in order to get their compensation. The states had to establish mini-courts in which a hearing examiner took testimony, ruled on admissibility of evidence, and made decisions. A hierarchy of appeals within the system developed, and a right of appeal to the courts. In return for limited benefits under the acts, injured workers were deprived of the right to sue in court for negligence, gross negligence, and punitive damages. Employers were required to participate in an insurance plan or to fund their own insurance for all accidents suffered by employees. In return they were relieved of all common-law liability.

After a half century of experience with workmen's compensation, it is reasonably clear that seriously injured employees have not been adequately compensated. One has only to compare the statutory benefits paid to employees with their recoveries against third parties who were sued at common law. In a typical case, an employee recovered $6,800 under the compensation act. A jury, however, found that his damages were $60,000.[7] Under even the most generous statutes an employee who is totally, permanently disabled recovers a maximum of two-thirds of his wages. From this recovery the injured employee pays his legal fees, medical witness fees, and other expenses of litigation. Many employees and their families have difficulty subsisting on their wages. With the additional expenses of care for a totally disabled person, it is unlikely that the worker and his family can maintain themselves on the compensation payments.

Is the cost to the public of administering the entire compensation system—consisting of a board, hearing examiners, medical examiners, claims investigators, lawyers, clerks, and other personnel, as well as the staff that administers the insurance program—substantially less than the cost of courts? No one has calculated the additional costs to the public of supplying welfare or charity to care for the families of injured employees who cannot survive on compensation benefits. These facts should be ascertained and evaluated before reaching any decision to substitute alternatives for court litigation.

There are scores of other federal and state quasi-judicial tribunals before which special types of cases are litigated. With the growth of the alphabetical agencies of the New Deal and new government regulations dealing with economic and social problems, administrative law tribunals proliferated. Their counterparts were established in the several states. All these bodies are alternative dispute-resolution devices that divert cases from the courts. The purpose of most such agencies was not to relieve the courts but to establish bodies with special expertise to handle specialized problems. The proceedings before such agencies as the Securities and Exchange Commission, the Federal Communications Commission, and the Interstate Commerce Commission are long, complicated, and expensive. Highly skilled lawyers, accountants, and experts are required to present evidence on these complex problems. Some of these regulatory bodies are financed in whole or in part by the industries they regulate. Few problems of equal access to justice inhere in the operations of such tribunals because the general public, composed of persons from all economic strata, rarely uses these administrative agencies. The parties who do appear before them can afford the counsel fees, expert witnesses, research, and all the other considerable expenses of litigation before these bodies.

Many industries include provisions for binding arbitration in their contracts. But innumerable disputes arise over the interpretation of these contracts. Courts must rule on motions to enjoin arbitration hearings, motions to compel parties to attend arbitration hearings, motions to consolidate hearings and to delay arbitration. After the arbitration has been concluded, courts must hear appeals from the awards of the arbitrators and petitions to enforce the awards.

Mediation, arbitration, and conciliation all have a place in the legal system. But they are not a substitute for courts. Nor is there reliable evidence that they are cheaper than courts. Mediation, conciliation, and arbitration are now available to disputants who wish to use these procedures in civil cases and who can afford to pay for these services. They depend on the willingness of the parties, unless statutes or rules of court mandate these procedures.

One form of compulsory arbitration that has been successfully used in a number of jurisdiction applies to civil cases involving only money damages. These cases are tried before a panel of lawyers. Either party, if dissatisfied, has a right to a new trial before a court. In the United States District Courts for the Third Circuit (Pennsylvania, Delaware, New Jersey, and the Virgin Islands) during a fifty-three-month period 4,010 cases went to compulsory arbitration. Of these only 60 required a new trial before a court.[8] Similar satisfactory results have obtained in other jurisdictions.

By a recent rule of court, the amount of money involved in cases which must be arbitrated in the Third Circuit was raised from $20,000 to $50,000. This is a practical device that will certainly relieve the federal courts of a great many cases. One must question the monetary limit. Even in an age of inflation, $50,000 is not petty cash. Is this another judicially sanctioned step towards institutionalizing the two-track treatment of the rich and the poor? On the other hand, if arbitration is fair and satisfactory for cases involving money damages of $50,-000, should it not be required for all similar cases, without a monetary limitation?

The cases recommended for diversion from the courts to other bodies that do not observe strict rules of evidence and procedural guarantees of rights, and do not have enforcement powers, involve, in the main, poor people and special interest groups. Mediation services for prisoners' complaints is widely recommended.[9] Most prisoners are indigent. A prisoner has already been deprived of many of an individual's most valued rights. To deny prisoners access to the courts deprives them, in effect, of all opportunity to assert any claims. It also deprives other prisoners of the benefits of court decisions establishing standards of treatment, declarations of prisoners' rights, and enforceable precedents declaring the obligations and limitations of jailers.

Chief Justice Burger suggests that problems of marriage, child custody, and adoption should be dealt with outside the courts.[10] These disputes involve those most valued relationships that should be guarded with all the protections of the law. Certainly the right to the companionship of one's own child is more important than any commercial contract or claim for money. An inappropriate or ill-considered adoption can wreak havoc on the entire life of the adoptee and the natural parents.

It is also frequently suggested that criminal courts are an inappropriate forum for dealing with intrafamilial violence. Few of these cases are prosecuted. Those that are taken to court are often treated as minor offenses regardless of the injuries inflicted. Tragic results occur when unchecked abuse culminates in serious injuries or homicide. A recent study indicates that criminal prosecution is the best corrective for intrafamily violence.

Mediation is proposed as a means of lessening hostilities in marital disputes, saving the battling spouses money, and providing a quick, fair result.[11] However, there are pitfalls for the unwary spouse who proceeds to mediation without representation. Admissions to a mediator are not privileged and can later be used against the incautious spouse in a court trial. Mediators are not licensed or regulated by the state. They are rarely insured, so that the unwitting spouse has no recourse if the mediator misrepresents the facts. The mediator cannot enforce his decisions. In most divorce cases, the parties recognize that their marriage is at an end. The fight is over a division of property, support, and custody of the children. With respect to the financial aspects of divorce, the more affluent spouse, usually but not always the husband, has a continuing obligation to contribute to the support of the children. He seldom can make a final property settlement in one payment but must do it over a period of time. In the event either party fails to live up to the award of the mediator, it will still be necessary for the other spouse to retain counsel and go to court to enforce the award or agreement. With respect to custody, no order or agreement is ever final but can be reconsidered by the courts in the light of changed circumstances and the best interests of the child. The courts will inevitably be involved in these problems even after mediation or arbitration.

The juvenile court was originally created as an alternative dispute mechanism designed to avoid the rigors and legalism of the criminal courts. It may properly be considered another form of diversion or alternative dispute-resolution device. After more than eighty years of functioning without rules, with few lawyers, and with judges who viewed themselves as big brothers, the juvenile court has been found to be detrimental to the very children it was intended to help and violative of their constitutional rights. There has been no analysis of the cost of the juvenile court bureaucracy—with its intake interviewers, social investigators, clerks, and school-liaison personnel—as compared with criminal courts hearing nonjury cases.

Mediation has also been recommended for environmental disputes. John Larsen, vice-president of Weyerhauser Company, a major forest-product concern, states that the nation can no longer afford to take environmental issues to court. But Leah K. Patton, an officer of the Institute for Environmental Mediation, points out that mediation is being "oversold and underutilized." Dr. Myra L. Kanstadt, a professor of community medicine, points out that only in a court of law will all the facts in an environmental dispute be revealed.[12] Significantly, litigation often results in settlements in which polluters agree to pay substantial fines.[13]

Several jurisdictions have attempted to remove medical malpractice cases from the courts by referring them to arbitration panels composed of doctors and lawyers. These efforts have generally proved to be unsatisfactory.[14] The constitutionality of providing special courts for one class of defendant is questionable. Dentists, lawyers, engineers, architects, and other professionals sued for malpractice might reasonably demand special tribunals composed of their peers to rule upon their cases.

Arbitration is a widely recommended alternative to litigation. Arbitration has had a long and honorable, if not particularly successful, history in the field of labor relations. States have experimented with many legal devices to strengthen arbitration. Many states have outlawed strikes by certain government employees and have mandated binding arbitration. All too often intransigeant employers and employees have thwarted the intent of the legislature and the wishes of the public. Ultimately, when mediation and arbitration have failed, the parties have had to resort to the courts.

It must also be remembered that the most vocal proponents of arbitration and mediation are arbitrators and mediators who earn a livelihood from the fees they charge the disputants. A typical example of such special pleading is an article in *Newsweek*[15] by Stanley J. Lieberman, the founder of the American Mediation Service. He writes, "Too often litigation works only to the advantage of the lawyer whose bag of tricks is bottomless. . . . The next time your lawyer says 'Sue the bastards,' tell him you would rather mediate."

Mediators charge what the traffic will bear. Conciliators often are employed by charitable or communal organizations. The public pays for their services indirectly. The American Arbitration Association has a set fee schedule based on the amount of each claim and counterclaim.[16] Thus, parties who seek to use arbitration as a substitute for litigation not only have to pay counsel fees but also pay for the arbitrators. This effectively precludes indigents and poor people from using the services of arbitrators.

Among the innovative schemes to divert cases from the courts is the California "rent-a-judge" statute.[17] Under this practice, civil cases are referred to an impartial referee. The referee is usually a former or retired judge. The referee's finding is the "finding of the court." The parties share the cost of the referee. The plan has been lauded as "private settlement for the public good" and denounced as "secret justice for the privileged few"[18] who can afford to pay for their own judges.

Much more careful evaluation of these programs is needed. Some types of arbitration and diversion may be cheaper than court trials, but until accurate information is obtained, the public and the legislatures cannot make an intelligent decision as to the desirability and economics of these programs as well as the protections and remedies they provide. The ultimate test of the desirability of each alternative program should be whether it affords access to equal justice to all members of the community.

Far less consideration has been given to devising means to ease the burdens of the appellate courts. Aside from a bill to create a special federal court to decide cases involving conflicting decisions by the various federal courts of appeals,[19] and a proposal to limit petitions by prisoners and to reduce the access of persons on death row to the United States Supreme Court,[20] few proposals have been made to reduce the number of appeals. If the appellate courts are to correct trial errors, clarify the law in the light of rapidly changing conditions, and provide guidance and precedents for litigants and lawyers, they must have the time to consider and write opinions in cases of wide public importance. As we have seen, the appellate courts are not adequately fulfilling that function.

Law schools have been charged with responsibility for the litigiousness of American society. I believe that in most instances clients, not lawyers, are responsible for the proliferation of civil cases.[21] The principal reforms suggested are to teach lawyers "negotiation and mediation techniques."[22] Since more than 90 percent of all civil cases are settled, lawyers must have learned these skills even though they were not taught them in law school.

Lawyers, judges, and legal scholars are genuinely concerned with the problems of overcrowded courts and delay. They call for innovations.[23] The need is clear. It has been evident for years. In 1971, a knowledgeable reporter recommended "abandonment by judges and lawyers of archaic delay-producing procedures—restructuring of the legal profession and the law schools to channel more and better trained lawyers, judges, and supporting personnel into the trial courts."[24] But to date practical remedies to implement these goals have not been proposed.

# CHAPTER XII

---

# A
# FEW MODEST
# PROPOSALS

As to my own part, having turned my thoughts, for
many years, upon this important Subject, and maturely
weighed the several Schemes of other Projectors, I have
always found them grossly mistaken in their computation.

—Jonathan Swift

What is needed is intelligent examination of the
consequences that are actually effected by inherited
institutions and customs, in order that there may be
intelligent consideration of the ways in which they are to
be intentionally modified in behalf of generation of
different consequences.

—John Dewey

The portrait of the American legal system presented here, limned
with warts and all, does not conform to the textbook physiognomy
of due process and equal justice for all. However, the very blemishes
described may be seen as a triumph of the vitality of the rule of law. Had

this belief not animated the public and the legal community, the system would probably have collapsed under the weight of numbers and manifest inequities. Nonetheless, it continues. People rarely flout court orders or seek self-help for injuries done them. Those convicted of crime serve their sentences. Even in prisons there is, for the most part, what Austin called a habit of obedience to law.

The social, economic, and technological upheavals of the past generation, although painful and destructive of many customs and beliefs, have not shattered the American polity. There has been no breakdown of law and order and no repudiation of the faltering processes of democracy in favor of the specious promises of dictatorship. The American legal system, which provides a peaceful alternative to violence in the pursuit of a more equal and just community, has been a substantial factor in maintaining the stability of American society. The price of this success has been a rush to the courthouse and the resulting increase in the demands and burdens placed upon the courts.

The challenge in the last decades of the twentieth century is to make equal protection of the laws not merely a nominal right but an actual, feasible, available means of redress and defense for every person. To do this, procedures must be simplified and expedited without jeopardizing constitutional rights and privileges. Courts and legal services must be available equally to rich and poor, young and old, corporations and individuals. The costs of justice must be borne equitably.

There is no quick fix—no cheap, easy device for ensuring equal justice. Neither platitudes nor panaceas will suffice. There are both immediate and long-range reforms in practice and procedure and in the structure of the legal community that, if adopted, should promote these goals. I cannot present a blueprint for rebuilding the legal system. Rather, I offer a rough map charting several roads to be taken by courts, judges, lawyers, and scholars.

Some flagrant inequities of the litigational process could be remedied at once by rule of court or the enactment of simple statutes, since they do not involve changes in legal principles or substantive law. These reforms involve (1) trial scheduling, (2) costs and fees, (3) the right to counsel of civil litigants who are unable to pay legal fees, (4) the right of all civil litigants and criminal defendants to counsel of their choice, (5) competence of lawyers, (6) quality of the judiciary, (7) appellate procedures, (8) insularity of the courts, and (9) information with respect to the operations of the courts in affording equal protection of the laws to all parties.

(1) Since due process requires that a party be given a hearing, it is essential that courts cease assembly-line processing of cases and grant every litigant a hearing sufficiently long to present a meaningful claim or defense.

More equitable allocation of trial time is the first step towards achieving equality for all litigants. No judge can hear and decide 100 cases or even 30 cases in one day. Few, if any, cases should require weeks or months of trial time. A limit of 10 or, at most, 15 cases per judge per day should be established and observed for all types of cases, including misdemeanors, small claims, and juvenile hearings. Such a trial schedule would allot barely twenty-five minutes per case. Less time than that is a mockery of justice.

It may be argued that even these few minutes are too much, that the backlog will become overwhelming, that the constitutional requirement of a speedy trial in felonies will be violated because there will not be enough judges to hear these cases. The obvious way to accord a modicum of equal justice is to shorten the unduly long trials. By scheduling one major trial every two or three days and informing counsel that if the schedule cannot be met, lengthy cases will be deferred, it is likely that many cases that would otherwise have consumed weeks of trial time will be concluded in much less time.

Such scheduling would induce many civil litigants to settle purely monetary claims. In other cases counsel would probably stipulate to facts not seriously in issue, shorten the direct testimony and cross-examination of fact witnesses, and agree to the use of written reports by experts instead of lengthy oral testimony that in essence repeats the substance of the reports. The not inconsiderable ingenuity of able counsel now directed to prolonging and complicating trials would of necessity be devoted to the task of simplifying and expediting trials. Compulsory arbitration for civil cases involving only money claims, without limit as to amount, would relieve the courts of an enormous number of time consuming cases and enable judges to hear cases involving significant rights that are now rushed through juvenile and felony courts.

(2) Access fees bar many poor litigants from court and contribute only a pittance to the support of the courts. They should be abolished. In some jurisdictions this can be done by rule of court. In others, a statute will be required. Costs that actually reimburse the court for the time spent on the trial should be imposed on the parties in the discretion of the court, taking into account the following factors:

a. the actual cost of trial time expended on that case;
b. the frivolous or substantial nature of the claim or defense;
c. delaying tactics in both pretrial discovery and trial;
d. the amount in issue; and
e. the ability of the parties to pay.

(3) Trials in which a party is unrepresented, except for simple small monetary claims that should be heard by arbitrators, deprive those parties of a meaningful hearing. Provision of free counsel for indigents is now mandatory in all but the most minor criminal cases, such as traffic violations and summary offenses. Free counsel should also be provided for indigents in civil cases that involve substantial rights. Such cases include any claim or defense of constitutional rights and familial rights such as custody, marriage, divorce, and alimony, as well as claims for entitlements, rights, and benefits such as social security, disability compensation, welfare, and pensions.

Counsel at affordable fees should be available to indigents and to poor but nonindigent persons with the assistance, when needed, of partial public subsidy. The cost of paying for counsel in whole or in part, although substantial, need not be an undue burden on the taxpayers. It could be defrayed in large part by a fund derived from costs imposed on civil litigants in accordance with the standards set forth above. At present the public subsidizes the litigation of countless parties who can well afford to pay for the use of the courts. In many states victim compensation funds are derived in major part from small fines imposed on convicted criminal defendants. The imposition of actual court costs on those who can afford to pay would yield substantial funds to finance counsel fees for those who have significant claims and defenses and cannot afford necessary counsel fees to assert these rights.

This is but one of many ways in which counsel for the poor could be provided and paid without imposing additional taxes on the public.

Little thought has been devoted to this problem. The legal community has limited its concern for providing counsel for the nonwealthy to urging the government not to cut the niggardly funding for counsel for the indigent.[1]

(4) All persons accused of crime are now constitutionally entitled to an adequate legal defense. If the accused cannot afford counsel fees, he must be provided with legal representation at public expense. Meaningful representation, not simply a pro forma compliance with the law, requires more than a warm body with a law degree. Every litigant, including indigents, should have a meaningful relationship with his lawyer. Counsel must confer with his client long before trial and prepare the case adequately. This requires time and trust. Few defender or legal services offices allow staff attorneys sufficient time to establish such a relationship and prepare each case. It is the practice of most courts to appoint counsel paid by the public for indigents. Appointed counsel may be a private attorney, the public defender, legal aid, or some other legal services organization. If private counsel is appointed, a judge, not the litigant, selects the attorney. All too often the choice is dictated by politics, friendship, the desire to help a needy lawyer, or to give a young lawyer experience. Such counsel, foisted upon the client, rarely has a relationship of trust with his client. Every litigant, regardless of economic status, should have the right to choose his own counsel.

Countervailing arguments are that every indigent will request F. Lee Bailey or the local lawyer with the greatest reputation, that such lawyers will not be available, and that they will be too costly. Free counsel and partially subsidized counsel could be chosen by poor litigants from a list of attorneys who are willing to take cases at the fee schedules established by the court and who meet qualifications of experience, competence, and integrity, the qualifications to be scaled according to the gravity of the criminal charges or the complexity of the civil litigation.

Whether appointed counsel is less expensive than a defender or legal services lawyer is another fact that is simply not known. Such agencies may or may not be cheaper on a per case basis than private counsel. Most such agencies have large administrative staffs and overhead that small law offices do not have. Some clients may prefer a legal services lawyer; many do not. Frequently, a more sophisticated and articulate defendant

will say, "Judge, I don't want a defender, I want a real lawyer." To force
a poor litigant to be represented by an attorney he does not want and
in whom he has little confidence significantly differentiates between the
poor and the nonpoor and undermines the claim that the legal system
provides equal justice to rich and poor.

(5) Providing counsel for poor litigants is essentially a meaningless
effort and pointless expense if those lawyers are not adequate. Wealthy
litigants are usually represented by the most able lawyers. Leaders of the
bench and bar agree that a great many lawyers are incompetent. For the
most part, such lawyers represent poor and indigent clients, compound-
ing the inequalities of the litigational system.

Legal education, like schooling at every level, is under attack. Judges
and lawyers are asking the equivalent of "Why can't Johnny read?"
They want to know why graduate lawyers admitted to the bar can't try
cases. The complaints are widespread and serious. Judge Irving R. Kaufman of the United States Court of Appeals for the Second Circuit
writes:

The twin aspects of the competency problem—actual incompetence and ethical
myopia—have their roots in the American system of legal education. While law
schools have stressed conceptual skills, they have placed insufficient emphasis on
the practical training in litigation techniques and ethical sensitivity necessary to
turn out competent trial lawyers.[2]

Law schools have a monopoly on legal education. An aspiring lawyer
can rarely "read law" in a lawyer's office, take a bar examination, and
be admitted to practice. Graduation from an accredited law school is a
requirement for admission to the bar in most jurisdictions. Thus, law
schools are directly responsible for the successes and failures of the legal
profession.

For years law schools dismissed complaints by judges and practitioners, declaring that professional schools are not trade schools, that the
function of a law school is to teach the student "to think like a lawyer,"
that the nuts and bolts of practice can easily be learned in a few months
after graduation from law school. The ablest law graduates who go into
large law firms do learn the practical aspects of a specialized practice
from older members of the firm. However, those graduates who enter
small firms, set up their own practices, or are employed by government

agencies and by legal services organizations, make many shocking and avoidable mistakes at the expense of their clients, the court system, and the public. Although many bar associates provide excellent courses in continuing legal education, offering specialized courses by expert practitioners on recent developments in specialized areas of substantive law and practice, these programs cannot compensate for basic inadequacies of legal education.

It is little wonder that recent graduates are ill-prepared for practice when some of their professors, although brilliant and learned, are utterly ignorant of the rudiments of practice. Professor Alan Dershowitz of Harvard Law School writes:

I had never actually tried a case at that time, having gone straight from law school to a pair of judicial clerkships and then on to teach at Harvard Law School. . . . Having made my decision [to represent his first client] I did not have the foggiest notion of where to begin. They didn't teach that sort of thing in law school.[3]

In a case tried before me, the defendant, a tenured member of the faculty of a leading law school, was apparently unaware of basic rules of practice, constitutional law, and legal ethics. This defendant was represented by a colleague, also a tenured member of the same faculty. The defendant had rented a house to three professional women. The neighbors sued to enjoin the lease, pleading a restrictive covenant that limited use of the premises to a single family of the Caucasian race. The covenant was clearly unconstitutional as racially restrictive and violative of the rights of privacy of the tenants. This fundamental issue was not raised by the defendant. Instead, a specious issue of failure to make service was pleaded, even though defendant acknowledged having received a copy of the complaint. While the case was before the court, the defendant wrote a letter to me (the judge) without sending a copy to plaintiff or plaintiff's counsel and then attempted to negotiate a settlement with the plaintiff without notifying either counsel, all of which were gross breaches of ethics.

Recently a number of law schools have acknowledged deficiencies in legal education. Dean James Vorenberg of the Harvard Law School reports, ". . . one of the most important changes in our educational program in recent years is the development of a broad range of clinical courses. . . . They enable students to deepen their understanding of law in theory and in practice by exposure to the tensions between the two that arise from performing working roles in the legal system."[4] Many of these "clinical" programs were adopted as a response to the activist students who demanded "relevant" courses.

The dean further lauds "a three-week Trial Advocacy Workshop taught by judges and lawyers who volunteer to come to Cambridge for a few days each year." Three weeks scarcely provides an adequate introduction to a difficult new skill. Law students who pay thousands of dollars a year tuition should not have to rely on the charity of judges and lawyers for their education. Significantly, Harvard Law School students complain that some professors maintain outside law offices and do not meet their teaching commitments and are not available to the students.[5]

Professor Mark Kelman of the Stanford Law School takes a less optimistic view than Dean Vorenberg of the new look in legal education. He is quoted as saying:

For most students, nothing that goes on in law school matters—it's simply a credential . . . The most common student here is getting none of the really new clinical training, none of the new, financially sophisticated courses, no law and economics, no nothing. What this place offers is a ritzy degree, and there's a legal requirement that you spend three years here to get it.[6]

Although law schools have borrowed medical terminology and now denominate some courses as "clinical," this training bears little resemblance to the medical model. The medical profession, unlike the legal profession, is not bifurcated into practicing physicians and academics. There is close cooperation between medical schools and medical associations. Most medical professors are practicing doctors, experts in their fields. Medical clinical programs require students to observe and work with practitioners. The curriculum of the medical schools, the pedagogic methodology, and the size of the student body are all matters in which the medical associations take great interest and on which they have a significant influence. Medical schools in the 1980s are experimenting with new curricula, introducing courses in the humanities and social sciences to deepen and broaden the understanding and awareness of young doctors.[7] By contrast, law schools are proliferating technical courses. Subjects like jurisprudence, legal history, philosophy, and comparative law are not even offered in many law schools. Where offered, they are not required courses and are rarely popular.

At present any graduate of an accredited law school who passes a bar examination and meets nominal standards of good character is admitted to practice law. Bar examinations, in the main, consist of computer-graded multiple-choice questions. These examinations do not test the applicant's ability to use the English language or to perform the basic tasks of a practicing lawyer.

Establishing new qualifications for eligibility to take a bar examination would eliminate the most egregiously inept lawyers. Such requirements should include participation as an assistant to a licensed attorney in at least one civil trial, one criminal trial, and one settlement conference; submission to the board of law examiners, in response to hypothetical statements of fact, a complaint, an answer, and a trial brief. Every applicant for admission to the bar should be required to draft a simple contract and an uncomplicated will, and to argue a simple motion before a bar examiner. These requirements would inevitably upgrade basic skills and assure that all litigants, rich and poor, are represented by counsel who meet reasonable standards of competence.

(6) Many judges are considered by their colleagues and members of the bar to be incompetent and/or lacking in integrity or judicial temperament. The only qualification for election or appointment to the bench is admission to the bar. Lawyers who have never tried a case or written a brief or argued an appeal are on the bench. Lawyers who have breached their duties to their clients are on the bench. Lawyers who have been convicted of crimes are on the bench.

The qualities of a good judge cannot be tested in advance or graded by an examination. To date no system of judicial selection has succeeded in screening out unfit candidates for judicial office or eliminating political considerations. Appointment or election of grossly incompetent, inexperienced judges and persons of proved lack of moral character could be prevented very simply by establishing by law minimum standards of eligibility to the bench. Such a statute should prohibit the appointment or election to the bench of anyone who has been convicted of a crime, other than a traffic violation, or suspended from the practice of law by a disciplinary body. It should require that every judge shall have engaged in the practice of law for at least fifteen years. Certainly these requirements should be uncontroversial. Since many judges who do not meet these minimum standards have been appointed and elected to office, legislation is needed.

In those jurisdictions in which judges are elected, solicitation of campaign funds from lawyers should be prohibited and strict limitations on the amount of money spent on election campaigns should be established by statute. Judicial salaries should be indexed to the cost of living in the community so that judges need not go hat in hand begging the legislature for a raise or importuning lawyers to lobby the legislature on their behalf.

(7) The appellate process is slow, cumbersome, and expensive. It fails to provide guidance on many important questions of widespread applicability. Appellate courts spend much valuable time reviewing the records of trials. In appeals that involve alleged trial errors, the record must be reviewed. Often, however, the only significant issue is a question of law. When the parties agree on the legal question or questions at issue and the trial court certifies that these are the only questions to be decided, the parties should be permitted to omit printing the record of the trial and to limit their briefs to these legal issues. A substantial percentage of appeals could be thus simplified, saving the parties money and materially reducing the time of appellate courts in deciding these cases. Opinions in such cases would be more useful to trial courts, lawyers, and litigants because the rulings would decide legal questions and not be limited to the often anomalous facts of the case.

Petitions for review addressed to the discretionary jurisdiction of the courts could also be greatly simplified. Only a tiny fraction of these cases are considered, but every petition must be accompanied by a full brief and record. Rules of court require every brief to contain a concise statement of the questions involved. The statement of the questions by the petitioner and the counterstatement by the respondent, with a short explanation of the significance of the issue, should be sufficient for the threshold determination of the court in granting or denying review. In those cases in which review is granted, the parties could then file full briefs and records. Such a practice would also save time of the justices and money of litigants.

Appellate opinions are the law of the United States, with the binding force of statutes. In order for members of the public to know their rights, obligations, and limitations, these opinions should, insofar as possible, be clear and concise. Many appellate opinions are unduly prolix and obfuscatory. Some judges appear to be writing disquisitions for law reviews and indulge in supererogatory erudition. A judicial opinion is a message addressed to the litigants whose case is decided, to the members of the bench and bar, and to the public. It should contain only the minimal facts necessary to understand the issue, a statement of the ruling, the reasons therefore, and the precedents that are controlling or are being overruled or limited. Judges must walk a fine line between oversimplification and overcomplication. Many judges are tempted to stray from the strait confines of this duty. The sweeping, memorable phrase that catches the public fancy sometimes proves irresistible. Notable examples are "Three generations of imbeciles are enough," a phrase presumably justifying compulsory sterilization of institutionalized mental defectives,[8] and "The petitioner may have a constitutional right to talk politics but he has no right to be a policeman."[9] This glib phrase limited the First Amendment rights of public employees. Such simplistic, overbroad generalities usually result in more litigation to define, to limit, and ultimately to overturn these decisions. The urge to write a learned treatise discussing not only law but other disciplines provokes confusion. A judge should be mindful of Occam's razor and not multiply ratiocinations and distinctions unnecessarily.

Most cases before the United States Supreme Court and the highest courts of the states are addressed to the discretionary jurisdiction of these courts. The Supreme Court's standard for granting review is whether the issue is of wide public importance or governmental interest. These are sensible, appropriate criteria but they are frequently not adhered to.

The practice in many jurisdictions permits a trial judge to certify to the appellate court that a case involves a significant legal question of widespread applicability heretofore not decided by an appellate court. The appellate courts are not required to hear such appeals addressed to their discretionary jurisdiction and frequently refuse to do so. When an appeal has been so certified, the appellate court should be required to accept the appeal and decide the question. All too often appellate courts year after year belabor problems that have already been decided and ignore important issues that continue to be litigated and appealed for want of a definitive ruling.

Pornography is not a problem that affects the economy, the social fabric of society, or large numbers of individuals. Censorship does, of course, involve fundamental First Amendment rights. In 1957, the United States Supreme Court established a reasonably comprehensible, fair standard that protected the First Amendment rights of individuals and publishers and the right of the public to free access to the written word.[10] In the succeeding quarter century the Supreme Court has reconsidered that question at least 157 times. It has decided forty-six cases with full opinions and issued eighty-three memorandum decisions.

Death penalty cases have also involved the Supreme Court, as well as the lower courts, in a myriad of conflicting, concurring, and dissenting opinions. The right of the state to take a human life is not really a legal question but one of public policy and moral values. In 1983, more than 1,000 persons, adults and children, who had been sentenced to death were awaiting execution. Because of the drastic and irrevocable nature of capital punishment, almost every such case is appealed to the United States Supreme Court. Much court time has been devoted to this one question without reaching a clear, consistent doctrine. If the Court continues to decide fewer than 150 cases with opinion each year, the appeals in death sentence cases could consume the entire time of the Court for more than six years even if no more death sentences were imposed by the trial courts. In the interests of judicial economy and efficiency, if for no other reason, the death penalty should be abolished. These are only two of many issues that the United States Supreme Court continues to reopen and obfuscate in order, it appears, to satisfy the perceived moods of the public.

Troublesome issues left in limbo include a question involving tax shelters undecided from 1947 to 1983,[11] the jurisdiction of bankruptcy courts (not decided at this writing), and the myriad problems involved in asbestos litigation. These issues affect large numbers of people and generate much litigation that could be avoided.

Difficult questions of discrimination and affirmative action are dealt with by devising multipronged tests, gradations, and classifications of rights and varying levels of review that create more problems of proof and jurisdiction than they resolve.

Judges devote much thought and time to writing opinions. Other judges, lawyers, and scholars are often highly critical of judicial opinions. "Ill-considered" is the most scathing comment; "learned," the most laudatory. When I was in practice, it seemed to me that the highest praise a judge conferred on a lawyer at oral argument was the comment, "You have been most helpful to the court." As a judge, I am grateful to lawyers who are helpful in enabling me to see the issues, their ramifications, and the likely results of the various options available to the court. The goal of judges in writing opinions should be to help the litigants, the legal community, and the public understand the decision, and the compelling reasons therefor, its precise parameters, and the path it charts for similar problems.

(8) The judicial mystique is aloofness. Beneath the black robes of office, judicial hearts are not supposed to ache with sympathy or throb with passion, judicial minds not to be concerned with practical problems but rather to focus on legal issues. Ethically sensitive judges do wisely remove themselves from politics. In conformity with the doctrine of separation of powers, they do not intermeddle with the duties of the legislature or the executive or proffer secret advice.

The problems of society, however, are not neatly compartmentalized. Some of the most understanding judges have had broad governmental and communal experience before going on the bench and are aware of the significance of their decisions. Others are not. The Supreme Court has reminded the public that what justices know as men they cannot ignore as judges. What the men and women of the judiciary know as human beings and what they do not know inevitably affects their judgments.

Issues brought before the courts arise out of the matrix of our enormously complicated, technological society. The learning explosion in the physical, biological, and social sciences in the past two centuries has infinitely expanded the accumulated knowledge of society. It has also Balkanized the intellectual world. Educated people are not simply divided into two worlds—the sciences and the humanities—as C. P. Snow declared. Each professional person, including lawyers, judges, and government officials, is imprisoned in his own field of expertise and rarely has the opportunity to explore the alien lands of other disciplines. It is more than three centuries since one man, Sir Walter Raleigh, could sit in one room and write a history of the world. Concomitant with the

increased breadth of total knowledge is the increased breadth of ignorance of every individual.

Judges who must decide so many and varied questions affecting great
numbers of individuals and society are handicapped not merely by lack
of information but by the narrowness of their training and backgrounds.
No one person can become an instant authority on psychiatry, lung
diseases, computers, accounting, reconstructive dentistry, aviation,
structural engineering, and hospital management—to name only a few
of the problems that I have had to rule upon in the past few years. Expert
witnesses, if they are competent and articulate, can supply much information. Documentary evidence is also instructive. The evidence in each
case is discrete and factual. It does not provide a philosophy of that
particular discipline or an understanding of the mind-set and limitations
of experts in that field.

Courts need informal interchange of ideas with other disciplines and
with other governmental agencies. With respect to other branches of
learning, it is not simply information but, more important, an understanding of attitudes and approaches to problems that is lacking. There
are many ways in which the traditionally parochial interests of judges
and lawyers could be enlarged to provide at least a conceptual framework
for approaching legal problems involving other areas of learning. This
serious need for greater breadth of understanding on the part of the
judiciary is barely recognized and has not been studied.

(9) The need of the legal system for information with respect to those
phases of its operations that affect the rights and remedies of all parties
has been noted again and again. It is abundantly evident that present
methods of undertaking legal and related studies have failed to provide
necessary factual data. Choice of subjects of study and funding are
aleatory and fragmentary. Rarely, if ever, is there an overview of the
needs of the legal system for information or investigation. Often projects
are proposed and financed by special interest groups. There is little
comprehensive planning and no establishment of priorities.

A National Center for Legal Research should be established to conduct continuing studies of problems of equal access to justice. Such a
center should not constitute a monopoly or present a monolithic, establishment point of view. There is a significant research role for private
foundations, law schools, and universities. But because these private and

quasi-private institutions have not addressed the urgent needs of the courts for factual information on which to base much-needed reforms, a public institution to undertake this research is required.

Cries for law reform come not only from the public but also from those engaged in every aspect of the legal system. Each seeks to remedy the problems with which he grapples. The United States Supreme Court, the intermediate appellate courts, and the trial courts ask for relief from their burdens. Lawyers for the poor go on strike. Lawyers for the rich advertise and retain public relations firms. Academicians blame private practitioners. Practitioners blame the law schools. Judges want to improve their image and their salaries. And the public demands better services. It is time for a broad review of a troubled system.

These suggestions are designed to correct gross inequities in the treatment of litigants at all levels of courts. It may be argued that they would result in a leveling down rather than a leveling up. It is true that a favored few litigants now do receive a full measure of legal rights and protections. Under carefully designed rules to effectuate the changes proposed herein, substantial due process rights would not be denied any party and such rights would be extended to many people now excluded from the protections afforded by the litigational system.

These proposals are not intended to be definitive solutions, guaranteed to provide swift, certain, and equal justice. Rather they are offered as suggested topics for investigation by experts and consideration by the public. The extraordinarily successful efforts of American courts and lawyers in extending legal protections to a large proportion of the population should not be abandoned in response to frantic, ill-considered clamor for panaceas. Economy and efficiency are desirable attributes for all institutions in both the public and private sectors. But they must not take precedence over the rights of the individual and the maintenance of a democratic society.

For more than two centuries, the American legal system has met the challenges and demands of a heterogeneous people—a dynamic, changing society—and problems of unprecedented diversity and seriousness while protecting and broadening the rights of the individual and preserving a peaceable, orderly, democratic government. With intelligent effort these values can be maintained and implemented so that the right to equal protection of the laws for all persons can be enforced.

# EPILOGUE

Preservation of the planet earth and prevention of nuclear annihilation are problems of such magnitude and urgency that discussions of the shortcomings of the American legal system may appear to be frivolous, if not futile. Those who through naivete, ignorance, or hope assume that catastrophe will be averted must continue the struggle to create and maintain a humane society. I, who have been schooled in the legal tradition, believe with Daniel Webster that "Justice is the ligament which holds civilized beings and civilized nations together." Justice is both a civilizing and a humanizing element in any society. In late twentieth century America, the concept of justice is predicated on the equal standing before the law of every person.

A generation of bruising litigation has established equal standing as a right acknowledged by the courts and accepted, though perhaps grudgingly, as an integral part of the national ethos. The implementation and enforcement of rights require access to the litigational process. The American legal community has been so occupied and bemused by increasingly refined, complicated, and time-consuming procedures in its elaboration of legal principles and practices that the warning of Marianne Moore has gone unheeded:

> "A pleasing statement, anonymous friend
> Certainly the means must not defeat the end."

The end goal of equal justice is no longer in dispute. It is being defeated not by evil will or malicious intent but by historical and incremental procedural means that are neither inevitable nor irremediable.

# NOTES

INTRODUCTION

1. Kevin Wallace is a fictitious name. The facts are true. Throughout this book, in all references to cases tried before me, the names of the litigants are fictitious, to protect their privacy and the reputations of their attorneys. The real names of the parties are used in referring to all other cases.

2. Some lawyers are women. A few judges are women. Many civil litigants are women. Most criminal defendants are men. Many victims of crime are women. To avoid the awkward use of the phrase "he or she" every time reference is made to a lawyer, judge, litigant, or crime victim, the masculine pronoun is used to refer both to males and females.

3. Morris Harrell, "The President's Page," 68 *American Bar Association Journal* 1184 (1982).

4. *New York Times*, January 3, 1983, p. 1.

5. *Report of the National Advisory Commission on Civil Disorders*, Bantam Books, Inc., New York, 1968, p. 22.

6. Benjamin Nathan Cardozo, *The Nature of the Judicial Process*, Yale University Press, 1921, pp. 63–64.

7. *New York Times*, December 20, 1982, p. E3.

8. Letter to the author from the Rockefeller Foundation.

9. *Management Statistics for United States Courts, 1982*, prepared by the Administrative Office of the United States Courts, U.S. Government Printing Office, Washington, D.C., hereafter referred to as U.S. Court Statistics.

CHAPTER I

1. *New York Review of Books*, June 3, 1983, p. 3.

2. *New York Times*, March 28, 1983, p. A12.

3. U.S. Court Statistics, 1980.

4. *New York Times*, January 17, 1983, p. A5.

5. "What Are Prisons For?" *Time Magazine*, September 13, 1983, p. 38.

6. San Antonio Independent School District v. Rodriguez, 411 U.S. 1 (1973).

7. Lois G. Forer, *The Death of the Law*, David McKay Co., Inc., New York 1975.

8.  *New York Times,* June 1, 1983, p. 1.
9.  These articles reported the following: A man was wrongly imprisoned twenty-four years; the Supreme Court refused to hear Abscam cases; a trial of Industrial Bio Test Laboratories was held in Chicago, involving fake lab tests; the Supreme Court agreed to hear an EPA air quality rule; the IRS ruled on rehabilitation tax credits; public distrust of criminal courts was spurring volunteer court monitors throughout the nation; a Puerto Rican kidnapper confessed; a federal judge ruled that the United States was liable for failing to prevent attack on civil rights workers in 1961; the Missouri Supreme Court refused to stay the execution of a convicted murderer; a California court sentenced a woman who killed her lover and a prostitute; the Arkansas school aid plan was held unconstitutional.
10.  Information as to the adequacy of compensation is not available in legal literature published in English.
11.  Cipriano v. City of Houma, 395 U.S. 701 (1969); Kramer v. Union Free School District, 395 U.S. 621 (1969).
12.  In South Carolina v. Katzenbach, 383 U.S. 301 (1966), the Supreme Court upheld the constitutionality of the act.
13.  Gray v. Sanders, 372 U.S. 368 (1963).
14.  The vast majority of adults accused of crimes are poor. In federal courts 90 percent plead guilty. In Pennsylvania, as in most states, more than 90 percent plead guilty. Fewer than 2 percent have a jury trial.
15.  *New York Times,* April 3, 1983, p. 24.
16.  James S. Kakalik and Abby Eisenshtat Robyn, *Costs of the Civil Justice System: Court Expenditures for Processing Tort Cases,* Rand Corporation, Institute for Civil Justice, Santa Monica, California, 1982 (hereinafter referred to as the Rand study). The National Center for State Courts does not have national statistics but reports that in Allegheny County, Pennsylvania, guilty pleas average forty minutes, nonjury trials two hours, and jury trials fifteen hours.
17.  "The Criminal Court: A System in Collapse," *New York Times,* June 26, 1983, p. 1.
18.  President's Commission on Law Enforcement and Administration of Justice, Task Force Report, *Juvenile Delinquency and Youth Crime,* U.S. Government Printing Office, Washington, D.C., 1967.
19.  James B. Stewart, *The Partners,* Simon and Schuster, Inc., 1983, p. 24.
20.  Philadelphia Court of Common Pleas Regulation 22-3. Although these figures reflect costs in Philadelphia, there is no reason to believe that the costs in other nonrural communities are not substantially similar.
21.  Stone, "The Insanity Defense on Trial," *Harvard Law School Bulletin,* Fall 1982, pp. 14, 17.
22.  For example, the United States Supreme Court appointed Abe Fortas, then a highly successful practicing attorney, to represent Gideon, an indigent defendant whose case resulted in the landmark decision, Gideon v. Wainwright, 372 U.S. 335 (1963), holding that persons accused of crime who face a prison

sentence are entitled to be represented by counsel.

23.  Ronald Olson of the Los Angeles firm of Munger, Tolles, and Rickhauser, past chairman of the American Bar Association litigation section, as quoted in an article by Morton Hunt, "Putting Juries on the Couch," *New York Times Magazine*, November 28, 1982, p. 70, at p. 88.

24.  This book does not purport to discuss theories of fairness, equality, or justice. Since Plato, philosophers have been attempting this difficult task. For recent efforts see, for example, Ronald Dworkin, *Taking Rights Seriously*, Harvard University Press, 1977; Herbert L. Hart, *The Concept of Law*, Oxford University Press, 1961; John H. Ely, *Democracy and Distrust*, Harvard University Press, 1980; Michael Walzer, *Spheres of Justice*, Basic Books, Inc., 1983; John Rawls, *A Theory of Justice*, Harvard University Press, 1972. None of these writers examines the operations of the litigation system. Note Rawls's comment, "By the principle of fairness it is not possible to be bound to unjust institutions, or at least to institutions which exceed the limits of intolerable injustice (so far undefined)." It is the contention of this book that the inequality of treatment of rich and poor litigants exceeds those bounds.

CHAPTER II

1.  Barton, "Behind the Legal Explosion," 27 *Stanford Law Review* 567 (1975).

2.  U.S. Court Statistics, 1981.

3.  *Philadelphia Inquirer*, April 20, 1983, p. 4A.

4.  Johnson v. Avery, 393 U.S. 483 (1969).

5.  Estelle v. Gamble, 429 U.S. 97 (1976).

6.  Morales v. Turman, 383 F.Supp. 53 (E.D. Tex. 1974).

7.  Rennie v. Klein, 653 F.2d 836 (3rd Cir. 1981).

8.  Newman v. Alabama, 349 F.Supp. 278 (M.D. Ala. 1972).

9.  "Settlement Ends Mine Dumping Suit," *New York Times*, April 25, 1982, p. 31.

10.  *New York Times*, April 3, 1983, p. 30.

11.  "Forcing Therapist to Pay," *National Law Journal*, January 17, 1983, p. 1.

12.  Robinson v. United States, 533 F. Supp. 320 (E.D. Mich. 1982); In re Swine Flu, 533 F. Supp. 703 (D.C. Utah 1982).

13.  *New York Times*, August 7, 1983, p. 29.

14.  See for example Richard Neely, *How Courts Govern America*, Yale University Press, 1981; and Alexander M. Bickel, *The Least Dangerous Branch*, Bobbs-Merrill Co., Inc., 1962.

CHAPTER III

1.  II, Henry VII, Ch. 12.

2.  *How Much Should We Charge for Justice*, a report of the New York Senate Select Task Force on Court Reorganization, 1978.

3. Berkowitz, "The Cost of Administering Justice," 26 *Rutgers Law Review* 30 (1972).

4. Ibid.

5. D. Weller and M. K. Block, *Estimating the Costs of Judicial Services*, Center for Econometric Studies of the Justice System, Hoover Institution, Stanford University, May 1979.

6. Rand study.

7. Alter, "The Case for Selling Justice," *Washington Monthly*, December 1981.

8. See for example Galpin v. Chicago, 139 Ill. App. 135 (1910) aff. 249 Ill. 334, 94 N.E. 961 (1911); Com. v. Giaccio 202 Pa. Super. 294, 196 A.2d (1963).

9. Ill. Rev. Stat. 1979 ch. 38 § 180-3; Ind. Ann. Stat. § 9-2227 (1956); Okla. Stat. Ann. 28 § 101 (1969); Tex. Code Crim. Proc. Ann. Art. 24.15 (1966).

10. See State v. Crook, 115 N.C. 769, 205E 513 (1894).

11. Williams v. Illinois, 399 U.S. 235 (1970).

12. Gideon v. Wainright, 372 U.S. 335 (1963); Burns v. Ohio, 360 U.S. 252 (1959); Williams v. Oklahoma, 395 U.S. 458 (1969); Douglas v. California, 372 U.S. 353 (1963); Ross v. Moffitt, 417 U.S. 600 (1974).

13. Gilmore v. Lynch, 404 U.S. 15 (1970).

14. *New York Times*, November 28, 1982, p. 48.

15. Boddie v. Conn., 401 U.S. 371 (1971).

16. U.S. v. Kras, 409 U.S. 434 (1973).

17. Ortwein v. Schwab, 410 U.S. 656 (1973). The Court justified the imposition of this fee because it contributed to defraying the expenses of the state court system.

18. Lassiter v. Department of Social Services, 452 U.S. 18 (1981).

19. Michelman, "The Supreme Court and Litigation Access Fees," 19 *Duke Law Review* 527 (1973).

20. Sir Frederick Pollock and Frederic Maitland, *History of English Law*, 2nd ed., Lawyer Literary Club, 1959, p. 597; Spector, "Financing the Courts through Fees, Incentives, and Equity in Civil Litigation," 58 *Judicature* 330 (1975).

21. Tatum v. Regents of Nebraska, *U.S. Law Week* 3883 (1983).

22. *New York Times*, March 31, 1983, p. 1.

CHAPTER IV

1. *Philadelphia Inquirer*, November 17, 1981, pp. 1D, 8D.

2. *National Law Journal*, September 20, 1982, p. 11.

3. *National Law Journal*, Law Office Management Supplement, March 1983, p. 9.

4. Ronald F. Pollack, "Lawyers Flock to the Rich, Shun the Poor" (Commentary) *Rocky Mountain News*, June 27, 1983, p. 39.

5. *Palo Alto Weekly*, June 23, 1982, p. 9.

6. *Wall Street Journal*, February 3, 1983, sec. 2, p. 33.
7. *Philadelphia Inquirer*, August 16, 1981, p. D1.
8. *National Law Journal*, September 20, 1982, p. 4.
9. The legal clinic chain of Joel Hyatt in 1983 had 117 clinics providing prepaid legal services. The chain was retained by 15,000 new clients each month. *New York Times*, May 9, 1983, p. D1.
10. Jack Ladinsky, "Careers of Lawyers, Law Practice, and Legal Institutions," 28 *American Sociological Review* 47, 54 (1963). See also, Jerold S. Auerbach, *Unequal Justice*, Oxford University Press, New York, 1976, describing the economic, social, and ethnic differences between the two groups of lawyers.
11. *Wall Street Journal*, May 31, 1978, p. 46.
12. In re Fine Paper Antitrust Litigation (E.D. Pa.), Memorandum Decision March 3, 1983.
13. *New York Times*, November 14, 1982, p. A24.
14. *Philadelphia Inquirer*, November 15, 1981, pp. 1A, 12A.
15. Coblentz, "A Glut of Lawyers," *Newsweek*, June 27, 1983, p. 17.
16. Judge Charles Richey of United States District Court for the District of Columbia laments that he often cringes at the lack of advocacy skills displayed by attorneys appearing before him, 52 *U.S. Law Week* 2064 (1983).
17. Note, "Neighborhood Law Offices," 80 *Harvard Law Review* 805 (1967).
18. The litigation involved National Student Marketing Corporation. Class actions were brought on allegations of securities fraud in 1972. Seven civil suits were brought, as well as charges of securities violations. Final settlements were reached in 1982 by United States District Judge Barrington D. Parker of the District of Columbia. For accounts of this litigation see In re National Student Marketing Litigation 368 F. Supp. 1311 (D.C. 1973); Lipsig v. National Student Marketing Corp. 663 F.2d 17D (D.C. Cir. 1980), and *National Law Journal*, September 20, 1982, p. 4.
19. These are fictional names for real people. The facts have been slightly disguised to protect their privacy.

CHAPTER V

1. See Michael Harrington, *The Other America*, Macmillan Publishing Co., Inc., New York, 1962, for a discussion of the two separate and unequal societies in the United States.
2. *New York Times*, July 6, 1983, p. A10.
3. Judge Jacob D. Fuchsberg of the Court of Appeals of New York was sharply criticized; a resolution to recall Chief Justice Rose Bird of California was adopted by the California Republican Commission, alleging that she led a majority of four justices in allowing blatant gerrymandering (*New York Times*, February 1, 1982, p. A8) and further that she "undermined morale among judges, court staff and law enforcement personnel" (*New York Times*, November 15, 1982, p. 13); Justice Rolf Larsen of the Supreme Court of Pennsylvania

was subjected to an investigation on charges of unethical conduct (*Philadelphia Inquirer*, May 15, 1983, p. 1). The Ohio Bar Association and the chief justice and the supreme court of Ohio have been accused of improprieties (*National Law Journal*, March 28, 1983, p. 1).

4.   Statement of Justice James Leff of New York, quoted by Jack Newfield in a series of articles, "The Worst Judges," *Village Voice*, September 26, 1974, pp. 5 et seq.

5.   *American Bar Association Journal*, May 1982, p. 544.

6.   Certain types of cases can only be heard in federal courts: bankruptcy, patent, maritime, federal taxation, antitrust, matters arising under federal laws, petitions brought by federal prisoners, prosecutions for violation of federal laws, and appeals from decisions of federal regulatory agencies. Other matters can be heard only in state courts. A vast variety of cases can be brought in both federal and state courts; the choice in such cases rests with the plaintiff's lawyer.

7.   See Joseph C. Goulden, *The Benchwarmers*, Weybright and Talley, 1974.

8.   Speech delivered at Louisiana State University, Baton Rouge, March 11, 1983. *New York Times*, May 16, 1983 p. A14.

9.   Harold W. Chase, *Federal Judges: The Appointing Process*, University of Minnesota Press, 1972.

10.   Occasionally an outstanding woman or nonwhite was appointed to the federal bench. For example, Judge Florence Allen, who was appointed in 1934, was the only woman on the United States Court of Appeals until the 1960s, when Shirley Hufstedler was appointed. Judge William O. Hastie, a black lawyer who was a graduate of Harvard Law School and a former governor of the Virgin Islands, was appointed to the Court of Appeals in 1949. For a discussion of the racial, religious, and gender- and status-based prejudice in the organized bar and bench, see Jerold S. Auerbach, *Unequal Justice*, Oxford University Press, New York, 1976.

11.   National Association of Women Judges newsletter, Summer 1983, p. 3.

12.   Grossman, "Social Backgrounds and Decision Making," 79 *Harvard Law Review* 1551 (1966).

13.   Jenkins, "A Candid Talk with Justice Blackmun," *New York Times Magazine*, February 20, 1983, p. 20, at p. 23.

14.   Elliot E. Slotnick, "The American Bar Association Standing Committee on Federal Judiciary: A Contemporary Assessment," 66 *Judicature* 385 (1983).

15.   65 *Judicature* 311 (1982).

16.   For example, Judges Clement F. Haynsworth and George Harrold Carswell were routinely and almost automatically approved for appointment to the United States Supreme Court. Only after public exposure of their decisions as federal judges by a small group of activist lawyers and law professors did the committee reconsider its approval. Significantly, both judges had been approved without question for the lower federal courts where they served. Federal Judge Alcee L. Hastings was tried on criminal charges of corruption and found not

guilty. He is under investigation with a view to impeachment. *New York Times,* June 6, 1983, p. A10.

Other federal judges have behaved unjudiciously, unfairly, and corruptly. See Anthony Lewis, "Courts in Contempt," *New York Times,* March 24, 1983, p. A31. Some have been forced to resign. Among those who resigned under fire were Judges Martin Thomas Manton, Albert Williams Johnson, and John Warren Davis.

17.  91 *American Bar Association Reports* 159 (1966).

18.  Berkson, "Judicial Selection in the United States," 64 *Judicature* 176 (1980).

19.  Fitzpatrick, "Depleting the Currency of the Federal Judiciary," 68 *American Bar Association Journal* 1236 (1982).

20.  *Philadelphia Inquirer,* July 14, 1983, p. 4B.

21.  Goulden, *The Benchwarmers.*

22.  Judge Archie Simonson was recalled in an election in 1977 after commenting on a case involving an attack by several juveniles on a female student in a high school stairwell, "The way girls dress nowadays, they deserve it."

23.  *Rocky Mountain News,* June 27, 1983, p. 6.

24.  One of the damning accusations against Supreme Court Justice Fortas was the fact that he accepted stipends from a foundation allegedly controlled by organized crime. Recent revelations that Supreme Court Justice Felix Frankfurter received supplemental support from Justice Louis D. Brandeis, a very wealthy, close friend, have provoked much comment. Many in the legal profession consider such support improper.

25.  Schoenbaum and Goldspiel, "Answering Unjust Criticism: First Aid for Battered Courts," 21 *Judges Journal* 39 (1982).

CHAPTER VI

1.  Rand study.

2.  In Hickman v. Taylor, 329 U.S. 495 (1946), the Supreme Court upheld the discovery rules permitting these extensive pretrial procedures, declaring, "Thus civil trials in federal courts no longer need be carried on in the dark. The way is now clear, consistent with recognized privileges, for the parties to obtain the fullest knowledge of the issues and facts before trial." Similar procedures obtain in most states.

3.  *New York Times,* June 14, 1982, p. B1.

4.  *New York Times,* March 31, 1983, p. 1.

5.  *New York Times,* July 28, 1982, p. A20; *New York Times,* July 31, 1982, p. 1.

6.  "See You in Court: Our Suing Society," *U. S. News and World Report,* December 20, 1982, p. 58.

7.  *Asbestos Reporter,* April 22, 1983, p. 6439.

8.  *New York Times,* April 17, 1983, p. F15.

9. Hearings before the Temporary National Economic Committee, 76th Cong., 1st Session, at p. 614 (1939).

10. Borkin, "The Patent Infringement Suit," 17 *University of Chicago Law Review* 634 (1950).

11. Noah, "Opinions for Sale," *Harper's,* February 1983, p. 28.

12. Long criminal jury trials similarly cause much of the delay and backlog in criminal courts.

13. *Finances and Operating Costs in Pennsylvania's Courts of Common Pleas,* National Center for State Courts, Northeastern Regional Office, North Andover, Massachusetts, September, 1980.

14. *National Law Journal,* September 20, 1982, p. 43.

15. Siegel, "Without a Lawyer the Poor Can't Complain," *Civil Liberties,* June 1983, p. 5.

16. *New York Times,* February 13, 1983, p. 1.

17. *New York Times,* January 30, 1983, p. E7.

CHAPTER VII

1. Argument in Eddings v. Oklahoma, 455 U.S. 104 (1982), 50 *U.S. Law Week* 3363.

2. Gideon v. Wainright, 372 U.S. 335 (1963), Powell v. Alabama, 287 U.S. 45 (1932).

3. Douglas v. California, 372 U.S. 353 (1963). But an indigent does not have the right to free counsel to pursue a motion for new trial. Com. v. Conceicao, 51 *U.S. Law Week* 2638 (1983).

4. See Bandy v. U.S., 364 U.S. 477 (1960); Bitter v. U.S., 389 U.S. 15 (1967).

5. Miranda v. Arizona, 384 U.S. 436 (1966).

6. Eskeridge v. Washington, 357 U.S. 214 (1958).

7. Pennsylvania Prison Society press release, May 13, 1983.

8. Hunt, "Putting Juries on the Couch," *New York Times Magazine,* November 28, 1982, p. 70.

9. Vinson, "The Shadow Jury: An Experiment in Litigation Science," 68 *American Bar Association Journal* 1242, at p. 1246 (1982).

10. *New York Times,* September 12, 1982, p. 69.

11. *New York Times,* September 10, 1982, p. B4.

12. *New York Times,* April 25, 1982, p. E11.

13. U.S. Court Statistics, 1981.

14. *Center for Jury Studies Newsletter,* Vol. 4, No. 4, July 1982.

15. *New York Times,* November 4, 1982, p. 28.

16. *New York Times,* November 28, 1983, p. 53.

17. *New York Times,* January 16, 1983, p. 42.

18. Donald J. Newman, *Conviction: The Determination of Guilt or Innocence Without Trial,* Little, Brown and Co., 1966.

19. See Wicker, "Defending the Indigent in Capital Cases," 2 *Criminal*

*Justice Ethics,* Winter/Spring 1983, p. 2, describing the inadequacies of the legal defense provided for many of the 900 people sentenced to death. The defense of those charged with lesser crimes is even less adequate.

20. "Budget Ills Cripple Defense of Poor, Lawyers Say," *New York Times,* November 14, 1982, p. 28.

21. Morris v. Slappy, 51 *U.S. Law Week* 4399 (1983).

22. Miller v. Pate, 386 U.S. 1 (1967).

23. Harry W. Jones, Ed. *The Courts, the Public, and the Law Explosion,* Prentice Hall, Inc., 1965, p. 85.

24. David Rothman, *Conscience and Convenience,* Little, Brown and Co., 1980.

CHAPTER VIII

1. *Juvenile Delinquency and Youth Crime,* Task Force Reports, President's Commission on Law Enforcement and Administration of Justice, U.S. Government Printing Office, 1967.

2. In re Gault, 387 U.S. 1 (1967), Kent v. U.S., 383 U.S. 541 (1966).

3. Compare the description of the operations of juvenile courts in the 1980s by Peter S. Prescott in *The Child Savers,* Alfred A. Knopf, Inc., 1981, with those of Anthony Platt in *The Child Savers: The Invention of Delinquency,* University of Chicago Press, 1969, and this writer in *No One Will Lissen,* John Day Co., 1970, and Charles Schinitsky, "The Role of the Lawyer in Childrens' Court," 17 *Record of the New York City Bar Association* 10 (1962).

4. Prescott, *The Child Savers,* at p. 108.

5. *Harvard Law Record,* March 11, 1983, p. 5.

6. *New York Times,* June 12, 1983, p. 60, describing the program of Columbia University Law School.

7. McKeiver v. Pennsylvania, 403 U.S. 528 (1971)

8. Birch Bayh, *Juveniles v. Justice: A Chapter in Legal Rights for Children,* a symposium, edited by the staff of *Columbia Human Rights Law Review,* R. E. Burdick, Fair Lawn, N.J., 1973.

9. Jonas B. Robitscher, *The Powers of Psychiatry,* Houghton Mifflin Co., 1980.

10. Johnson v. Zerbst, 304 U.S. 458 (1938).

11. Kent v. U.S., supra.

12. In re Gault, supra.

13. See DeBacker v. Brainard, 396 U.S. 28 (1969); In re Winship, 397 U.S. 358 (1970); McKeiver v. Pennsylvania, supra; Fare v. Michael C., 442 U.S. 707 (1979).

14. In a few scattered cases, children have been accorded some protections. For example, Federal Judge Russell G. Clark of the United States District Court in Kansas City, Missouri, has entered a consent decree requiring important safeguards and standards with respect to foster homes, including prohibition

against corporal punishment. *New York Times*, March 27, 1982, p. 23.

15.   Alice M. Rivlin, director of the Congressional Budget Office, reported that
13 percent of all seventeen-year-olds are functionally illiterate and that in minority youth the figure might be as high as 40 percent. Nearly 40 percent of
seventeen-year-olds cannot draw inferences from written material, only one-fifth
can write a persuasive essay, and only one-third can solve a mathematics problem
requiring several steps. *Philadelphia Inquirer*, April 29, 1983, p. 3A.

It has been my experience that functional illiteracy is a common characteristic
of young adult male offenders and male juveniles. I have never encountered an
illiterate female offender under the age of seventy.

16.   For a similar saga of a child lost in the mazes of the New York City juvenile
justice system, see the report on Dwayne Lee Gosso, *New York Times*, October
17, 1983, p. B1.

17.   The *Diagnostic and Statistical Manual of Mental Disorders*, American
Psychiatric Association, 1968, describes running away as a mental disorder as
follows: "308.3. Runaway reaction of childhood (or adolescence): Individuals
with this disorder characteristically escape from threatening situations by running away from home for a day or more without permission. Typically they are
immature and timid, and feel neglected at home, inadequate, and friendless.
They often steal furtively."

18.   Com. v. Sadler, 301 Pa. Super. 228, allocatur den. Oct. 13, 1982.

19.   *New York Times*, March 20, 1983, p. 61.

20.   *Civil Liberties*, February 1983, p. 9.

21.   Alan Sussman, Stephen J. Cohen, *Reporting Child Abuse and Neglect*,
Ballinger Publishing Co., Cambridge, Mass., 1975.

22.   Judge Maxwell Davison, "Child Abuse: The Pennsylvania Experience,"
*Pennsylvania Law Journal Reporter*, June 7, 1982.

23.   *Philadelphia Inquirer*, May 1, 1983, p. 1B.

24.   Howard James, *The Little Victims*, David McKay Co., New York, 1975,
p. 308.

25.   Naomi Chase, *A Child Is Being Beaten*, Holt, Rinehart and Winston,
Inc., New York, 1975, at p. 211.

26.   Joseph Goldstein, Anna Freud, and Albert J. Solnit, *Beyond the Best
Interests of the Child*, Free Press, New York, 1973.

27.   *Philadelphia Inquirer*, February 14, 1983, p. 1, at p. 2.

28.   Stanley v. Illinois, 405 U.S. 645, 656 (1972).

29.   Walton, "Why Women Hate Their Gynecologists," *Philadelphia Inquirer
Magazine*, April 10, 1983, p. 34, at p. 36.

CHAPTER IX

1.   In most states, there are also local courts that hear small claims and
misdemeanors and traffic violations. Many claims involving relatively small sums
are heard by arbitrators. From all these decisions there is usually, by way of
appeal, a right to a new trial in the trial court of general jurisdiction.

2.   The nomenclature is confusing. In some jurisdictions such as New York,

the trial court is called the Supreme Court and the highest court is called the Court of Appeals.

3. In the United States Supreme Court the vast majority of filings are addressed to the discretionary jurisdiction of the court by petitions for writ of certiorari. Only a small number of cases are appealed as a matter of right.

4. This chapter is concerned only with appeals from decisions of state and federal courts. Administrative agency rulings often have equally significant effects on the lives of the people involved. The right of appeal from these orders is hedged with many restrictions as to the scope of review, the nature of the remedy, and the qualifications and procedures of the reviewing tribunals. For a discussion of the review of administrative decisions denying federal benefits see Skoler, "Hard Times, Soft Justice," *Human Rights*, Winter 1983, p. 26.

5. U.S. Third Circuit Court of Appeals statistics.

6. Harry Kalven, Jr., and Hans Zeisel, *The American Jury*, Little, Brown and Co., 1966.

7. See for example Thomas Church Jr., *Justice Delayed: The Pace of Litigation in Urban Trial Courts*, National Center of State Courts in Cooperation with the National Conference of Metropolitan Courts, Williamsburg, Virginia, 1978.

8. I participated in the posttrial discussions in Darryl's case because court approval is required for settlement of a minor's case. In similar cases involving adults, the court usually does not know what happens after trial or why.

9. *Philadelphia Inquirer*, February 15, 1983, p. 3B.

10. I was involved in one of the many hearings in this series of cases.

11. Berkebile v. Brantley Helicopter, 337 A.2d 893 (1975)

12. Douglas v. California, 372 U.S. 353 (1963)

13. Eskridge v. Washington, 357 U.S. 214 (1958).

14. Com. v. Turner, 338 U.S. 49 (1949).

15. Com. v. Turner, 371 Pa. 417 (1952).

16. *Legal Intelligencer*, November 30, 1982, p. 1.

17. The courts discourage frivolous appeals by imposing costs and fees on such appellants. Asberry v. U.S. Postal Service, 51 *U.S. Law Week* 2315 (1982).

18. Most petitions for certiorari are denied in approximately two months. The following cases are but a few of the many denied review in five weeks or less in May 1982: Booth v. U.S., 81-1927 pet. filed 4/19/82 den. 5/17/82; McGrath v. State University, 81-1935 pet. filed 4/19/82 den. 5/24/82; McCarty v. U.S., 81-1932 pet. filed 4/16/82 den. 5/24/82; Saint Prix v. U.S., 81-1975 pet. filed 4/23/82 den. 5/24/82; Cotton Belt Ins. v. U.S., 81-1981 pet. filed 4/12/82 den. 5/17/82.

19. SB 645 98th Cong., 1st Session. For discussions of this proposal see Hoffman, "Caseload, Conflicts and Decisional Capacity: Does the Supreme Court Need Help?" 67 *Judicature* 29 (1983); and Brennan, "The National Court of Appeals: Another Dissent," 40 *University of Chicago Law Review* 473 (1973).

20. *New York Times*, February 21, 1983, p. B1

21.   Hamilton, Rabinovitz, and Szanton, Inc., *Cutting the Overhead Costs of Resolving Asbestos Claims: A Time for Action,* Los Angeles and Washington, November 1982.
22.   Caire v. Stassi, 379 So. 2d 1056 (1980) cert. den. 449 U.S. 871 (1980).
23.   Balter v. Ethyl Corp., cert. den. 452 U.S. 955 (1981).
24.   Vaught v. Lee Vision Center, Inc., 444 U.S. 941 (1979). See also R & T Construction Co., Inc., v. St. Louis, San Francisco Ry. Co., cert. den. 444 U.S. 941 (1979).
25.   Dacey v. Naruk, 445 U.S. 941 (1980).
26.   Estes v. Met Branches, 48 *U.S. Law Week* 4119.
27.   See for example Boeing v. Van Gemert, 444 U.S. 913 (1979).
28.   See for example Wolfman, Silver, and Silver, "The Behavior of Justice Douglas in Tax Cases," 122 *University of Pennsylvania Law Review* 235, 236 (1937), in which the authors write, "More significant than merely highlighting contradictions among cases, however, Justice Douglas' indiscriminating approach obscures conflicting factors within a given case, so that he fails to come to grips with their details and significance and rarely clarifies the actual determinants of his votes." The authors analyzed 290 tax cases decided between 1939 and 1973. Certainly Justice Douglas never had time to comb through these cases, arising under different circumstances, at different times, and in different contexts, to compose and resolve inconsistencies.
29.   Bob Woodward and Scott Armstrong, *The Brethren,* Simon and Schuster, Inc., 1979.
30.   Richard Neely, *How Courts Govern America,* Yale University Press, 1981, at p. 201.
31.   Spaeth, "Achieving a Just Legal System: The Role of State Intermedial Appellate Courts," 462 *Annals of the American Academy of Political and Social Science* 48, at p. 55 (July 1982).
32.   Baldwin v. Hale, 1 Wall. 223 (1864).

CHAPTER X

1.   See O'Brien, "The Seduction of the Judiciary: Social Science and the Courts," 64 *Judicature* 8 (1981).
2.   See Ballew v. Georgia, 435 U.S. 223 (1978), in which the Court admitted that studies, later severely criticized, formed the only basis other than "hunch" for the decision.
3.   Resnik, "Managerial Judges," 96 *Harvard Law Review* 376, 404 (1982).
4.   Wilson, "Changing Criminal Sentences," *Harper's,* November 1977, pp. 16, 17. See also two widely quoted books recommending presumptive sentences and mandatory sentences: Marvin Frankel, *Criminal Sentences: Law Without Order,* Hill and Wang, 1972; and Twentieth Century Fund, Inc., *Fair and Certain Punishment: Report on Criminal Sentencing,* McGraw-Hill Book Co., 1976. The recommendations in these books were made without any supporting factual data.
5.   *New York Times,* March 6, 1983, p. 4E.

6. Stuller, "Putting Prisons to Work," *American Legion Magazine*, January 1983, p. 26.

7. See Solem v. Helm, 463 U.S. 77 L.Ed.2d 637 (1983), holding that under the Eighth Amendment sentences must be proportionate to the crime.

8. During the academic year 1981–82, the *Harvard Law Review* and the *Yale Law Journal* published six articles that were funded by research grants, as well as several that had been speeches for which stipends or honoraria were paid. Many articles are funded by more than one grantor. See for example Henkin, "Rights Here and There," 81 *Columbia Law Review* 1582 (1981). The author acknowledges support from two foundation grants and additional support from two other foundations. Most of these law review articles analyzed Supreme Court opinions or specific legal doctrines. None involved factual research.

Innumerable authors of books on legal subjects are also funded by several sources. Many of these volumes rely almost exclusively on published information. See for example Paul D. Carrington, Daniel J. Meador, and Maurice Rosenberg, *Justice On Appeal*, West Publishing Co., 1976, discussing the increase in the work load of the appellate courts and making recommendations. Other than published statistics on the number of appeals in selected courts, the authors do not offer any new information. The grant acknowledgment for *Justice on Appeal* reads as follows: "The writing of this book was assisted by a grant from the National Institute of Law Enforcement and Criminal Justice. Additional funds were provided by the National Center for State Courts pursuant to a grant from the Law Enforcement Assistance Administration. . . . the authors are also indebted to Columbia University Law School for its generous support during the year 1972–73 . . ." John H. Ely, *Democracy and Distrust*, Harvard University Press, 1980, a scholarly disquisition on theories of appeal reconciling strict construction with judicial activism and providing a synthesizing concept of "interpretivism," was substantially funded. The author acknowledges help from "the Ford Program for Basic Research at Harvard Law School, which provided support during 1976–1978, and the Woodrow Wilson International Center for Scholars at the Smithsonian Institution, where I spent the academic year 1978–1979." The author also acknowledges lectureships at several law schools.

Joseph Goldstein, Anna Freud, and Albert J. Solnit, *Beyond the Best Interests of the Child*, Free Press, 1973, a short book that refers only to published legal documents and provides no new data, contains the following acknowledgments: "For financial assistance (travel, study, and research group): the Field Foundation, the Ford Foundation, the Foundation for Research in Psychoanalysis, the Freud Centenary Fund, the Anna Freud Foundation, the Grant Foundation, the Institution for Social and Policy Study, the Andrew Mellon Foundation, the National Institute for Mental Health, and the New-Land Foundation."

9. Miranda v. Arizona, 384 U.S. 436 (1966).

10. Los Angeles Department of Water and Power v. Manhart, 435 U.S. 702 (1978).

11. Abel, "Dispute Institutions in Society," *Law and Society Review*, Winter 1973, at p. 288.

12. Sheldon and Eleanor Glueck, *One Thousand Juvenile Delinquents*, Harvard University Press, 1934.
13. Williams v. Florida, 399 U.S. 78 (1970).
14. Apodaca v. Oregon, 406 U.S. 404 (1972).
15. Ballew v. Georgia, 435 U.S. 223, 246 (1978), concurring opinion joined by Chief Justice Burger and Justice Rehnquist.
16. Zurcher v. *Stanford Daily*, 436 U.S. 547 (1978).
17. Kalven and Zeisel, *The American Jury*.
18. Letter from Willard J. Hertz of the Ford Foundation to this writer dated May 26, 1978.
19. Lois G. Forer, "One Judge's View of the Split Verdict in Civil Cases," *Pennsylvania Law Journal-Reporter*, August 31, 1981, p. 1.
20. Mills and Bohannon, "Jury Characteristics: To What Extent Are They Related to Jury Verdicts?" 64 *Judicature* 22 (1980).
21. Parkinson and Buckles, "Court Analysis of Court Systems: A Case Study," *State Court Journal*, Winter 1978, p. 13, at p. 15. This research was funded by the Missouri Council on Criminal Justice and completed by the National Center for State Courts.
22. Howard James, *Crisis in the Courts*, David McKay Co., Inc., 1968.
23. Charles E. Silberman, *Criminal Justice, Criminal Violence*, Random House, 1978.
24. William Broad and Nicholas Wade, *Betrayers of the Truth*, Simon and Schuster, Inc. 1982.
25. See, for example, Butterfield, "The New Vietnam Scholarship," *New York Times Magazine*, February 13, 1983, p. 26, indicating that beliefs thought to be based on fact are the product of inaccuracies, misperceptions, and outright lies.
26. Malcolm M. Feeley, *Court Reform on Trial*, a Twentieth Century Fund report, Basic Books, Inc., 1983, at p. 73.
27. Brown v. Board of Education, 349 U.S. 483 (1954).
28. Furman v. Georgia, 408 U.S. 238 (1972).
29. Gregg v. Georgia, 428 U.S. 153 (1976).
30. See, for example, Korematsu v. U.S., 323 U.S. 214 (1944), upholding the right of government to relocate Americans of Japanese ancestry from the West Coast to camps in Arizona, based on a wholly unsubstantiated fear that these citizens simply by reason of ancestry were disloyal Americans who presented a clear and present danger to national safety.

CHAPTER XI

1. *Lawyer's Digest*, April 1983, p. 7.
2. The Bible, Chaucer, Shakespeare, and Dickens, to name only the literature that every American should be expected to have read, present scathing criticisms of the law and lawyers. Dickens's novels, of course, are replete with detailed accounts of lengthy costly court cases.

3.  Henry J. Friendly, *Federal Jurisdiction: A General View*, Columbia University Press, 1973.

4.  See Schnader, "A Short History of the Preparation and Enactment of the Uniform Commercial Code," 22 *University of Miami Law Review* 1 (1967).

5.  Thatcher, "From Lawsuits to Out-of-Court Solutions," *Christian Science Monitor*, November 29, 1978, pp. 14, 121.

6.  *Alternative Methods of Dispute Settlement: A Selected Bibliography*, Special Committee on Alternative Means of Dispute Resolution, American Bar Association, updated May 1982.

7.  American District Telegraph Co. v. Kittleson, 81 F.Supp. 25, rev. 179 F.2d 946 (8th Cir. 1950).

8.  Broderick, "Compulsory Arbitration: One Better Way," 69 *American Bar Association Journal* 64 (1983).

9.  See Reynolds and Tonry, "Professional Mediation Services for Prisoners' Complaints," 67 *American Bar Association Journal* 294 (1981).

10.  Address to the Pound Conference, 70 Federal Rules Decisions 79 (1976).

11.  *National Law Journal*, August 30, 1982, p. 1.

12.  *New York Times*, May 29, 1983, p. 16E.

13.  For example, U.S. Steel pleaded no contest and agreed to pay a $175,000 fine, *Lawyer's Digest*, April 1983, p. 7.

14.  Note the unsatisfactory situation in New York, where there is a backlog of 1,400 complaints against New York doctors in the State Health Department office, *New York Times*, February 21, 1983, p. B1. See also Mattos v. Thompson, 491 Pa. 385 (1980), holding unconstitutional the Pennsylvania medical malpractice act of December 14, 1979, P.L. 562N. 128, 40 P.S. §§ 1301.101 et seq., providing that such cases be arbitrated instead of tried in court because it was found that arbitration was "incapable of providing the prompt determination and adjudication of medical malpractice which was the goal of the Act."

15.  Stanley J. Lieberman, "A No-Lose Proposition," *Newsweek*, February 21, 1983, p. 14. Many diatribes against lawyers and litigation are issued by suspect sources. See a letter in the *New York Times*, June 15, 1983, p. A26, by Robert Coulson, president of the American Arbitration Association. Thomas W. Conklin writes about "The Tort of Unreasonable Litigation" in 18 *For the Defense* 101 (1977) discussing hypothetical cases in which plaintiffs sue for damages in bad faith or maliciously. The author is a member of the International Association of Insurance Counsel and Defense Research Institute.

16.

| Amount of Claim | Fee |
|---|---|
| $1 to $20,000 | 3% (minimum $200) |
| $20,000 to $40,000 | $600, plus 2% of excess over $20,000 |
| $40,000 to $80,000 | $1000, plus 1% of excess over $40,000 |
| $80,000 to $160,000 | $1400, plus ½% of excess over $80,000 |
| $160,000 to $5,000,000 | $1800, plus ¼% of excess over $160,000 |

Where the claim or counterclaim exceeds $5 million, an appropriate fee will be

236    

NOTES TO PAGES 201–214

determined by the AAA. (American Arbitration Association rules as amended and in effect April 1, 1982.)

17. California Code of Civil Procedure § 638 et seq.

18. 66 *Judicature* 6 (1982).

19. § 645, 98th Congress, 1st Session. For a critical evaluation of this bill see Hellman, "Caseload Conflicts and Decisional Capacity: Does The Supreme Court Need Help?" 67 *Judicature* 29 (1983).

20. See Barefoot v. Estelle, 51 *U.S. Law Week* 5189 (1983).

21. In certain types of class actions the lawyer for the plaintiff class is, in fact, the moving party and receives the largest monetary recovery. However, these cases often serve a wider public purpose by holding the defendants financially responsible for illegal and undesirable practices.

22. Vorenberg, "Notes from the Dean," *Harvard Law School Bulletin*, Spring 1983.

23. See address of United States Judge Irving R. Kaufman at a meeting of the Palm Beach Round Table, *New York Times*, February 11, 1983, p. B8.

24. Leonard Downie, *Justice Denied*, Praeger Publishers, Inc., 1971, p. 211.

CHAPTER XII

1. When private counsel is appointed for indigents in Washington, D.C., the rate of pay is $30 an hour for time spent in court, *New York Times*, September 1, 1983, p. B10. Similar rates prevail in other communities. Contrast this compensation with fees of $181,306 paid to the board members of the Legal Services Corporation appointed by President Reagan, *New York Times*, September 1, 1983, p. A21.

2. Irving R. Kaufman, "Attorney Incompetence: A Plea for Reform," 69 *American Bar Association Journal* 308, 311 (1983).

3. Alan Dershowitz, *The Best Defense*, Random House, 1982, pp. 16–17.

4. Vorenberg, "Notes from the Dean," *Harvard Law School Bulletin*, Spring 1983.

5. Cowan, "Reaction Mixed to Council Questionnaire," 76 *Harvard Law Record*, May 6, 1983, p. 5.

6. Margolick, "The Trouble with America's Law Schools" *New York Times Magazine*, May 22, 1983, p. 21.

7. Dr. Richard S. Ross, medical dean at Johns Hopkins University School of Medicine, explained, "We at Hopkins would like to reverse the trend toward early specialization and overemphasis on science as preparation for medicine, giving undergraduates the opportunity to pursue a liberal education." *New York Times*, May 8, 1983, p. 21.

8. Buck v. Bell, 279 U.S. 200, 207 (1927).

9. McAuliffe v. New Bedford, 155 Mass. 216, 220 (1892).

10. Roth v. U.S., 354 U.S. 476 (1957).

11. Commissioner of Internal Revenue v. Tufts, 51 *U.S. Law Week* 4518 (1983).

# INDEX